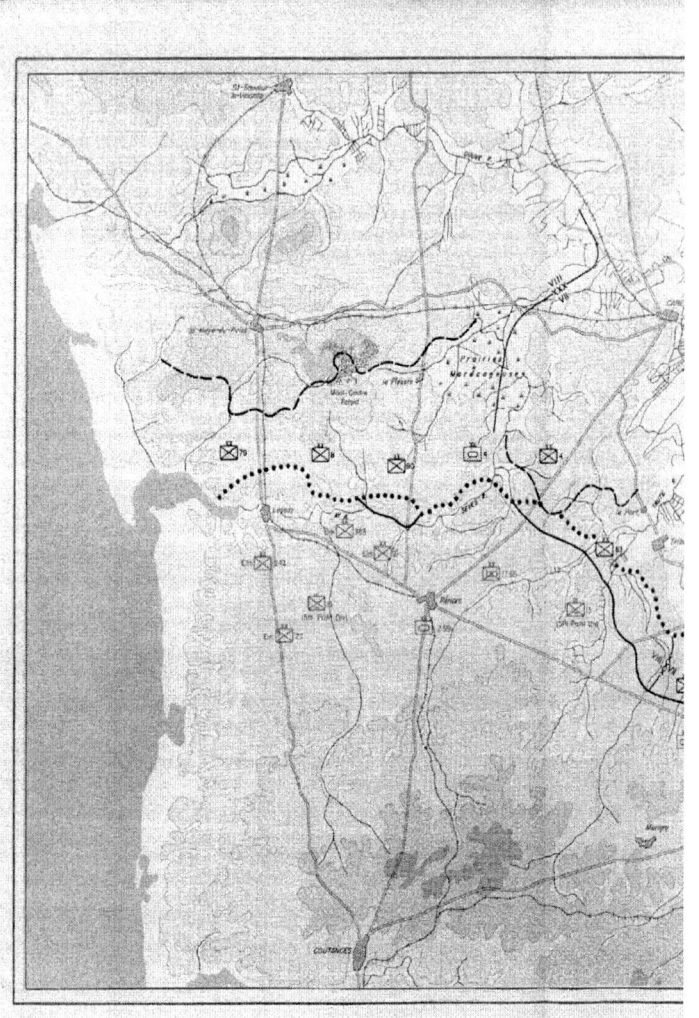

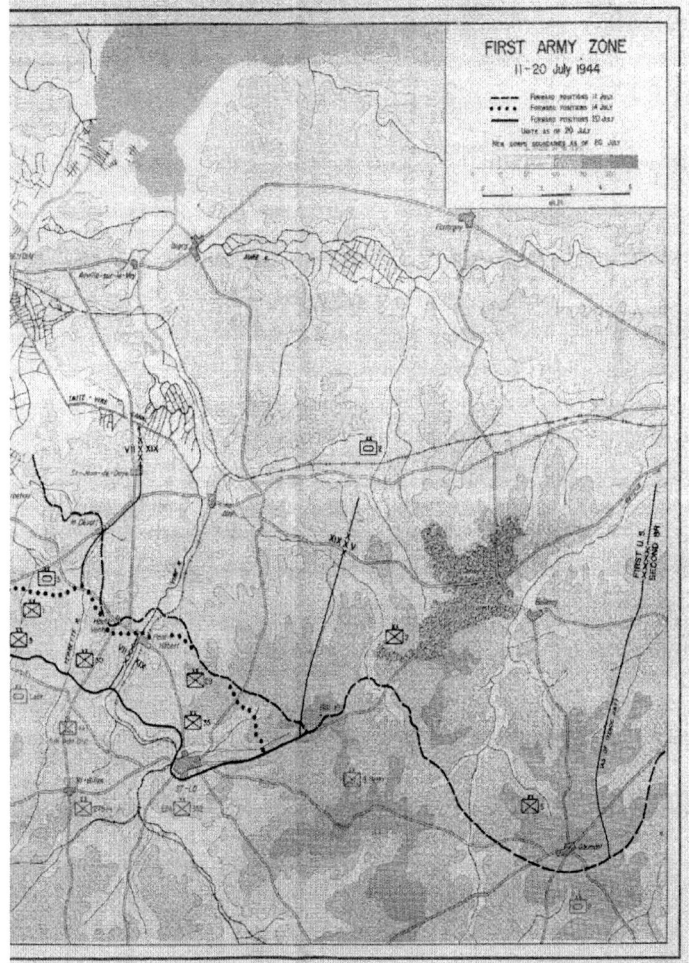

Roads Without Birds

Crucifix of Notre Dame

Roads Without Birds

Memories of Normandy, 1944

Edited by

Ann Echols
Solange Gracey
Anne Marshall Huston
James A. Huston

Airleaf Publishing

airleaf.com

© Copyright 2005, 2006, James A. Huston

All Rights Reserved.

No part of this book may be reproduced, stored in a retrieval system, or transmitted by any means, electronic, mechanical, photocopying, recording, or otherwise, without written permission from the author.

ISBN: 1-60002-018-6

Cover Illustration

This is from an original Christmas card design, "Christmas, St. Lô" by the Catalan-American artist Pierre Daura in 1947. Recalling the Massacre of the Innocents, it depicts the city of St. Lô, in Normandy, site of an intense battle in July 1944. Rays of light, alluding to the Star of Bethlehem, illuminate the way for a family as it flees against the backdrop of a bomb-ravaged church, while the young child in its mother's arms reaches out to touch an image of the Virgin and child.

Frontispiece

Amidst the destruction of Notre Dame, St. Lô, the great crucifix stands unscathed.

Preface

A few years after the end of World War II, I was revisiting Saint-Lô in Normandy to observe some of the work of reconstruction. Browsing through a bookstore there I noticed a book titled *Les Routes sans Oiseaux*—"Roads Without Birds." Immediately I recalled how, as our battalion was advancing toward Saint-Lô in July 1944, someone remarked, "Have you noticed, no birds along here."

"That's right," I answered, "and you would think ordinarily there would be lots of them in all these hedges, trees, orchards, meadows, and everything."

"Of course."

"I guess they don't like all the artillery fire and everything going on around here. They don't like it."

I bought a copy of the book. It turned out to be a very moving account of the reactions of a group of local inhabitants, refugees, to the warfare around them after the 6th of June. It was written by an author who was living in Normandy, Raoul Dujardin. An English translation of that book is offered as Part Two of this collection.

Part Three comprises short memoirs of several other people who recall their own experience as young inhabitants who were in the paths of the battles in this area in '44.

Three chapters from my earlier *Across the Face of France* make up Part One. These recall the parachute drop around Ste. Mère Église, the landings on Omaha

Beach and Utah Beach, and the intensive bombing of Saint-Lô, all on the 6th of June and the days following.

Upon my return home in April 1946 from the war in Europe, I proceeded to Bloomington where I ensconced myself in a room in the tower of the Indiana University Memorial Union Building and spent several days in writing up my recollections of our battles in Normandy. Perhaps that was a way of contributing to a "drying out" from the war and returning to civilian life.

Later, with considerable revision, including changing from first person to third person and adding a lot of documentation, that became the basis for Part One of my wartime history of our battalion—3rd Battalion, 134th Infantry Regiment, 35th Infantry Division—*Biography of a Battalion* (published in 1950, republished by Stackpole Books in 2003). Now the original first-person narrative is presented as Part Four of this work.

I wish to acknowledge with thanks Flammarion of Paris and Mme. Raoul Dujardin, for permission to publish this translation of *Les Routes sans Oiseaux*. And we thank Mme J. Masselin for providing the memoir of Jean Masselin with permission to publish, and the following for providing their memoirs with permission to publish: Madeleine Levannier, *La Meauffe*, Yvonne Gautier, *Pont Hebert*, and Bernard Chardine, *Conde-sur-Vire,* and we thank Claudine Remy for her assistance in translating these personal memoirs.

A special note of thanks is due Martha Daura for her permission to use the drawing by Pierre Daura, "Christmas St. Lô, 1947," for our cover illustration.

In our reading and writing of military history we often neglect the fate of the civilian population caught in the violence and dislocation of warfare. We hope that this will give some appreciation of how the war in Normandy appeared to the local inhabitants as well as to advancing soldiers.

James A. Huston
Lynchburg, Virginia U.S.A.

Contents

Preface ix

Part One: D-DAY, THE SIXTH OF JUNE 1

    From: *Across the Face of France* by James A. Huston

  1. Sainte-Mère Église 3
  2. Omaha Beach and Utah Beach 22
  3. The Bombing of Saint-Lô 58

Part Two: LES ROUTES SANS OISEAUX 81

    By Raoul Dujardin

    [Translated by Ann Echols and Solange Gracey]

Part Three: PERSONAL RECOLLECTIONS 249

  1. Madeleine Levannier, *La Meauffe* 251
     [Translated by Claudine Remy]
  2. Jean Masselin, Medical Student 258
     [Translated by Claudine Remy]
  3. Yvonne Gautier, *Pont-Hébert* 268
  4. Bernard Chardine, *Conde-sur-Vire, la Potinière* 275
     [Translated by Claudine Remy]

Part Four: WITH AN INFANTRY BATTALION
IN NORMANDY 283

   A Personal Narrative 283

      By James A. Huston 283

   1. Hedgerows and Sunken Roads 285
   2. "Assemble at Emelie" 314
   3. "Attack! Attack!" 331
   4. On to Saint Lô 349
   5. Moving along: Conde-sur-Vire 365
   6. "Bloody Sunday" 380
   7. Pinched Out Across the Vire River 393
   8. Detour to Mortain 407

PART ONE

D-Day, the Sixth of June

From: *Across the Face of France*

by

James A. Huston

Ste. Mere Eglise

1
Sainte-Mère Église

On the night of June 5, 1954, people of Sainte-Mère Église, in the French department of Manche, on the Cotentin Peninsula, joined by friends, relatives, and visitors, crowded into the big Quonset hut known as the "Hall Americain" for a *manifestation folklorique*. The occasion was the eve of the tenth anniversary of the town's liberation by American paratroops. Folk dancing groups, all in colorful costume, from

Normandy, Alsace, Vosges, Bordeaux, and Scotland, performed dances typical of their regions. The crowd gave enthusiastic approval to each number.

A light rain was beginning to fall as people moved out to the streets at the conclusion of the folk dancing. A new floodlight played upon the tower of the old church near the Quonset hut and streetlights caught colorful decorations on the lampposts along the street. While people waited impatiently for the ceremony commemorating the liberation to begin, the light rain turned into a downpour. Yet the crowd stood firm to await the meeting at the center of the town of the two torches of liberty—one French, the other American.

At last a small procession came down the street from the direction of the town hall. It was made up of a drum and bugle corps, a color guard with flags of France and the United States, and a detachment of boys, about ten years old, dressed as American paratroopers. Their make-up was complete even to the blackening of their faces. Several of the boys probably were born during the year of liberation—and doubtless the celebration of their tenth birthdays was not too far from the celebration of the tenth anniversary of the liberation. Now the French torch, beginning at the cemetery near the church came with the procession down Route Carentan. Soon another torch appeared from the opposite direction. It was a flame which had been lighted in Washington, D.C., carried by airplane to Paris, and then by highway, through Carentan, to Sainte-Mère Église. Representatives of the American Legion were carrying this torch. After they met, both torches moved at the head of the procession to the town hall where the crowd soon concentrated.

Floodlights lighted up the town hall and the highway marker in front of it—the "0" kilometer marker on the "Liberty Highway." The inscription on the front of the marker next to the street reads:

N°0
Voie
de la
LIBERTÉ
1944

And on either side there are inscriptions, one in French and the other in English, which read:

Ste Mère Église
This was the first town
to be liberated
on the Western Front
5-6 June 1944
Saga of the All-American

The last line is a tribute to the 82nd Airborne—the "All American"—Division. This is the starting point of the "Way of Liberty," which runs back to Cherbourg, and in the opposite direction all the way to Bastogne, with this special marker at every kilometer. A plaque centered at the forward edge of the grounds of the town hall reads:

En Hommage
Aux Français de Ste Mère Église
Qui Ont Donné Leur Vie
Pour Racheter Notre Liberté

For an hour the men stood holding the torches in the unrelenting, heavy rain, without wavering. And the people who had filled the street remained there until their special midnight mass was concluded. Colored decorations and flags were everywhere, and in spite of the rain their color stood out brilliantly in the darkened scene. The voices of a boy choir drifted out across the streets from the town hall to hearten dampened spirits. From the central doorway of the town hall, the priest celebrated mass—a memorial service for those who had died in the war, and an occasion of thanksgiving for the liberation. Here and there a few Americans could be spotted in the crowd—here a major who had jumped with the 82nd Airborne Division ten years ago, now stationed in Germany, there an American newspaper correspondent—but residents of the town and their friends and relatives made up most of the crowd. Thoughts of the exciting and joyous and tragic events of that night just ten years ago seemed to add a chill to the already cold night rain for all of the gathered crowd who could remember.

In the years following, many former members of the 82nd Division returned to Sainte-Mère Église, some for another observance of the anniversary of liberation, others passing through when they could. Then, in 1961, local citizens watched the filming of scenes for the

American motion picture *The Longest Day*, and felt the shock of reliving, seventeen years later, the high tension of June 6, 1944.

The Germans arrived at Sainte-Mère Église on June 18, 1940—four days before the French government signed armistice terms with the Nazis. Here the German army immediately began to push preparations for an invasion of England. After weeks of doubt and delays, it finally appeared that the great attack was scheduled for September. But it failed to come off. By the end of 1940 an army for offensive operations had become an army of occupation. The weeks of hostile military occupation turned into months and then years. Soon it became clear that all plans for an invasion of England had been abandoned. In fact, it was becoming evident that the Germans themselves now faced the prospect of meeting an invasion from the other direction.

On May 10, 1944, at eight o'clock in the evening, German officers came to Alexandre Renaud, mayor of Sainte-Mère Église, to ask for ten motor vehicles and for all available horses and men in the area. At first Renaud thought that the request was being made to assist some night maneuvers for the occupying forces, and he protested that this was a violation of the armistice agreement. But half an hour later he learned that the German unit was leaving Sainte-Mère Église for Vauville. The mayor was only too glad to cooperate in the evacuation of his town.

During the next few weeks a rising tenseness could be sensed among the people of Sainte-Mère Église.

Talk of an Allied invasion, and liberation, was in the air. The place of the promised Allied landing had not been announced, but a nervous anticipation was running through the German soldiers in the feeling that Normandy was a likely place for the cross-channel attack to strike. By the end of the month the Germans had flooded the marshes along the Merderet River. Local citizens were inquiring anxiously of each other, "Where are the English?" All seemed to assume that it would be the English who would land here to effect their liberation. The growing certainty on the part of the Germans that an invasion was coming in the Cotentin Peninsula quickly was communicated to the populace.

At nine P.M. on June 5 a broadcast of the BBC came clearly over local French radios—in French—"The poet makes verses...clouds hide the moon...the window is open...the garden will be blooming...it is warm in the desert." *"It is warm in the desert"*—for certain leaders of the Underground this was the alert signal. Curiously, German agents had succeeded in infiltrating several French Resistance groups, and on June 1 and 2 they had picked up twenty-eight of the BBC prearranged signals directing the Resistance to stand by for code messages for execution of sabotage plans. This information had gone to the central SS intelligence in Berlin, but there had attracted little serious attention. The German Western Command headquarters and Fifteenth Army intercepted some of the later BBC broadcasts on the night of June 5, but this made little difference to the German alertness. It appears that Field Marshal Erwin Rommel's intelligence officer put little stock in the warnings, for he thought it would be absurd for the Allies to make an advance announcement of their invasion over the BBC.

Later that night the heavy roar of bombardment along the coasts and great numbers of low-flying aircraft proclaimed that this was it. Official accounts suggest that the first American paratroopers dropped near Sainte-Mère Église between 1:30 and 2:30 A.M. on June 6. Local citizens still insist that the first American paratroopers arrived there between 11:00 and 11:30 P.M. on the fifth. (There was an hour's difference in the time—Britain was on British Double Summer Time.) Soon it seemed that the country was alive with these soldiers from the clouds.

More planes could be seen skimming through the clouds and across bands of moonlight. The crescendo of German *flak* and the burst of anti-aircraft shells disturbed the steady, monotonous roar of aircraft. A house near the edge of Sainte-Mère Église caught fire. Soon the flames seemed to light up the whole countryside, and the burning house became a reference point for more plane-loads of paratroops. Anxious Germans and hopeful Frenchmen watched in awe. By the firelight they could see clearly the big white canopies, legs dangling beneath, as their assailants and liberators descended upon them. One parachutist could he seen coming down directly toward the house. Frantically he tried to maneuver his shrouds—and then with a terrifying scream he dropped directly into the fire to be burned alive.

Several paratroopers came down in the area between the church, the doctor's house across the street where the Germans maintained their local headquarters, and the cemetery. A number of big shade trees here presented something of a hazard for a night parachute landing under any conditions. In such proximity to the German headquarters this factor took much greater significance for the individuals for whom the height and speed of the airplane and the winds had been such at the moment of their jump into the darkness as to bring them down at precisely this point. One man drifted right past one of the big trees, and his 'chute caught on the upper branches. There he swung back and forth like a pendulum as he worked rapidly to try to get out of his harness. But Germans on the ground spotted him. Their frightened hearts had no room for mercy. From several yards away a machine gun opened fire. The hands dropped to the side and the body went limp.

Shortly afterward two other paratroopers came down in neighboring trees. They too were killed by machine-gun fire as they dangled helplessly in the air. A German soldier cried out to some Frenchmen who had gathered near the church, "Tommies parachutists, alles kaput!"

Quite to the contrary, these were American parachutists, and their numbers were increasing. Sounds of the little mechanical "crickets" which they carried for identification seemed to be coming from everywhere. Two or three men descended on the top of the church, and had to let themselves down by the ropes which they carried. One man, caught on the church steeple, "played dead" until hauled down and taken prisoner two hours later.

But the men who came down at or near the church, or near the southeast edge of Sainte-Mère Église represented but a small fraction of the Americans coming down by parachute into Normandy that night. Only one of the three parachute regiments assigned or attached to the 82nd Airborne Division did have a reasonably good pattern on the zone scheduled for it. This was the 505th Parachute Infantry which, together with division headquarters, landed in a fairly good concentration one-half to two and one-half miles east of Sainte-Mère Église—between the town and the Merderet River. Other elements of the 82nd Airborne Division were scattered for forty miles up and down the Cotentin Peninsula, as much as fifteen miles to the north and twenty-five miles to the south of the intended drop zones near Sainte-Mère Église, and from within two miles of Utah Beach inland fifteen miles to the vicinity of Saint-Sauveur-leVicomte.

Some twenty-five to thirty plane-loads of men of the 507th Parachute Infantry came down in the watery marshes along the Mederet River. While some marshlands were known to border the "river" (actually it is a creek), tall, thick grass had hidden the deep water. In the darkness it was difficult to distinguish swamp from meadow. As a result many paratroopers, heavily laden with equipment, soon found themselves struggling for their very lives in several feet of water and thick undergrowth. The problem of finding equipment and assembling thus was magnified many fold.

American paratroopers in Normandy that night were, as the old army saying phrased it, "Scattered from Hell to breakfast." But the instructions to troop carrier and airborne units were not to return to base with a loaded plane. If a pilot could not find his exact drop zone, his paratroopers were to jump anyway. The airborne forces further were instructed and trained to fight wherever they might land. Clearly a great many of them did just that.

One of the time-honored principles of war is the "principle of mass"—the concentration of combat power at the decisive place and time. The descent of the 82nd Airborne Division on the Cotentin Peninsula was hardly in a concentrated pattern. Yet it was largely successful. Possibly it was successful in part because of the fact that it was *not* concentrated. Thanks to efforts of members of the French Resistance, communications lines had been cut and local German commanders found it most difficult to coordinate the actions of their units. Then came the distractions of the scattered paratroop drops. Well-planned counterattacks against paratroop concentrations were of little avail when no sizable concentrations could be located. A German unit might be sent off in one direction, only to hear firing break out in quite another, as small groups of American paratroopers faithfully carried out their instructions to fight wherever they happened to land.

Some concentration of forces on the part of the Americans was necessary, nevertheless, before any key objectives could be taken and held. Actually the 82nd Airborne Division was able to carry out only one of its three assigned missions—and that was accomplished by the one regiment which had had a very good drop pattern northwest of Sainte-Mère Église. That regiment's job was to capture the town.

In this case the aircraft had been scattered, just as had those carrying the other regiments, as they approached the drop zone, but they had been able to circle back and permit the paratroopers to jump accurately at the place marked by the pathfinders who had preceded them. Assembling quickly in the early-morning hours, about a fourth of the men of the 3rd Battalion, the unit assigned with the specific mission of going into the town, moved swiftly toward their objective. The battalion commander, Lt. Col. Edward C. Krause, ordered his men to use only their bayonets, knives, and grenades, as they moved through the streets. Any firing of weapons in the darkness could be identified at once as enemy. Actually few enemy troops remained in the town.

Their equipment and uniforms giving them the appearance of men from another planet, the paratroopers surprised Norman farmers as well as German soldiers wherever they happened to encounter them. Some of the local populace took all the invaders to be Negroes, for they had blackened their faces; strange haircuts and face paint on others created the impression that they were Indians.

At one house a soldier went up to ask for some water. A rather apprehensive housewife opened the door. She was taken aback when she heard the strange-looking creature ask for some water in the French of her own familiar Norman diction and accent! How could this be? She wondered. Was this not an American? Indeed it was, but it happened that he was from Louisiana, and there he had learned to speak French with the accent and colloquialisms of the language of Normandy.

Some time later in the day, near the little farm village of Reigneville, another group of Americans was looking for some water. M. Lemenuel had just stepped out into his yard when he noticed someone signaling to him to come. He went over to find seventeen American soldiers, faces blackened with soot, crouching behind the hedgerow. "Have you water?" one of them asked. The Frenchman did not understand. The soldiers then made signs with their hands of drinking. Lemenuel went to get some cider, some wine, and some Calvados. The soldiers hesitated momentarily, tasted the drinks warily, and then drank them all down. Then they departed.

Shortly afterward a lone paratrooper, lost from his unit, arrived at the Lemenuel house. Sure that Germans were in the vicinity, Lemenuel hid the lost soldier in the cellar under a wine cask. (It turned out that he remained here nine days.) Presently the group of paratroopers returned. Now they were hungry. The French farmer went toward the house to get some bread and eggs and wine. But then Germans appeared all around. They were coming to search the farm. They were shouting and swearing and threatening. "Tommies are here. You are *kaput!*" they said. The Frenchman went with them to visit the house, and even the storeroom where the lone American was hiding under a cloth, holding his breath. At last the Germans gave up the search and moved off. Suddenly there was a burst of fire, and a German captain fell. The Germans hunted in vain for whoever had fired.

A few hours later an American paratrooper again came to the door of Lemenuel's house. He wanted to know where his comrades were. Lemenuel told him to come in quickly, for Germans were all about. The Frenchman led the soldier hurriedly down to the cellar. Just now the farmer's wife went out to feed the poultry. Their young son Paul and their pretty fifteen-year-old daughter Pierrette went out on the doorstep. A burst of fire rang out, and Pierrette fell to the ground. Lemenuel told the newly arrived American to run out the back way, and then he went to see what had happened. When he got outside Lemenuel saw the Germans coming into the yard. He showed them his daughter who lay bleeding from bullet wounds in her abdomen. They responded with an indifferent "C'est la Guerre."

Pierrette, the gay, pretty daughter of the Lemenuels, moaned weakly, "The Boches, they have killed me." A few hours later she died.

Other D-Day missions assigned the 82nd Airborne Division had included the securing of crossings of the Merderet creek near la Fière and Chef du Pont. Here marshlands along the Merderet appeared to be especially troublesome—though the marshes are not generally as extensive as they then appeared to be. (Ten years later, one could stand on the bridge west of Chef du Pont and count nearly two hundred cattle grazing in the broad meadows on the east bank of the stream—and directly in front of the big dairy plant.) Temporary bridgeheads at la Fière and Chef du Pont could not be held against the stronger German forces which were able to form against the small bands of paratroopers holding them.

The woman who operated the café across the street from the railroad station years later recalled vividly the arrival of the paratroopers. She had gone to sleep, only to be awakened between one and two A.M. by the airborne invasion. Almost at once she guessed that American parachutists were coming. The Germans had left this area a week or so earlier, so that she felt confident of American success here. Unfortunately for the Americans, Germans returned to attack, and paratroop forces had not been dropped in such a pattern as would permit an effective build-up of a bridgehead to the west of the Merderet. The small groups holding the crossings at la Fière and Chef du Pont therefore had to give up those places for the time being.

At the end of D-Day the situation of the 82nd Airborne Division around Sainte-Mère Église remained obscure and tenuous. Apparently the beach landings had been successful, however, and the 101st Airborne Division, while somewhat scattered, had landed in much better concentrations than the 82nd. The 101st had been able to take its objectives, including Saint-Martin-de-Varreville and Pouppeville, and to secure the vital exits to these beaches which would permit the troops landing by sea to move inland. These tasks had been accomplished relatively quickly. But it was not until the next afternoon, June 7, that forces coming in from the beaches were able to link up effectively with the airborne forces at Sainte-Mère Église—and during the interval, Sainte-Mère Église was under heavy counterattack. Believing a German armored thrust to be building up, Maj. Gen. Matthew B. Ridgway, commander of the 82nd Airborne Division, was able to get word to the corps commander, Maj. Gen. J. Lawton Collins. General Collins immediately ordered a task force from the 704th Tank Battalion to proceed directly to Sainte-Mère Église. The tanks rolled into the town early in the afternoon. Alexandre Renaud recorded it as follows: "A great cry went up: 'The tanks! The route to the sea is free, the coast is ours!' They were small tanks, but for us they were beautiful; they were great. At their observation posts on the turrets, the crews looked at us, majestically as gods, powerful as giants. They were Victory; for us they were Deliverance!"

On the walls of a café on the main street of Sainte-Mère Église, a series of three colorful, impressive murals depict the liberation. One represents the night, and it pictures paratroopers dropping over the town while aircraft fly overhead and a house burns below. In the second it is daytime; the American soldiers are on the ground, and again airplanes are flying overhead. In the third American tanks are shown rolling through the streets; forces from Utah Beach have made contact and liberation is complete.

The zero marker of the Way of Liberty, in front of the town hall, is another effective daily reminder of the liberation. The heraldic emblem of Sainte-Mère Église itself, carved and painted on the outer walls of the town hall, now contains another element—figures of American paratroopers, descending under open parachutes. The official stationery also carries the parachute symbol. In the local bookstore one may find picture postcards, souvenirs of Sainte-Mère Église, which show drawings of pretty girls descending by parachute. The central square now is Place du 6 Juin, and the main street in 1960 was renamed Avenue du 505me Infanterie.

The most impressive indication of all, perhaps, of the esteem in which the American paratroopers are held is to be found in the church. As in so many towns of this area, the old stone church dominates Sainte-Mère Église, and its architecture, dating from the twelfth century, is common in this region. It is an old building, but the big stained-glass window over the main door is a new feature. The central figure in the window is a full-length picture of Mary, the mother of Jesus, holding the Christ child in her arms. On either side are figures of American paratroopers descending on Sainte-Mère Église! The window was designed by Paul Renaud, son of the mayor, who was a lad of fourteen at the time of the liberation.

Fortunately the early capture of Sainte-Mère Église spared this town the destruction from ground battles and aerial bombardment which became so general for towns throughout Normandy. It is true that German artillery, from positions in the village of Azeville to the south, kept Sainte-Mère under fire for three days (until local inhabitants discovered that the German artillery was being directed by observers in the church steeple), but the resulting damage was relatively light.

Liberation had come quickly and dramatically to Sainte-Mère Église, the first town in Western Europe to fall to Allied arms in the great liberation. It was the beginning of a series which was to run into thousands as Allied armies—often with much greater violence—drove the Germans out.

Reconstruction here was not the problem which it proved to be elsewhere. Truly, the economic dislocation which accompanied occupation and war was serious, but even that was less severe for Sainte-Mère Église than for many other communities. The loss of livestock had unfortunate consequences for this important dairy region, but still this was country where good food generally could be produced in quantity, and people usually could eat reasonably well.

A decade after liberation, Sainte-Mère Église bore few physical marks of the war which swept through and around it. Today Sainte-Mère Église is the old church, with American paratroopers immortalized in the stained-glass window. It is a group of people laughing and talking over glasses of wine as they sit in the café beside the big murals of the airborne liberation. It is the highly respected pharmacist, Alexandre Renaud, the former mayor, who goes about his work of filling prescriptions as he greets a stream of customers and friends, and it is his good wife and son, who radiate the same hospitality. Sainte-Mère Église is the restaurant down the street where local workers gather for their noon meal. It is the little dress shop which displays fashionable lace blouses and chic dresses from Paris. It is the local butcher and the bakery. It is the town hall and the school and the home for the infirm. It is personable young Dr. Jean Masselin, treating the ills of patients who come to the office in his house, or getting hurriedly into his car to bring medical care to people for miles around, and it is his attractive Parisian wife and their six children. Sainte-Mère Église is an active, thriving town of about 1,300 friendly, good humored, industrious, patriotic people. Physical scars of war have been erased, but people who lived through it will never forget the liberation, nor will inhabitants in the future, surrounded by monuments and reminders, be likely to forget it either.

Are the stories of Charles Martel, Charlemagne, William the Conqueror, and Napoleon of a completely different order of things than the campaigns and battles of 1944? Or, in years to come, will the exploits of American parachutists on the Cotentin Peninsula in 1944 rise in men's esteem to match the most daring feats of the most celebrated warriors who ever passed through the country? Probably they will; for Sainte-Mère Église, American parachutists were indeed only "a little lower than the angels."

D-Day, The Sixth of June

Tanks landing on Omaha Beach on the 6th of June

Ceremonies at Utah Beach commemorating the landing

2
Omaha Beach and Utah Beach

Omaha Beach, that stretch of sand lying before a backdrop of bluffs between Vierville-sur-Mer and Colleville-sur-Mer, prominent in 1944 as a stage for the intense action of amphibious invasion, now stands in contrasting emptiness. Then the beach was secondary to the events taking place on and around it; now it commands primary attention for itself. It is like a great theater, with vivid scenery still visible under a raised curtain, after the conclusion of a tragic drama, when all the actors and all the spectators have gone away and a few caretakers go about their tasks nonchalantly. Omaha Beach now claims for itself the dark wrecks of boat hulls and the ruins of blasted pillboxes. The thunder of gunfire, the roar of motors, and the sharp exchanges of agitated voices all have given way to the soft breaking of the waves upon the sand. Still the bluffs attract a certain bit of the respect that was theirs when they provided sites for hostile observers and gun emplacements. On a hillside near the east side of the site of the landings, a monument commands the whole beach. It is the monument of the 5th Engineer Special Brigade—one of the units which shuttled back and forth with amphibious trucks (DUKW'S) and landing craft to deliver supplies from ships to shore. The monument's foundation is a concrete pillbox which commanded the beach on D-Day.

D-Day, The Sixth of June

Down the beach to the west, down the road from Saint Laurent-sur-Mer near the little settlement known as Les Moulins, stands a French monument to the American soldiers who fought on this beach. It is not far from that part of the beach designated "Dog Green" on D-Day—where Company A of the 116th Infantry suffered nearly 75 per cent casualties, including virtually all the officers and noncommissioned officers, in crossing the 150 yards of open beach toward the draw which was to serve as their exit.

On the bluff is the cemetery, a spot of solemn beauty overlooking the sea. Officially this now is designated the American Normandy Cemetery, but it still is referred to here as the St. Laurent Cemetery (although it actually is closer to Colleville than it is to St. Laurent). Here are 9,385 graves, each marked by a cross or a star of David carved in Italy of Carrara marble. The gleaming white crosses, "row on row," stand out sharply against the rich green grass on which they rest.

A monumental central mall, laid out like a formal garden, divides the fields of crosses. Workmen still are busy tending the grounds, but major construction is finished, so that the scene impresses its dignity and beauty on all who visit there. On the mall, near the east end, are the "Garden of the Missing;" then a big semicircular memorial colonnade with huge maps showing the campaigns in Normandy and into Germany; a circular court, paved in stone and bordered by dark evergreen shrubs; a rectangular reflecting pool, and then a long rectangular court of grass leading to a small stone chapel. The chapel stands near the center of the four sections into which the burial grounds are divided. Two high flagpoles, each flying the Stars and Stripes, flank the mall.

This inscription is carved on the frieze of the memorial colonnade:

THIS EMBATTLED SHORE, PORTAL OF FREEDOM, IS FOREVER HALLOWED BY THE IDEALS THE VALOR AND THE SACRIFICES OF OUR FELLOW COUNTRYMEN

As one walks by the rows of crosses, he may find himself looking for names of soldiers he knew or otherwise have some association for him. There is Private First Class Flager of Michigan, who died on this beach on D-Day. There is another, Private Murray of Pennsylvania. There are the names of other men who were killed on D-Day over near Sainte-Mère Église, men of the 82nd and 101st Airborne Divisions, and pilots of troop carrier groups—names such as Schinkveth, Boehm, Smith, Doerges, Shipley, Rivas, Bruno. Here is the grave of Technical Sergeant Richard H. Weiser of Nebraska, a member of the 134th Infantry who was killed on July 17 as his unit approached Saint-Lô. And rather frequently one notices a marker with the inscription, "Here rests in honored glory a comrade in arms known but to God."

The chapel is a small, circular building. A series of stone columns goes all the way around, enclosing a small room containing a black marble altar. In the ceiling of the dome is a mosaic depicting a soldier, a ship, an airplane, and angelic figures representing the spirit of liberty, against a background of sky blue. Outside, on the frieze, another carved inscription appears:

THESE ENDURED ALL AND GAVE ALL THAT JUSTICE AMONG NATIONS MIGHT PREVAIL AND THAT MANKIND MIGHT ENJOY FREEDOM AND INHERIT PEACE

One wonders, do these noble expressions carry real meaning, or do they represent the hollow sentiments of someone who had to put up a tribute which would be more or less reassuring to visitors who would come here questioning why all this sacrifice had to be? Or, perhaps people too anxious to dismiss such expressions are looking for ways to ease their own responsibilities. If those words are to have any meaning at all they must apply to the living no less than to the dead. Soldiers seldom express themselves in such language. As cold, seasick, nervous men huddled together in their landing craft, approaching this beach on June 6, 1944, it is quite doubtful whether many of them were thinking, in any precise way, about such abstract sentiments as patriotism, liberty, or justice. Most of them simply felt that here was a job that had to be done, and it had fallen to them to do it, and they wondered how long it would take to get it over, and they wondered with some apprehension what awaited them on the shore. They were sure that many of their number would be killed within a few hours, yet most probably did not seriously think of themselves as really likely to share such a fate. At the same time there probably was some very deep unexpressed feeling, a vague feeling about the defense of their homeland and loved ones, and perhaps some undefined conviction that they were sailing against injustice and tyranny—a basis which, with the discipline of training and the social pressure of the comrades around them, made it possible to face the ordeal which they knew lay ahead. But such sentiments seldom became articulate. Instead there was almost complete preoccupation with things going on outside, with attention to equipment, to small talk and banter, to nervous buffoonery, and then complete silence except for the waves and the boats.

Farms and villages in the beachhead area still bear scars of war, though most damaged buildings have been restored and life goes on much as before. Though directly in the path of the D-Day attack, Saint Laurent and Colleville escaped serious damage. Here and there the ruins of a war-torn building may be found, now and then a new wall testifies to the repair of war damage and the pock-marks of machine gun and rifle bullets remain on the sides of some of the buildings. All the church steeples are new, for the old ones were victims of the highly accurate naval gunfire which sought the German observation posts on D-Day. Vierville suffered more serious damage than Saint Laurent or Colleville, but even there the damage was nothing like the general destruction that one finds in places like Caen or Saint-

Lô. Possibly those little towns of Vierville, Saint Laurent, and Colleville owe their survival to the bad weather on the morning of D-Day which restricted Allied air support, and to the fact of their very location so close to the beach that they fell into American hands on D-Day and the day after.

American influence persists in this area—and not always in the most complimentary terms. Years later, a group of workers along the road between Colleville and the cemetery paused briefly to discuss their recollections of the "debarquement." One of them was able to speak a little English, and he was anxious to try it out. Curiously he introduced almost every phrase with, "Holy Christ!" Other professions of profanity and obscenity made up a sizable part of his English vocabulary. Clearly, he resorted to such language profusely because otherwise he would have been able to speak hardly any English at all. It turned out that he was a boy of thirteen, living on a farm east of Colleville, when the invasion came. Attracted to the American soldiers, he attached himself to one of the companies and won a permanent assignment to kitchen police. He had learned his English in a G.I. kitchen.

These youthful French volunteers later were to be found in many American units going across France. They had no authorization, but if they appeared to be without a family in the vicinity, the G.I.'s were glad to have them come along to do all kinds of odd jobs. Often they were picked up and carried along by infantry companies or battalions without any reference to higher headquarters. A boy of about fourteen joined the 3rd

Battalion, 134th Infantry, during the "race across France" east of Orléans. The men had fitted him out with some ill-fitting clothes and a steel helmet. During a temporary pause in the pursuit, when personal neatness was being re-emphasized again, the division commander descended on the battalion for a surprise visit. The first thing he saw when he entered the partially ruined building which was serving as a command post was the French boy. There he stood in his sloppy uniform, without leggings or boots, wearing a civilian belt and knapsack, shirt tail out, peering out from under that big steel helmet like a lookout in a pillbox. The general stopped in his tracks, spun around, and in the most bellicose language demanded from the lad an explanation for such unmilitary behavior. The boy had not been around long enough to pick up even the most common terms of profanity, so that he had not the slightest idea of what was happening; nor had he learned to be impressed by stars. He stood there in amazed silence. Then he gave one of those infuriating shrugs of the shoulders and turning down of the lips by which the French signify complete lack of comprehension and concern, and turned and walked away. This was the signal for everyone who could to disappear. A quick explanation of the boy's status seemed to appease the general partially, but it probably also was the termination of effective use of this kind of special service personnel in the division.

Along the road just outside Saint Laurent an old man cutting grass with a sickle recalled how he had been here on D-Day. He was living in the same house, but in 1944 he had some Germans as uninvited guests. No warning, of course, could be given to the civilian population (other than the tips to Resistance leaders via BBC broadcasts) before the beach assault, so that it all was as much a surprise to the local inhabitants as to the Germans. The old farmer told of the excitement of D-Day, and how his house was hit by shell fire, but not totally destroyed.

Several other small towns lie along the main coastal highway, the road running in this sector from Bayeux to Isigny, paralleling the Vierville-Saint Laurent-Colleville road two to four miles further inland. These towns include Mosles, Formigny, Longueville, and la Cambe. Like those nearer the sea, these towns too escaped any general destruction. Formigny stands at the junction of roads leading to Vierville and Saint Laurent, and the Germans fought for it so bitterly that American units were not able to enter until the morning of June 8. Yet this defense was in the fields in front of the town, and not so much in the town itself. Once the defense was broken, the Germans withdrew on through the town to take up positions again some three kilometers to the south. As a result the town was spared heavy destruction.

It seems incredible, in this age of radio, radar, high-speed aircraft, and fast patrol boats, that an invasion the size of that of the Allies could have come across the English Channel and caught a supposedly alert German army by surprise. Yet that is what happened. A fortuitous combination of circumstances resulted in a surprise more complete than anything for which Allied leaders ever dared hope.

In planning for the invasion of England in 1940 (Operation Sea Lion), German officers had arrived at the same conclusion as had the British and Americans in determining the timing of the most favorable conditions for a cross-channel attack. Both had decided that landings should take place on the beaches about three hours after low tide, at early dawn, though with enough daylight to permit naval and air bombardment of coastal defenses in advance, and with a half-moon to give some light for the handling of the invasion fleet during a crossing of the channel at night. These conditions occurred together only for a period of three days once a month. During June, the fifth was the beginning of this three-day period. It should have been clear to the Germans, on the basis of their own planning, that the period of June 5-7 would be an especially dangerous one. Yet the weather and other factors operated against German vigilance, and an Allied fleet of more than six thousand ships was able to leave the ports of southern England in broad daylight and then proceed during the night to within a few miles of the French coast without any interruption and without the Germans knowing about it.

German intelligence had been able to get accurate information about the strength and disposition of forces in southern England. Through the activities of a private operative in Turkey, Berlin even had learned the date for D-Day. The Luftwaffe had been able to continue aerial reconnaissance, including photography, over the ports of southern England up to May 24. Analyzing the results of this reconnaissance, the German Naval Command in Paris concluded that the Allies had not yet assembled enough ships to carry the anticipated invasion. On June 4 the Naval Command had reported to the Luftwaffe Special Command, "At the present moment, no immediate major invasion is to be expected."

Perhaps the most important element contributing to the surprise was the one which worried Allied leaders the most—the weather. The same stormy weather which caused General Eisenhower to postpone the invasion twenty-four hours also caused German security forces to relax their watch. Steaming through the heavy seas then running in the English Channel, the Allied invasion fleet encountered no dreaded mines, no reconnaissance or attack aircraft, and no naval outposts —until it was so close to the French coast that warnings could not be relayed to major coastal defense units before Allied armies were hitting the beaches in full force.

Because of Allied air superiority and unfavorable weather, the German Third Air Force, charged with reconnaissance over the Channel and with anti-invasion bombing of the English coast, had been unable to carry out its mission. No reconnaissance planes were covering the Channel on the night of June 5-6, even though this was, except for the unfavorable weather, what could have been considered a critical period. The naval forces also failed to go out on that fateful night. Moreover the Allied air forces in their pre-invasion bombing had succeeded in destroying much of the radar net and the communications system which the Germans had carefully set up along the French coast.

The German radio listening service did pick up a number of clues suggesting that invasion was imminent —broadcasts of the BBC to the French Resistance, continuous weather reports to major American combat units, the concentration of large formations of aircraft in the area north of London. All this was enough to move Field Marshal Gerd von Rundstedt, the German commander in chief in the west, to order an alert for all coastal sectors in the Fifteenth Army—in the Pas de Calais region. The Seventh Army, in Normandy, was not alerted until 1:30 A.M., and by this time, Allied parachute units were already landing. After receiving reports at 2:15 of the airborne landings, von Rundstedt within fifteen minutes issued orders to move the 12th SS Panzer Division forward toward Lisieux, and for the Panzer Training Division, then northwest of Orléans, to prepare to move. At this point the Wehrmacht High Command (OKW) intervened to order both panzer divisions to remain in place. Reports sent back by light naval forces sent out to meet a concentration of Allied vessels which had been picked up on a German radar screen at Port-en-Bessin shortly after three A.M., further convinced von Rundstedt that a major landing was in the making. But further appeals to the High Command for release of the panzer divisions at that time were to no avail.

Hitler, then at Obersalzburg, was permitted to sleep undisturbed. He did not learn of the attack until the regular noon conference with his staff.

The High Command did not release the 12th SS Panzer Division until early afternoon on June 6. By this time Allied air domination had become so complete that it was not possible to move major units until nightfall. The result was that the movement of this division was delayed for almost a whole day—the critical first twenty-four hours during which Field Marshal Rommel had insisted all along the battle would be won or lost.

After some preliminary planning during the previous year, Hitler had decreed in March 1942 that defenses of the European coast be organized in such a way that any invasion could be beaten at or near the water's edge.

The following summer he had called for the construction of bomb-proof gun emplacements and concrete pillboxes which would provide interlocking bands of machine-gun fire across beaches all along the coast in front of this great "Atlantic Wall" which, when finished, would comprise a new "Siegfried Line" of 15,000 concrete strong-points to be garrisoned by 300,000 troops. Material shortages and lack of labor had slowed the work, so that it never approached the completeness which Hitler had envisioned.

As it developed, the disposition of German troops represented something of a compromise between two divergent views on the best way to defend the French coast. Von Rundstedt held that the only way to defeat the expected Allied invasion was to defend the coast relatively lightly, and to concentrate in the interior sizable mobile reserves which could counterattack to throw the enemy back into the sea after the place and strength of the landing was made known. The Germans were not strong enough to defend everywhere, he thought, so that if they did not hold out major reserves for counterattack, they would not be able to hold anywhere. The General Staff upheld Von Rundstedt in this view. Rommel insisted, on the other hand, that the Germans' only hope for repelling the invasion was to defeat it on the beaches. He believed that the issue would be decided in the first twenty-four to forty-eight hours. Hitler shared the view of Rommel.

Rommel's view did not prevail altogether, but the defensive organization tended to be in that direction. Even Rommel did not plan to put every man in a blockhouse or trench overlooking the beaches, but he wanted to maintain mobile reserves close to the front line where they would be available for local counterattacks within the critical first twenty-four hours. He was only partially successful in gaining his way.

Rommel opposed the von Rundstedt notion of a mobile defense, not on any doctrinaire grounds, but on the basis of practical experience. He saw that the Allies would be weakest at the moment of their landing, when units and weapons could not be controlled as effectively as after reorganization and movement inland. Here the English Channel afforded the greatest natural obstacle that could be found, and the beaches and bluffs and the draws leading up from the beaches provided ideal sites for additional obstacles and for gun emplacements and other defensive works. But what seemed to impress Rommel more than anything else was the Allied command of the air. His experience against Allied air superiority in North Africa had convinced him that reserves held out in the interior would not be able to move. It was not a question, as he saw it, of which type of defense was preferable; it was a question of which was possible. If major troop movements were to be made impossible by the Allied air forces, then there was no alternative to deploying the troops at or near the beaches. With neither naval superiority nor air superiority, the Germans had two strikes against them from the very outset.

But if the prepared defenses along the Normandy coast were much weaker than plans had called for, and much weaker, even, than Allied leaders had thought, the men who went ashore on Omaha Beach that June 6 found them formidable enough. The concrete bunkers and casemates were sufficiently sturdy, and in particular places sufficiently numerous to constitute very serious hazards for any invader.

In the strongly defended sectors the concrete pillboxes and shelters, considered "bombproof," had walls and tops of a standard thickness of six feet, six inches. Some of them were ten feet or more thick. In less strongly defended areas, three-foot-three-inch "splinter-proof" pillboxes and shelters had to do. In the areas selected for the American assault, sixteen coastal batteries of four to six guns each were in position to fire.

Already postponed in its sailing twenty-four hours because of bad weather, the Allied invasion fleet was riding through heavy seas, nearing the coast of Normandy, when D-Day broke gray and cool over the English Channel. Some six thousand ships and smaller craft here comprised the greatest invasion fleet of all time. Assault waves were scheduled to hit Omaha Beach at 6:45 A.M. The ships had left the English ports (for the second time) early on June 5. By about 2:30 A.M. on the sixth day they were arriving at the assembly areas about seven miles off the coast. Soon the assault troops began unloading from transport ships into the smaller landing craft which would carry them to the shore. About 5:30 the assault craft began moving toward the beach, while naval units took up formations to support the landings by gunfire. Some sporadic firing from German coastal batteries began about five minutes later, and just fifteen minutes after that the Allied battleships, cruisers, and destroyers opened up their thunderous preparatory fires on the beaches and bluffs.

Except for the bad weather, the channel crossing had, up to this point, been quiet. Winds were reaching a velocity as high as twenty-five miles an hour, and waves as high as six feet were running in channel. The sky was gray, and low-hanging clouds made air support difficult. Yet for the operation as a whole the weather undoubtedly had contributed a great deal to the complacency and ineffective actions of German security units.

So far, it has been said, all had gone well. But soon after the landing craft began their seven-to-ten mile run to the beach, several things began to go wrong. The heavy seas were too much for a number of the landing craft, and at least ten of them, loaded with infantry, were swamped on the way in. Much hope had been placed in some duplex-drive amphibious tanks which were being counted on to land armored support for assault units on the beach. Twenty-nine of these tanks were launched about six thousand yards off the shore, but they began to sink almost at once. Only two of the tanks were able to "swim" to the shore, and three others arrived only because the LCT (landing craft, tank) carrying them had been unable to lower its ramp at sea, and so carried them all the way in. Moreover the field artillery which was being counted upon to support the infantry attacks inland failed to reach the shore in effective numbers.

As the landing craft moved in close to the beach, the men in some of them, waiting to wade ashore, were disheartened by the splatter of machine-gun bullets against the steel ramps of the craft. Some of the soldiers, loaded with heavy combat equipment, went over the side, and in some cases they dropped into water over their heads. Others dashed down the ramp through a hail of bullets to seek refuge in the deep water behind some of Rommel's exposed beach obstacles. A number of men fell wounded on the beach, and lay helplessly to be drowned in the rising tide. Some "froze" under the heavy fire at the water's edge, and ultimately crawled in with the tide.

Generally those who were able to keep moving—those who hurried, as best they could, resolutely through the fire to the bluffs or an intervening sea wall—fared better.

Other difficulties developed in effecting the landing. Poor visibility and a west-east current along the beach led to some errors in landing. The errors were not great, but they did lead to confusion, to scattering of some units, and in some cases to dangerous bunching of men. Mislandings, together with the heavy German fire, made reorganization of units on the beach virtually impossible.

Carefully laid plans for the landing of specific units at specific spots on the beach, and close time schedules to govern the landings of reinforcements, quickly went awry. The arrival of succeeding waves on the beaches before the first had cleared only confounded the confusion. Wounded and dead men lay all along the beach, and other men lay motionless, pinned down by the heavy fire, to become mingled with men of other units landing after them. Yet when it seemed that surely the whole effort must bog down, a few determined leaders—officers and enlisted men—by the very force of their personalities picked up small collections of men and began to move inland up the draws and slopes.

When such detailed plans as those which had been drawn for the assault on Omaha Beach go astray, the question naturally arises whether there was any value in making such plans. The one thing most certain among the uncertainties of an attack of this kind is that the operation will not go according to the detailed plans. In a broader sense, one may find some merit in thorough battle planning simply from the fact that this planning involves a careful consideration of all the factors involved. When some new factor is introduced and all the plans have to be thrown out, adjustment to the new situation nevertheless comes about more easily and with greater assurance simply because those concerned already have considered carefully all the other elements, and they are familiar with the basic data. However, in the stricter sense of mapping detailed plans for each boatload and each platoon of the assaulting forces, such as had been done for the Omaha Beach force, "prior planning" may actually work to the disadvantage of the effort. In this case the plan left little place for flexibility and improvisation, although it is improvisation which generally pays off in this kind of operation. Most of the assault units here ran into very heavy fire and suffered serious casualties and confusion. Detailed briefings on identification of landmarks and beach exits were of little avail, for most of the units did not land where they were supposed to anyway. One wonders whether the confusion and the casualties could have been any greater without any small-unit plans at all. It is conceivable that a deliberate policy of flexibility and improvisation might have accomplished more at much less cost.

For instance, most of the small units of the assault wave immediately encountered strong resistance on the beaches. The one notable exception to this was the fortuitous landing of four boat sections of Companies E

Roads Without Birds

and F of the 16th Infantry. They landed some distance to the east of the place designated and a good distance from other elements of the same regiment. They hit a blind spot in the German defenses, and those men were able to get across the open beach with only two casualties. But for a long while no one else was in a position to take advantage of this situation. Instead, other boatloads continued to land in the face of withering fire and to become intermingled with units already pinned down. Might it not have been practical to send patrol boats carrying infantry patrols in advance to seek out soft spots in the defense? Then when an undefended spot had been found, signals could be hoisted at the base of the bluff and radio messages sent back to direct succeeding waves to pour ashore where they could exploit the enemy's weakness. Inland objectives could be given the company commanders after they were already on the way in, or even after they had landed and reorganized. Naval guns or aircraft might even mark beaches and inland objectives with colored smoke, after the landing craft already were underway.

As it was, movement off the beaches did not even begin for over an hour after the first landings. In a critical hour between 10:30 and 11:30 close-supporting naval fire became more effective, and assaulting infantry forced a penetration of some of the defenses. By noon it seemed that the beachhead would be held—barring a strong counterattack—but progress was slow throughout the day. By the end of the day most of the immediate defense areas had been overcome, Vierville-sur-Mer and Saint Laurent-sur-Mer had been taken, and though the Germans still held Colleville-sur-Mer, sizable American forces virtually surrounded it. Though defenses in the area had not been completed in the way Rommel had hoped, the effectiveness there of the effort in breaking up the assaulting units suggested that Rommel's system of defense had much to recommend it. If Rommel had had the panzer division that he wanted for counterattack, it might have made a big difference, at least for the time being.

One further factor that had been helpful for the Americans was the British and Canadian assaults which had been going on simultaneously on the beaches a few miles to the east of Omaha designated "Juno," "Gold," and "Sword." The British had broken through the coastal defenses in several places, so that the Germans did not dare shift any defense units or local reserves from the Caen area to the American zone.

Meanwhile, the landings on Utah Beach on the Cotentin Peninsula, had been proceeding more smoothly. There, errors in landing had played a more decisive, and more fortunate, role than on Omaha Beach.

This peninsula often had been the site of invasion before. In 1106 Henry I of England landed at Barfleur to march against his brother, the Duke of Normandy; Edward III landed near there in 1346 with the army which later won fame at the Battle of Crécy; the English seized Cherbourg in 1418; the Comte de Montgomery, the Huguenot leader who had taken refuge in England, landed at La Hougue at the head of an ill-fated English army of five thousand men in 1574; men from an English fleet again seized Cherbourg in 1758. But no earlier invasion could compare with that of 1944 either in magnitude or in the impact which it had on the whole population.

On Utah Beach the 8th Infantry of the 4th Division (with the 3rd Battalion of the 22nd Infantry attached), under the command of Colonel James A. Van Fleet, led the way. H-hour was 6:25 A.M.—ten minutes earlier than Omaha. Here the waters were more sheltered by the Cotentin Peninsula than at the other landing sites, and the landing craft moved in toward the shore with little difficulty.

Accompanying the first wave of the 4th Division's assault forces on Utah Beach was Brigadier General Theodore Roosevelt, colorful son of the illustrious first President Roosevelt. He had begged General Omar Bradley for an assignment with the invasion—after already surviving landings in North Africa, Sicily, Italy, and Corsica—and General Bradley had decided that the greatest service which Roosevelt could perform on D-Day would be to go in with the leading wave of this untried division to steady the men under fire on the beaches. Among the first men to reach the Beach was General Roosevelt. To their surprise, the men of these leading units had reached land without arousing serious German counter-fire. The General flattened himself on the sand, in the midst of a group of soldiers, and surveyed the land ahead with his binoculars. "By Jove!" he exclaimed, as he crawled up a low sand dune for a better look.

One of the soldiers near him sang out, "My God! We're in France!"

But Roosevelt was not listening. Half to himself, and half to his aide, he muttered, "We've missed it. There has been a mistake. We are in the wrong place!" Then he started swearing while he considered quickly what ought to be done. On the one hand was the practical impossibility of redirecting the whole invasion to the place where they were supposed to land, two thousand yards up the coast. On the other hand he recognized the difficulties involved in trying to find other exits from the beach across the inundated swampland, or of trying to find the causeways that the paratroopers were supposed to be securing opposite the landing site designated in the plans. Roosevelt noticed a causeway leading through the marshes directly ahead. Immediately deciding that the only thing to do now was to go for it, he called the two battalion commanders who had landed with the assault wave, and told them to do just that. Some intervening concrete blockhouses were knocked out, and the 4th Division was on its way inland.

Apparently coastal landmarks had become obscured in the smoke of the preliminary naval gunfire, and for this and other reasons such as coastal current, the assault waves hit the beach some two thousand yards to the south, that is, to the left, of the intended place. Surprisingly enough, men going ashore on Utah Beach found little German resistance. Leading companies quickly overcame the few pillboxes and the small German garrisons holding field fortifications near the beach exits. But when a battalion moved up the beach to the north to extend the beachhead, it ran into strong resistance—at the place where the landing was *supposed* to have come!

Although casualties on Utah Beach were light and the landings relatively easy, there were still casualties. Death and pain still were present. Some of the landing craft hit mines and sank. German artillery and machine-gun fire was sporadic, but that made it no less fatal for the soldiers it happened to hit. As the boats carrying men of the 2nd Battalion, 8th Infantry, approached the shore, some of them came under machine-gun fire. Officers led the way in jumping over the sides into the waist-deep water. Weapons held high over their heads, the men waded in. But then machine-gun fire found some of them again. Some fell dead in the water; others fell wounded, and drowned in the surf. Other men reacted with the natural tendency to stop and get down. Lieutenants shouted to them to keep moving. Some of them carried satchel charges which would be used to blow up the pillboxes ahead, but first they had to reach them. It is always easy to forget the old rule, "Move forward out of artillery fire," and officers had to keep urging them on. One young lieutenant got some of his men to shore, but others held back. He went back to them, shouting, "For God's sake, if you want to live, move forward!" And just at that moment a German artillery shell burst beside him and cut through his head.

No bluffs dominated Utah Beach, such as those at Omaha. Only a sea wall and some low sand dunes stood between the beach and the fields beyond. The greatest obstacles were the lowlands which had been flooded so that troop movements were restricted to the roads across them. Paratroopers of the 101st Airborne Division had seized the causeways through the inundated areas, and units of the 4th Division hurried across them. Within two to three hours the beach area had been cleared and landings of reinforcements had become virtually routine.

As scores of bombs fell around his house near the coast during the pre-invasion bombardment, Pierre Lenourry had more reason than the danger of the bombs to be in a cold sweat. His wife had just given birth to a baby girl. A neighbor woman had been in earlier to help, but now she had gone. Pierre felt an awful helplessness as bombs shook the house violently, and he crawled from under an overturned wardrobe which had pinned him down momentarily, and found broken stones scattered over his wife's bed and over the beds of two other children, four and two, who slept peacefully through the thunderous bombardment. He looked at his wife, pale and weak from loss of blood, and then at the new baby, crying feebly in a baby carriage near its mother. It was impossible to call a doctor or even neighbors. They would just have to wait here as best they could. At last daylight came and Pierre stepped outside to see if he could find some help. He ran directly into some American soldiers who had just come ashore. Wary of who were their friends, they pointed their rifles at him. He raised his hands and shouted "Français, Français!"

Then he began telling them about his wife. But they did not understand him. They took him along until he met some other soldiers, but they paid no attention to him either. Much to his consternation he soon found himself behind barbed wire with German prisoners on the beach. He chafed there for an hour, and then a soldier took him to an officer for a long interrogation, and back he went to the barbed wire. Hours passed, while his worries about his family and anger at being held prisoner with the "Boches" grew. Presently he was surprised at the arrival of half a dozen of his friends and neighbors—also to be confined as prisoners! In the evening they were put aboard a boat, where they faced further interrogation and searching. At high tide they were transferred to a cargo ship. For four days they were passed around from one ship to another, and then on June 10 they wound up in England. There Pierre and his neighbors had to remain for five weeks before he could get back to see how his family was. Fortunately he found his wife and all three children well. During the celebration of the tenth anniversary of the D-Day landings, the little girl born in the midst of the bombardment near Utah Beach was celebrating her tenth birthday.

Colonel Edson D. Raff arrived on the beach late in the afternoon of D-Day with elements of the 82nd Airborne Division's "seaborne tail." These included some glider infantrymen and a company of tanks. His job was to get these tanks through to the 82nd, now fighting near Sainte-Mère Église, and in addition to clear glider landing areas north of the village of Les

Forges (south and southeast of Sainte-Mère Église) where glider artillery was scheduled to land that evening. This was a novel tactical use of airborne forces. Generally it was assumed that airborne forces would go into an area and hold a position to clear the way for a link-up with surface forces. But in this case units had been sent in by sea to secure an area for airborne troops to land. It might have been far simpler to send the airborne artillery in by sea in the first place. All it had to do was to get within range and establish communications in order to give effective artillery support. Artillery did not have to be linked up with the parent unit on the ground, it could just as well have moved in behind units of the 4th Division. But the schedule had been set up, and apparently it had to be followed through come hell or high water. And the selected landing sites were at the very place where important German troop concentrations now were to be found. Colonel Raff made several efforts to break through, but after the loss of three tanks, gave up the effort. But no word went out to the glider units scheduled to land here. Precisely on schedule, at 7:00 P.M., the tow planes roared in low over the area, and about sixty gliders cut loose to go down into a storm of German machine-gun and anti-aircraft fire. Many crashed, and others were captured as soon as they landed. The artillerymen and pilots who survived the landings and escaped capture joined Colonel Raff's force to form a makeshift defense for the night.

On Utah Beach itself casualties on D-Day had been relatively light. The total for the whole 4th Division

Roads Without Birds

were fewer than two hundred—not many more than those suffered by two companies in the first forty-five minutes on Omaha Beach. Sainte Marie du Mont had been taken quickly and there began an argument which still goes on—whether Sainte-Mère Église, liberated by the 82nd Airborne Division but not yet linked up with the beachhead, or Sainte Marie du Mont, liberated by the sea landing forces, should be honored as the first French town to be liberated in this great invasion.

With the fall of Carentan on June 12, the Allies held a consolidated beachhead seven to ten miles deep, extending from Quineville, on the Cotentin Peninsula, about seventy miles, to the east bank of the Orne River. Already, in the first six days of the operation, 326,547 men, 54,186 vehicles, and 104,428 tons of supplies had been brought in over these beaches.

Though German resistance in the days ahead grew stronger, and obviously many days of bitter fighting through the difficult hedgerow country lay ahead, complete Allied victory now was a matter of time and casualties—costly but certain. In spite of underdeveloped defensive works and the complete tactical surprise which the Allies had achieved, they found that German resistance could not be overcome easily. Almost immediately the Allied time schedule was upset. The beachheads were supposed to be consolidated, according to plans, on D-Day; that did not come about until six days later. Cherbourg was supposed to be taken by D plus 15 (earlier plans had indicated that it should be taken in a week); the peninsula was not cut until June 18 (D plus 12), though three divisions launched a strong attack to the north early the next morning, and the port city fell on June 26. This was only five days behind the tentative schedule, but it was an important five days. A violent four-day storm which struck the beach areas on June 19 had left Omaha and Utah beaches, as well as the British beaches, strewn with wreckage. Artificial harbors and landing craft were disabled and over-the-beach supply operations had to be virtually suspended. This had made all the more urgent the capture of a major port, though as it turned out the Cherbourg port facilities had been so badly demolished that the port could not be put into operation until July 19, and its full capacity was not restored until October. Sainte-Lô, according to original plans, was scheduled to fall to V Corps by about D plus 9; the capture of that town came on July 18, after six weeks of heavy fighting through the hedgerows. Caen was a D-Day objective for the British, but it was not finally cleared of German defenders until July 10.

During the critical first six weeks of battle in Normandy, the Germans fought tenaciously, but without the reserves they needed to make an effective counterattack. Fortunately for the Allies, the German Fifteenth Army during this whole period remained pinned down in the Pas de Calais, northeast of the Seine River, because the German commanders feared that the Allies planned another landing in that area. The Allies were at pains to encourage this miscalculation and by the time the Germans finally were convinced that the landings were to be confined to Normandy, it was too late to shift the troops necessary to seal off the beachhead.

Here another decisive factor again came into the picture—Allied tactical air superiority. This above everything else limited the troop movements that could be made, once a decision to do so was taken. It was this which had moved Rommel to insist on a static defense at the water line. In his report as Supreme Commander of the Allied Expeditionary Forces, General Eisenhower had some strong criticisms for Rommel's defensive policy. Eisenhower reported as follows:

> Meanwhile, the enemy found himself in a dilemma. He had pinned his faith on Rommel's policy of concentrating upon the beach defenses, and when they failed to prevent the establishment of the Allied beachheads, he lacked any alternative means of combating the threat offered. Rommel's confidence in his mines and concrete was indeed to have disastrous results for the German Army. There being no system of defense in depth, when the beaches were forced the enemy lost the initiative and never subsequently succeeded in regaining it. The hand of von Rundstedt, endeavoring to remedy the errors of his lieutenant, became apparent after the first 2 or 3 weeks of the campaign, when desperate attempts were made to form a mobile armored striking force in reserve; but it was too late.

But later in the same report, Eisenhower suggested how right Rommel was—right in assuming that the invasion would have to be defeated on the beaches, because Allied air superiority would not permit the movement of strong reserves rapidly enough to make decisive counterattacks. When the Allied troops hit the beaches of Normandy, only two bridges over the Seine below Paris remained intact. By July 20 it was reported that "there were no rail bridges left standing nor any rail line uninterrupted in the area bounded by the Loire River, the Seine River and the Paris-Orléans gap." It took the German 275th Infantry Division a week to travel the 150 miles from Fougères to the front. Two panzer divisions, shifting from the east, traveled from Poland to France in the same time it took them to move from eastern France to Normandy. Men of a German air force unit left The Hague by train on June 18 and, after a circuitous tour through Holland, Belgium, the Rhineland, and eastern France, were unable to reach the battle area until July 3.

The Normandy beachhead was won at a high cost in blood, but casualties were rather less than had been feared and considerably less than the United States Army had suffered on a number of earlier occasions. American losses on D-Day totaled approximately 4,700, including about 1,235 killed and the remainder wounded and missing. The two airborne divisions suffered 2,500 of these casualties and the V Corps, which landed on Omaha Beach, suffered about 2,000 killed, wounded, and missing. (Losses of the Union Army at Antietam in the Civil War on the single day of September 17, 1862, amounted to 12,410—2,108 killed, 9,549 wounded, 753 missing.) In the first eleven days of battle in Normandy, June 6 through June 16, total American casualties rose to 3,282 killed and 12,600 wounded. (Serious as these casualties were, it might be noted again that in *three* days of battle at Gettysburg the Union casualties alone totaled some 23,000—3,072 killed, 14,497 wounded, 5,434 missing, and again in the Meuse-Argonne offensive in World War I, Americans suffered an *average* of over 17,000 casualties a *week* for seven weeks.)

During 1954, all France joined in the celebration of two anniversaries—the fortieth anniversary of the battle of the Marne and the tenth anniversary of the Liberation. Everywhere posters were to be found calling attention to the celebration. A common poster was one showing the white silhouette of the traditional rooster emblem of France on a background of bright red and blue, and within the white area a church standing on a green meadowland; the caption was: "One Country, Two Anniversaries."

The National Committee of the Two Anniversaries, sponsored by the War Veterans Ministry, issued a folder recalling events of the wars and showing a map of France with the date for the traditional celebration of the liberation of each major city. The folder opened first to a letter from President René Coty, flanked by a small reproduction of the general order for mobilization for August 2, 1914. The president's letter was as follows:

> If history is the memory of peoples, as Foch liked to say, the commemoration of their great

national hours is imposed by conscience as well as by sentiment. This year bids us to celebrate at the same time the fortieth anniversary of the Battle of the Marne and the tenth anniversary of our Liberation.

It is good that in each town and village of France and the French Union all the citizens, who owe their freedom to the sacrifices of their fathers and brothers, commune in the same fervor. Our thoughts go toward those who, faithful to Joffre's order of the day, "Be killed in place rather than fall back," and toward their juniors who, in the night of oppression, dared, sometimes at the price of martyrdom, to be the advance guard of the victorious Allied Army.

To all those soldiers, to those heroes of liberty, the Nation will express, in the communion of festivals, its recognition and fidelity.

On the other side was a reproduction of a bill containing the message which General Charles de Gaulle broadcast from London in 1940, which began, "France has lost a battle! But France has not lost the war!"

A drawing on the anniversary folder depicts the famous taxicab caravan that rushed reinforcements from Paris to the front in the critical battle of the Marne. Photographs recall outstanding French contributions to victory in World War II, episodes which often have escaped the attention of American accounts of the liberation of France. A picture of July 1940 shows General de Gaulle reviewing Free French forces in London; of the eleven volunteers who can be identified in the photograph, ten were killed later in the battles for liberation. A photograph of August 1940 shows Éboué, the fabulous colored governor of Tchad, in Equatorial Africa, who remained steadfastly loyal to the Free French. Another shows troops of the 1st Free French Division in action at Bir Hakeim, on the Western Desert in the spring of 1942; here 3,600 volunteers of this division under General Pierre Joseph Koenig, held off the assaults of two German armored divisions for two weeks—"They lost 800 of their men, but Rommel did not get to Suez." Another shows Free French forces of the expeditionary corps which fought in Italy under Marshal Alphonse Pierre Juin. Then there is a picture showing a contingent of the *Maquis* marching through the village of Oyonnax, where they descended from the mountains to display the French tricolor on Armistice Day, 1943. Another shows a crowded invasion beach of Normandy in June 1944, the beginning of the liberation, in this case a British sector, Gold Beach, near Arromanches-les-Bains. Another picture shows the arrival of General Jacques Leclerc and his 2nd French Armored Division in Paris in August 1944, and another shows troops of the First French Army, under General De Lattre de Tassigny, marching through the snow in Alsace, toward Belfort, during the period December 1944 to January 1945. Then there is a picture of Jean Moulin, founder of the National Council of the Resistance, and leader of the Resistance until his arrest and execution in 1943.

The tenth anniversary of the *debarquement* was the occasion for celebrations throughout Normandy.

D-Day, The Sixth of June

Sunday, June 6, was Whitsunday, and holiday crowds gathered everywhere for the memorial exercises. Highways were heavy with traffic, and trains were crowded. Some 361,000 Parisians left the capital city by train alone for the holiday.

In towns of Normandy, festivities continued all night, from midnight to five A.M. on that tenth anniversary of the invasion. In the back of the minds of the people now celebrating was a hope and prayer that their country might never again suffer an invasion nor an occupation nor a liberation.

Roads Without Birds

St. Lo: Before the bombing

St. Lo: After the bombing

D-Day, The Sixth of June

St. Lo – The Sameness of Destruction

3
The Bombing of Saint-Lô

On the banks of the Vire, between the Torteron and the Dollée, on its acropolis, to the medieval walls, the capital of Manche displayed its monuments…

In its neat and bright streets, its inhabitants led a peaceful, calm, and leisurely life of provincial happiness…And all around it, in rich meadows clinging to the low, rolling hills, milk cows grazed; and in the fair, blue days of fresh springtime, the perfumed snow of apple blossoms fell.

The war passed there!

Of the little city of 11,000 souls reflecting in the clear waters of the Vire, nothing remains.

Everywhere craters, ruins, blackened stones…

Only a little while ago, gay, abundant life, singing, laughter…

Today silence, tears.

Death…

—Manche 1945

More than a decade after the furies of World War II swept beyond Saint-Lô to the south and east, this old Norman town carried on in the midst of its struggle for revival. Even as men spoke of rearmament and threats of new wars, citizens of Saint-Lô bent their efforts toward mending broken hearts and restoring crumbled buildings in the hope of recapturing something of that tranquil life which they had learned to love in earlier years. Impressive results rewarded those efforts; but the work of reconstruction had a long way to go.

After ten years, a row of attractive new apartment houses stood, like a few gold fillings in a mouth full of cavities, along the edge of the Place du Champs de Mars; but people continued to live in one-story prefabricated barracks or huts, and some families still lived in the caves below the ruined church of Notre Dame. Bright new shops were open for business on the first floor of the new apartment buildings, but a number of the shops, stores, and business offices, like the dwellings, were in one-story temporary buildings of wood or masonry. The whole city had taken on something of the appearance of a temporary military post, or a temporary town around a big dam-building project. Here the work of construction went on at every side, every day. Temporary housing had to be found not only for all the families whose homes had been destroyed, but also for the hundreds of construction workers who had come in from Paris and other cities.

A traveler seeking a room for the night might yet find one at the Hôtel de la Gare or the Hôtel de l'Universe—just as before the war—except now his room would be in a one-story, wooden, prefabricated barrack. But now one also could find an excellent modern room in a new hotel near the center of the city.

Children already in high school could remember their city only in ruins. Young people now out of high school retained the vivid memories of the terror of its destruction. So incongruous, so grotesque, so fantastic —a few minutes, two decades ago, have had enduring effects for so many years. What happened? What turned this peaceful city, set in the midst of farming country, into a charred and broken ruin? What attraction did this picturesque city hold for the god of war?

Excitement was running high in Saint-Lô by eight P.M. on that June 6 in 1944. Already it had become clear that Allied armies had landed on the beaches of Normandy and the people could look forward now with real hope for early liberation from German occupation. But surely more prominent in the discussions of people of Saint-Lô as they sat about their dinner tables that evening was the air raid which had struck the city at 4:30 that afternoon. American fighter-bombers had attacked the railroad and power stations—without very much damage to either. Though some might have wondered if the planes would not return to complete the destruction of those objectives, others hoped that the early arrival of the liberating armies would make even such further pinpoint bombing unnecessary. The Germans had nearly all left, so that now no apparent reason for bombing remained.

At eight P.M. that evening the deputy mayor of Saint-Lô, Georges Lavalley, late for dinner, was hurrying along the street from the city hall. The roar of aircraft engines drew his attention skyward where he saw fourteen American Flying Fortresses overhead. Then, to his dismay, they began dropping their bombs. Gone were any efforts at pinpoint bombing of specific installations; now the bombs seemed to be falling completely at random. It seemed that the whole city was marked for destruction. But the deputy mayor had little time to ponder these considerations. Very soon he found himself in the midst of a bomb pattern. Deafening explosions and streaks of flame seemed to bring the whole world falling about his head. Before he could move to take shelter, he was hurled among broken stone and collapsing walls into complete darkness. Miraculously he had escaped serious injury, but he found himself trapped in what he thought was a deep cellar. Shortly afterward another tremendous bomb explosion blew the rubble away and freed him. To his surprise, he discovered that he had been hurled to the *upper* story of a nearby house, where the debris which fell over him had cut off the light so completely (in Saint-Lô it is still quite light at eight P.M. in June) that he had imagined himself in some underground cave.

A local journalist recalls that about five o'clock on the afternoon of that sixth of June a little girl by the name of Fabre, the youngest child of the organist at the Notre Dame church, stopped him on the street. "What are you going to do?" she had asked. "What do you advise? Is it necessary to leave?"

"It is very difficult to give any advice," he had answered as he thought how the girl's questions must have reflected the indecision that she had heard at home. "If you leave, where will you go? Perhaps there will be some danger everywhere. As for us, we are not going to leave."

A few hours later the little girl and all her family, seeking protection in a basement, were burned beyond recognition.

Shortly after the air attack struck at eight o'clock, the newsman answered his door to find the little girl of a woman who worked for them. The child was frightened and crying. She managed to say, "The house has fallen. Momma sent me to get you. Little brother Jacques and Simone are underneath."

Several men joined in the search among the rubble. They worked rapidly and carefully, stone by stone, as night fell. They found some broken toys, then an empty, crushed crib. Holding out little hope of finding the children still alive, they worked on. Someone shouted that he had felt a foot. It was little Simone—covered with blood. She cried out softly as they put her gently on a blanket. Now they redoubled their efforts to find Jacques. Darkness was complete now, but the men could see by the light of nearby fires. Once again they heard a little cry, and then a call, "Mamma!" Jacques wanted to know what had happened; then he wanted to be let alone so that he could go back to sleep. They wanted to hurry with the children to the hospital. But Simone was already dead.

Unlike the light raid in the afternoon, this attack by heavy bombers had brought serious casualties and destruction. Most of the bombs had fallen in the center and the south of the city, and fires continued to spread the destruction long after the bombers had departed. Some enterprising photographer caught a picture of that scene which, in its way, is as awe-inspiring as the well-known picture of St. Paul's in London standing in the midst of the burning city after the German raid there. In this photo, half-destroyed houses and debris-filled streets appear in the foreground, while in the background is the dim silhouette of the two towers of the church of Notre Dame standing tall and defiant amidst the flame and smoke of burning ruins. But unhappily, neither Notre Dame nor any other edifice was to survive.

The most terrifying raid of all struck between midnight and one A.M. Cries of the terror-stricken and of the dying were all but drowned out in the thunderous reverberations of bombs and the crackling of high flames. Hundreds sought refuge in the big tunnel which the Germans had been excavating in the rock of L'Enclos (the "acropolis"); others hurried to their cellars or crawled helplessly beneath tables. As often seems the case in a big catastrophe, death followed no regular pattern. A little girl cried in terror in the very center of the devastation, and then found that though the house was destroyed, all her family had been spared. Further away, a furniture merchant found two of his family dead. In the suburb of Saint Georges-Montcocq, on the hill at the northern edge of the city, all nine members of the LeBrun family perished; and old Father Georges Garnot, who had been the parish priest for forty-four years, was killed. In the prison, the Germans kept locked up nearly two hundred patriots whom they had arrested during the preceding months; when a series of bombs struck the building at 1:15

A.M., seventy-six of them died beneath the heavy stone.

M. Delaunay, later educational inspector for this district, reacted quickly when he heard the news of the D-Day landings on Omaha Beach. A war veteran himself, he thought immediately that it probably would be wise to dig a trench in his garden. He spent the morning doing this. When the first heavy bombing raid came at eight P.M., he and his wife and their eight-year-old daughter took refuge in the trench. The bombs did not fall close to them and with some relief they thought that the danger had passed. Then came the big midnight raid. Again the three huddled in the trench as fire and confusion burst all over the city. This time a bomb plunged directly into their house, and the explosion which followed left it in total destruction. (One piece of furniture was saved from the house—a glass-door bookcase with a bomb fragment lodged in its doors, which now rests in M. Delaunay's study.) Stone fragments and dirt fell all about the Delaunays as they waited out the raid in their trench. One bomb came down almost beside them, but it fell into a small creek so that they were protected from the blast. After half an hour of this, the airplanes went away. The Delaunays got up and started walking to the south. They were at a relatively safe distance when the next raid came.

One twelve-year-old boy happened to visit some friends on that fateful evening. When he returned to his home, he found the house in ruins. Every other member of his family had been killed. In the afternoon one man had remarked that whatever happened he wanted to remain in his home; that night his house was hit, and he and all his family were killed.

In a house not far from the Delaunays' a fifteen-year-old school girl, Jacqueline Lecaplain, was at home with her mother and father when the eight o'clock air raid came. Bombs seemed to be falling all about. One hit the house directly across the street. None hit her own house, but the concussion of those falling nearby blew out all the windows and hurled the furniture about on the floor. After that tempest of bombs, Jacqueline was too shaken and too frightened to go to sleep until about midnight when exhaustion overtook her. About the same time her mother stepped outside to listen. Since the news of the invasion early in the morning everyone was expecting liberation momentarily, and some thought that the air attack was the prelude to the coming of Allied ground forces. At least they hoped that was the case—not only would the arrival of Allied soldiers mean the end of German occupation, more important just now was the consideration that it would also mean the end of Allied air attacks. Hearing the sounds of motors in the distance, Mme. Lecaplain rushed back into the house to report excitedly, "The English tanks are coming!" (Apparently, here, as at Saint-Mère Église, it had not occurred to anyone that the Americans might be coming this way.) But a few minutes later the roar of heavy aircraft grew overhead, to be drowned out almost immediately by the thunderous explosions of another terrible bombardment.

Again the Lecaplain house escaped a direct hit, but again the bombs fell all around it, more furiously than before. Soon the interior of the house was completely wrecked, and some gasoline which the Germans had left in the attic began to burn.

Jacqueline thought that her parents were dead beneath the piles of furniture and plaster. In times of great danger one seems often to feel a natural impulse to run. Perhaps this is a reaction against the complete helplessness of action. Jacqueline ran out of the house. Other people were running by, and she ran after them. As each near bomb came screeching down she would fall flat on the ground to await its verdict and then run on until the next second of final judgment. Bright flashes lit up the field. Several times close bombs sent stones and dirt flying over her.

After a few minutes Jacqueline came upon a man and woman who were nearly frantic about their eighteen-year-old son. He had become separated from them and they were afraid that he had been caught by one of the bombs. Soon a priest came hurrying up. He said that the boy was lying in another field badly injured; the priest was afraid that the boy was dying, and he wanted to find the parents. Jacqueline directed him to them. The parents were nearly overcome when they heard the news. They could not bear to go and find the crumpled body of their son. Then two days later the boy was found—still alive. He was given medical treatment for about three weeks, and then the doctor decided that a delicate brain operation would be necessary in order to save his life. But after the operation the boy went mad. Later he died.

Again, as people fled through the fields at the south edge of Saint-Lô on that fateful night some of them heard wild screams coming from near one of the hedgerows. At first they thought that it was a dying animal, but they went to look just to make sure. They found a woman pinned beneath a big fallen tree; she was giving birth to a child. Several people rushed away to look for a doctor, while others tried to move the tree. In this case a doctor arrived in time to save her.

Some people, including some of the local school teachers, disappeared that night without a trace. Some may have been the victims of direct bomb hits. Some may have been buried beneath so many tons of rubble that they never were found. It is possible that some were dazed and suffered loss of memory, and wandered off—still to live.

At the height of the attack, bombs rained down at the rate of one a second for a period of twenty minutes. When these minutes which seemed an eternity at last passed, scores of trapped persons could be heard crying out in the night. But before rescue work could more than begin, more bombers arrived to feed the holocaust. Hundreds of bombers returned at three o'clock and again at five o'clock to spread their ruin and death.

By dawn Saint-Lô was a hell of fire and brimstone. Where the day before had stood the prefecture, the city hall, churches, houses, shops, the prison, the Palace of Justice, the medieval ramparts, the hospitals, schools, the municipal theater, hotels, and all the rest, now there was nothing but craters and rubble and smoke. Streets could not be recognized. Only the towers of Notre

Dame still stood but those, too, were to succumb in the succeeding day of warfare.

Survivors who could sought refuge in the hedgerows and sunken roads of the countryside that day. The Nazis permitted more than a thousand to remain in the tunnel for three days. For nearly two years the Germans had been working on this underground network with the apparent purpose of constructing an elaborate underground hospital. Now people eagerly sought its protection. A local surgeon performed urgent operations for seriously injured survivors there; a druggist organized the distribution of what food could be salvaged from the National Relief stores nearby and from the warehouses; a plucky baker continued to make bread, and a courageous milkman brought in milk. After three days, however, the generator which provided light and ventilation for the place failed, and Mayor Périers organized a complete evacuation.

Those killed on that horrible night of June 6-7 numbered only a few German soldiers, but they included 900 French citizens of Saint-Lô. Additional bombing on the days following brought the death toll to nearly 1,300. Without considering the even greater numbers of injured, more than 10 percent of the population of the city had been killed. But the wonder is that it was not 90 percent. As frequently is the case in a particularly violent but non-fatal automobile accident when people look at the wreckage and say, "How could anyone have survived that?"—so anyone who might have seen the ruins of Saint-Lô would have been moved to ask, "How could anyone have escaped that bombing?"

Often when people suffer the loss of loved ones or find themselves the victims of calamity, they demand to know *why*. Sometimes that question goes to the very problem of life itself, and explanations for the suffering of the innocent are never easy and seldom satisfactory. Surely the citizens of Saint-Lô must have asked a thousand times, why was their city marked for destruction? The question recurs: Was this bombing really necessary? Was this catastrophe the result of some shortcomings of the people? Was it the result of German activity and the inevitable consequence of modern war in that area? Or did it result from shortcomings of Allied military commanders— shortcomings in military intelligence; shortcomings in concepts of the capabilities, limitations, and proper uses of air power; shortcomings in moral responsibility for the conduct of war?

Truly enough, Saint-Lô stood at an important communications point for the defense of western Normandy, and the Germans had maintained important military headquarters (for the LXXXIV Corps and for Military Administrative Area A) there. But *all* German military units, save a few subaltern officers and guards, had withdrawn from the city *before* June 6. (At the same time, the inhabitants were *forbidden* to leave.) Most of the troops had left several days before, and the last units pulled out just the day before. This final withdrawal on June 5 may have represented a coincidence in timing, but one cannot escape the suggestion that the German command was anticipating the attack of June 6. This would imply two serious Allied errors of intelligence: (1) the failure of counter-intelligence in denying to the Germans information on the planned bombing of Saint-Lô; and (2) the failure of tactical intelligence to keep track of German troop movements, and thus to be unaware of the German evacuation of Saint-Lô. One prominent citizen of Saint-Lô spoke of a rumor which he had heard from an American air officer—that the Americans thought there were forty thousand Germans in Saint-Lô at the time of the bombing. If that was true, certainly there were serious shortcomings in Allied military intelligence. If shortcomings there were, it was Saint-Lô that suffered the consequences.

In a city of no more than twelve thousand inhabitants whose only activities which even generously could be called "industrial" consisted of a cider mill beyond the northeast corner of town and a paper mill near the northwest corner, the people had reason to think themselves beyond the scope of such saturation raids as had hit the great port of Hamburg or the great steel center of Essen. The railroad was only a secondary line connecting the Paris-Cherbourg, Paris-Granville, and Brest lines. No stretch of the imagination could include Saint-Lô among those industrial targets marked for destruction in the strategic bombing offensive. Strategic bombing is aimed at the enemy's capacity to make war; that is, its object is to cripple his economic war potential.

If the bombing of Saint-Lô did not fit into the category of strategic bombing, then it must have been tactical. Then, as now, the Air Force recognized three priorities for the use of tactical aviation: first, the gaining of air superiority by attacks against enemy airfields and aviation; second, isolation of the battlefield to deny movement of enemy forces into the battle area; and third, direct support (the Air Force now insists upon using the word "cooperation") of ground troops. Obviously the bombing of Saint-Lô was not aimed at the German air force, and certainly it was not made in response to calls from ground troops just then completing their assault of the beaches. Actually, the bombing of Saint-Lô fell into priority two: isolation of the battlefield; the air forces had been instructed to prevent movement through the city. Their method was not to send dive bombers to destroy the bridges and blow strings of craters in the roads where they pass through narrow defiles of hedgerows and elevated fields; rather their method was to send heavy bombers of the strategic air forces to obliterate the city—to make road blocks by spilling the rubble of homes and shops and schools and hospitals and churches into the cratered streets.

As for the actual military advantage obtained by the bombing, none impresses itself very readily. In his official report, General Eisenhower paid tribute to the success of the air forces in isolating the battlefield before D-Day, but his emphasis was upon the destroyed bridges across the Seine, not upon the destroyed cities at road junctions. Perhaps there was delay for the

Germans, but it is difficult to show that the destruction of Saint-Lô contributed substantially to that effect. It may have been inconvenient for the German mechanized and motorized columns to have to bypass the city, but it was far from impossible. The bombing did not prevent powerful German forces from meeting the invasion and contesting it hedgerow by hedgerow across Normandy. It did not prevent the crack Panzer Lehr Division from moving up for a sharp counterattack against the 29th and 30th Divisions as they fought toward Saint-Lô on the night of July 11. The bombing hardly could have been considered as making the ground attack toward Saint-Lô quicker or easier. As was found at Cassino and at Caen, rubble is just as easy to defend as are whole buildings, and indiscriminate aerial bombing of a city does little or nothing to assist the advance on the ground.

But the battling for Saint-Lô was done mainly among the hedgerows honeycombing the higher ground which rings it. It was not a fortified town nor was it situated in a good defensible position. Little fighting therefore went on in the streets. Some dive bombing in support of the ground troops, artillery fire, and mines contributed to the sea of destruction, but the significant destruction already had been accomplished by the heavy raids of June 6-7 and the days immediately following. After the 29th Division had occupied the high ground around Martinville to the northeast, and the 35th Division had taken Hill 122 and the high ground to the north, the Germans had withdrawn to the hills to the south of the city to continue their defense by artillery.

If Allied bombing was aimed at German troop concentrations, of course it failed, because the Germans had left. But even if they had not, most of them probably would have escaped. It was bitterly ironic that almost the only buildings not hit were those of Caserne Bellevue—the permanent French military post at the southern edge of the city which Allied intelligence maps indicated as the location of the "largest troop concentration billeting of German enlisted men." The insane asylum, just three hundred yards away, and the Ste. Geneviève School for Girls, and St. Joseph's elementary school, within two hundred yards, were totally destroyed—but not the military barracks. One other small installation escaped the bombing—the electric power station. This was only a distributing station for electricity coming from Lille, and as such would hardly be a major strategic bombing target, but presumably it would have been more appropriate for attack than were the public buildings, hospitals, schools, churches, and homes.

Least understandable of all for the local citizens is the fact that they received no advance warning. Even the local Resistance leader first learned of the bombing attacks when the bombs started falling. Even granting that it was necessary to destroy their city in order to interrupt German communications, they still cannot see why some warning to the population could not have been given. This question receives special emphasis when it is recalled that the Germans already had withdrawn anyway. Some still insist that no more than seven Germans were to be found in Saint-Lô at the time of the bombing. There were occasions when even enemy cities were given warning by leaflets of an impending raid. But this was a courtesy withheld from the allied cities of Normandy.

All this raises serious moral questions. Perhaps it is one of the major misfortunes of modern times that moral issues—particularly with respect to the conduct of war—have often been relegated to an inconsequential place. Yet the importance which nations professed to attach to the principles of international morality at the Nuremburg and Tokyo trials of war criminals would suggest that mankind still demands respect for moral law and still seeks its temporizing influence on the waging of war.

War becomes terribly depersonalized for its participants. An antitank gunner sees in an enemy tank only a dread machine bent on his own destruction—not a driver who is someone's son and someone's loved one; the air gunner sees only a dangerous, heartless machine in an enemy aircraft; even an infantryman sees in his sights—if anything—only an impersonal moving object, or some dangerous animal. So air officers coolly planning the destruction of Saint-Lô saw only a darkened area on a map; and the pilots and bombardiers saw only a cluster of impersonal buildings—they did not see the burned children, the dead priest, the mutilated women, the homeless refugees. To a considerable extent this impersonal attitude is essential even to carry on the necessary activities of such a grim business as war, for it would be disastrous for soldiers to wear their feelings on their sleeves. But it is too easy to permit this attitude to carry beyond the realm of the necessary.

Infantrymen are taught that in direct combat they seldom will see their adversaries; they must gain fire superiority by directing their weapons against all the areas *likely* to be occupied by the enemy. But can this same approach be carried over to aerial bombardment —that is, to bomb all the places where the enemy is likely to be—when this involves the destruction of cities and death and injury to thousands of the civil population whether friendly or enemy?

An unbroken spirit is, if anything, more difficult to maintain through bombings by friendly powers than by an enemy. It is more difficult because there is none of that attitude of defiance and of determination to fight back which builds up against the despair of enemy attacks. And in rebuilding, there is likely to be less of that determination to "show" the enemy what capabilities and energies still remain. It is the same as with a soldier who gets caught in friendly machine-gun fire; he finds that much worse than being caught by enemy fire, for all the means of removing the menace are not open to him, and he is overwhelmed with a terrifying helplessness, an inability to do anything in a positive way against that thing which threatens his destruction.

Tasks of evacuation and relief left by the bombing of Saint-Lô were almost overwhelming in their magnitude and complexity. Fortunately, some people had been able to leave the city before June 6. But most, not conceiving that their city could be a major bombing target, remained. The women patients of Bon Sauveur Asylum had been removed to an old château. The St. Paul Sisters of Chartres remained with the old people and the children of the Hospice, but they were located across the street from the entrance to the tunnel, and they were able to take refuge there while their medieval buildings were being destroyed.

The Germans would not permit anyone to leave immediately before June 6, but a few days after the bombing, mass evacuation began. More than four thousand went only to Le Hutrel, a small village just to the south, until they were driven farther on by the July battles. Other people remained—especially on the farms around the outskirts—until July 14, when, as the ground battles approached, they moved out with a few personal possessions to farm communities in the vicinity of Mortain, about thirty-five miles to the south.

Several families had begun preparations to move southward as soon as they heard about the landings on June 6, but then many of those who survived the bombing remained for several days in the hope that liberation was close at hand. The Lecaplain family remained in this hope until about the end of June. Then they caught a glimpse of a German newspaper which shattered their supposition that the Americans and British were in control of virtually all the area from the Seine through Brittany. Sensing that hard battles were yet to be fought, they joined many of the others in going to the Mortain area to live for a while with friends—only to find themselves once again practically in the front lines when the Germans launched their counteroffensive around Mortain a few weeks later.

The Delaunay family lived in the hedgerows south of Saint-Lô until about the first of July, and then they too moved southward toward Mortain. They carried with them only themselves, the clothes they wore, and very little else. En route someone gave them a wheelbarrow in which they could carry a few things, and with this they made their way to the home of some relatives. They remained there until the German counterattack, and then they went up to Granville, on the west coast of Normandy.

Wherever they went, the refugees shared some of the same experiences of precarious living under hostile surveillance. Frequently a group of refugees would settle at some farm, only to be dispossessed a few hours or a few days later when some German unit arrived searching for quarters. From time to time they would see one of their number executed. Again a town in their path would be bombed.

Naturally it was a great relief to these refugees, wherever they happened to be, when the American breakthrough came and they were able to pass through the lines. Always they affected enthusiasm in greeting their liberators, and they showered fruit and flowers on American tanks and trucks passing by. Yet a part of that enthusiasm was an affectation adopted for the purpose of sharing in the cigarettes and candy and food items with which the Americans were so generous. Their smiles sometimes covered a deep resentment against the mass bombing of their towns and homes.

Some families faced greater disappointment when at last they were able to return to their own homes. One family which had left from near Sainte-Mère Église, for instance, endured the uncertain life of refugees just living in the hope of going home again, and then after a long trip back to the north they had felt the exciting heartbeat of a return to home country as they approached their neighborhood—but then their anticipation had dissolved in tears as they came within view of their farm and saw the buildings now only a collection of charred ruins.

The return of the refugees to the ruins of Saint-Lô and the surrounding farms began about August 4—by which time Mortain itself was about to become a battle area again in the abortive German counteroffensive toward Avranches and the sea.

Mutual aid, cooperation, and outside assistance all helped life return to Saint-Lô. Two examples of the latter may be mentioned here: the Irish Hospital and Don Suisse. Out on the Rue de Bayeux stood the white wooden huts of the Irish Hospital, surrounded by trim green lawns. The French Services of Reconstruction built the houses, but they were completely equipped—wards, aluminum-lined operating room, laboratories, radiology rooms, maternity ward, dispensary—by the Irish Red Cross. Until December 1946 it was staffed by Irish medical personnel. The Swiss contribution was an institution called "Don Suisse," located on the hillside to the south of Notre Dame and the "acropolis." Its principal work began later, in April 1946, but it did valuable work in distributing clothing, shoes, furniture, kitchen utensils, and other necessities to the stricken families; in May 1947 it organized a nursery, a kindergarten school, and a sewing school, which it later turned over to the city. The resurrection of Saint-Lô was beginning.

PART TWO

Les Routes Sans Oiseaux

by
Raoul Dujardin

[Translated by Ann Echols and Solange Gracey]

Les Routes Sans Oiseaux
[Roads Without Birds]

I

Monday, June 5.

The farm was dropping off to sleep.

It was cold in spite of the advanced season and the sky was half-covered with clouds. The Germans were now making camp in the fields; so we were able to lock our doors; a forgotten gesture, an act of independence and liberty that I liked, knowing all the while that at the first call I would have to open up. Waiting for the day's end, why I don't know, I was the last to go upstairs.

In the morning a friend had said to me: "It will be very soon…"

This fellow was probably mistaken. The weather didn't seem encouraging. Two allied fighters had just flown over the village at this unusual hour of dusk. They were banking to see our houses and roads. After a rapid round they headed toward the coast.

The moon was rising. The first big planes arrived. You could feel their rumbling clamor from afar and soon they covered all the land. Their deafening arch moved toward the west in a continual, monotone movement, as if atmospheric. Adding to this impression, brief, red strikes of lightening of undetermined origin progressively lit up the sky toward the sea.

We spoke in low voices by a northeast window. In the shadows the leaves of a large elm tree rustled gently. Bombs were falling in the distance. Planes kept flying overhead. Sometimes they flew so low that you could see the enormous shadows of their wings between the trees. Then their motors would seem to turn faster. And the storm above the calm air that we breathed kept on. Where, on what shore, to what part of France were they going? This time it had to be the landing. But on what coast?

We didn't know that at that very moment we were already in the fight; that in our fields, on our roads, around our villages, silent men with blackened faces were advancing carefully with Tommy-guns in their fists. We couldn't believe that the big battle was beginning.

Since the air was a little cold we closed the window to retire for the night. In the darkness we listened to the unremitting and continual passing over of planes. Leaving for our last adventure, we remembered those who had crossed our skies and whom we had heard in bed from our darkened rooms during so many nights. It reminded us of all those who had crossed our skies for so many nights—the heavy fortresses bombarding Germany and Italy and the Goering bombers flying low, nearly grazing our chimneys on their way to destroy London in 1940. But this day the deployed force seemed infinite. The planes' whirring sound neither stopped nor weakened and finally soothed us by

Les Routes Sans Oiseaux

its sleep-conducing lull. While the fate of the world was playing itself out above us, sleep overtook us.

Perhaps it was the stopping of the colossal noise that awakened us. Dawn was coming. Fog was on the ground and stars in the sky. Given the strength of the air force, we thought that the landing should have been accompanied by an enormous artillery uproar. Toward the east we heard only indistinct and interrupted firing. Day was breaking gradually to the song of birds.

Marie saddled her mule and left to do the milking as usual. Soon she came running back. She had seen Americans in our fields. They had spoken to her and told her that they had come from the States to liberate us. In spite of my sore hip I followed the young woman as fast as I could.

Each parachute unit had its rallying point, its place of attack. But by error or the force of the wind, the soldiers had landed too far, beyond almost impenetrable lines. Without civilian help, many would have been captured or slaughtered. It would take pages to relate the deeds of some of our men who everywhere and under all conditions helped the soldiers by picking up the wounded, hiding the lost soldiers, and making them go right under the Germans' noses.

Under a large hedge of oaks there were four members of that glorious division whose mission it was to liberate Saint-Côme-du-Mont and Carentan. One of them appeared in front of us, aimed his Tommy-gun, but lowered it and grinned when he heard the word *"France."*

The first thing he asked me was to show him on the map where he was. At this he seemed disheartened. His approaching comrades were worried. They should have landed beyond the marshes. They looked at me somewhat suspiciously, but then I saw that they had confidence. They were young and agile men whose footsteps made no noise. They wore high brown boots and loose greenish uniforms with large pockets down the legs and chest from which were attached grenades, bundles, canvas-covered canteens, and satchels. They had automatic loaders and Tommy-guns hanging from their woven cotton belts and a sheathed dagger on their calf; and some were using heavy infantry rifles. Their overly large, bell-shaped helmets were covered with green mesh. They had wiped their faces that still bore the traces of burnt cork. They offered me several packs of cigarettes and then immediately went back to the hedge, where I followed them.

"Are there any Boches around here?" asked the first soldier.

Alas! The enemy, whose nearest camp was about a kilometer away, was on patrol everywhere, even right up to our village. A tall, skinny kid, perhaps the leader, explained to me in a singsong dialect that during the night he had found only three comrades. Then all four took up the search without getting too far from their landing spot. But they got no response to the little child's noisemaker that they called a cricket. They had not encountered any Germans.

"We are also looking for water. We're thirsty."

Marie had started milking right next to us. The soldiers were going to have warm milk. They smiled. One of them lit a cigarette. Another climbed the slope hiding among the branches to survey the neighboring fields.

Cows gathered around us; but their curiosity was already satisfied. They chewed their cud seriously as if to say that it was useless to try to understand. I can still see the innocent, heavy and happy cattle with their white spots, swatting away the flies from their eyes or suddenly turning around to lick their flanks with rough tongues. They would all die in the battle of the following days. They knew nothing and only awaited the diligent hands that would relieve their heavy udders. Around a pail full of foam, the four soldiers squatted to drink from their cups. Then they gave candy and chocolates to the servant girl and showed us a sack full of cans and other food under the hedge.

Ammunition, weapons, collapsible stretchers, and boxes of bandages had been dropped elsewhere, but we had to hunt for all of it in the countryside. On my way back I found a yellow and a green parachute. Others were white or red, each color indicating the type of load that they were carrying.

Friends were waiting for me at the house. They told me that they, too, had just seen some Americans. Luckier than I, they were able to help the Americans find a Tommy-gun and clips of cartridges that had fallen on an old road.

"The Americans are everywhere!" they said enthusiastically.

How strong and impatient we felt. However, the paratroopers were relatively few compared with Hitler's troops. Gathered in two farms outside the village, there were scarcely thirty in their group. In the morning I had come back to the hedge where the four soldiers were supposed to wait. They were not there. Had they been able to rejoin their comrades? I do not know. A few months later I was to learn that on that day about ten o'clock in the morning four paratroopers slipped onto the main road that reaches Carentan. A young farm servant had kept watch. Two German sentries who turned their backs from time to time were keeping vigil at the crossroad two hundred meters away. The four paratroopers had crossed the road at a favorable moment, but on the other side one of them had stopped to lean on a tree and carefully aim. He had fired. As one of the Germans was falling, the other turned around and took up his weapon only to collapse in turn.

"Goodbye," said the American to the farm servant, "thanks, young man." They had soon disappeared, agile as wild animals.

I was not a witness to heroic combats or fierce battles where elite troops sacrificed themselves in so many places, fighting down to the very last cartridge and ending with the knife. Everyone who saw them still marvels at their courage. And German soldiers in the Air Force who were sent to this sector to fight the allied paratroopers said with the tone of respect that they reserve for the mighty, "Americans soldiers, prima, Sir."

Les Routes Sans Oiseaux

As they passed by the farm, the Germans ostentatiously smoked cigarettes that they had taken from the injured and dead, and from prisoners. They had lost their affectation of politeness. The threat of a pistol accompanied each and every order. You get used to these ways.

In the morning and early afternoon of Tuesday, June 6, two bomber squadrons attacked Carentan, and a family of friends came some hours later to take refuge at our home. Laden with baggage and exhausted, they brought us yet another picture of the war. In their random, confused memories, they told us the names of the first victims that we knew.

It was forbidden to move about on the roads in cars or on bicycles, and everyone stayed at home behind closed gates. Many heavy squadrons still went by at night. Perhaps Saint-Côme-du-Mont was taken for we no longer heard battle. A strange calm, a huge silence scarcely broken by the noise of distant artillery, left us in a state of anxiety. Some claimed that the landing had been unsuccessful and that the Americans were retreating to the sea. The silver-colored light bombers that grazed our roofs seemed, however, to be masters of the sky.

In the stormy afternoon we went to the garden. Three Wehrmacht trucks went by on the road toward the village. Armed soldiers in helmets ready for combat were standing on the flat bed surrounded by iron ramps. One submachine gun short barrel seemed ready to shoot. Vehicles advanced slowly with men scrutinizing hedges and fields. Suddenly they stopped and a fusillade burst forth. Within moments some Germans ran and crouched with their enormous machine guns banging powerfully. Other machine guns responded. And then again there was silence. The soldiers dashed in small groups toward the village while the empty trucks started their engines.

We had hidden our cigarettes and canned foods given to us by the Americans. This was a good precaution because two soldiers soon came to ransack the house. They made us go upstairs ahead of them to the bedrooms and empty the contents of the wardrobes on the floor. They seemed furious and uttered a few words in incorrect French and in German commanding us, "Open everything!"

In their eyes you could see their regret for not having been ordered to kill us.

In the evening we were on our beds with blinds closed but windows open, letting in all the little noises and the cool night air, when the intense, more distant shooting began again. Soon flames crackled, and a fire cut out the silhouettes of trees and roofs in the sky. We understood the drama that was going on: Americans hidden in a farm had been discovered and had returned the German attack. To drive them out, the enemy was burning their haunt and shooting civilians that were trying to flee. The war, the immense war, this horrible war, was rolling its first surge right under our windows. And our house stood firm and tall like a sandcastle built by a child on the beach.

Saturday, June 10, we hid a little food because the Germans were taking everything. They would enter at any moment, open the cupboard, and ask for something to drink. There were Russians, Poles, and Czechs. On the first lines, toward Saint-Côme-du-Mont or Carentan, their paratrooper infantrymen who were trained to fight all battles and on whom Rommel had counted to break the allied assault, fought. Some were still passing by here on that day. They seized carts and wagons, horses, harnesses—we hadn't hidden the harnesses! Each of their demands was accompanied by the threat of a pistol and brought as reward the offer of a Camel or a Lucky Strike, which we politely declined. They were dirty and restless, with week-old beards. Around their necks they wore silk scarves cut from parachutes. Their uniforms seemed more practical then that of the Americans, but that was only in appearance due to the cleaner line of the multi-colored jacket and overalls that covered the green uniform. Actually this uniform offered few advantages. These soldiers didn't wear boots but high worn-out shoes.

"Many Tommies?" we asked.

"Ho! So so. Tomorrow—caput."

That evening we heard the first close artillery shell. It was one of the strongest emotions of the war, but hard to recall after so many others. You could hear this new, long whistling. You follow its path through the sky and its crushing metallic crash seems unexpectedly violent.

Shells? A kind of numbness grabs you. We were at the door listening to the distant noises of the battle as we did every evening. The shell whistled through the low clouds and soon exploded about a kilometer away.

And right away two or three others followed even closer. Windows shattered—another deplorable sensation—these first destroyed windowpanes! We had hurriedly brought down mattresses to the room that seemed the most sheltered. Other bursts of shells passed over us, to the right, to the left, and farther away. They hit the ground at random. Sometimes the silence lasted awhile. We would toss in our beds, and when we were close to falling asleep; suddenly the launching buzz would come a half-second before the mewing moment of landing.

June's short night seemed long. In the morning, just as after a bad storm, we went to see the damage around our house. It proved insignificant.

The shells had only made shallow holes in the dry ground. All around, the grass was turned up and the branches of the trees mangled. An apple tree hit in the trunk was cut right down. Meanwhile, in the village the wheelwright's daughter had just died. A shell fragment had hit her in the stomach as she was leaving the house with her parents in search of shelter. She had lived for several hours. She was a little seamstress who did day-work at our house. Always clean, sweet and smiling, even last Sunday for her brother's first communion, she had asked us for some flowers and then left happy with a big bouquet in her arms. Today was Sunday again. At the regular hour, in spite of the danger, the bell rang for Mass. At the service there were folks from the town and other villages and refugees in city clothes. German soldiers went through the church to go up into the steeple. In the harsh light of the broken stained glass windows, the priest was reciting prayers. You could hear footsteps in the cemetery. Planes were flying over. The bell ceased pealing.

At lunch time we were all seated at our long kitchen table as before. It was a peaceful moment. Our friends talked about their lovely house that had been destroyed and all the things they had lost, but in order to keep our courage and mood up, I had opened a bottle of good wine. I found a little cognac and a few cigars in an old stash. Maybe the war was going to pass around us and leave us at peace there in the house. Shells were no longer falling.

"Listen!"

Farther away on the road to Carentan, an artillery strike erupted. But the wind was not favorable, and the blasts were muddled and difficult to place. Suddenly two Germans, or rather two Russians in German uniform, entered. The first one sat down. He seemed drunk and poured himself a big glass of cognac. He was dark with slanted eyes, but accompanied by a comrade of another stock, very blond with a drooping moustache and blue eyes. The latter did not want to drink and remained standing, looking at us and listening attentively, to what we did not know. He seemed worried and in a hurry to leave. He made signs to his comrade and went to the window to listen again. He spoke quickly in a singsong language that I did not recognize, and then he appeared to become angry. The other was still drinking and squinting his dark eyes; but at the call of his friend he finally decided to get up to leave. This was a laborious exercise. He succeeded in saluting us with dignity, then drew his pistol with a wicked smile. The blond soldier twisted his wrist harshly, grabbed the weapon, and made him leave. They went off very quickly along the walls in the courtyard, one holding the other up. What were they up to? We thought that possibly they were deserters who were trying to cross the lines or to hide in the fields.

The calmed wind now let us identify the closer noise of automatic weapons near Carentan. Planes were machine-gunning the town. Since the Americans could be here this evening or tomorrow, it was important to hold on. We had the idea of rapidly digging shelters. We had lost precious time these past days.

To work! My friends were bad excavators but were spurred on by good will and excitement of danger and hope. They dug and sawed round logs. A girl with delicate hands skinned her fingers. Her father was in a sweat. The hole got bigger. The artillery that thundered in the distance was not getting closer.

At nightfall, overcome with fatigue, we were eating in silence when a big army motorcycle turned around and stopped in front of the door. A non-commissioned officer jumped out of the sidecar and bounded into the kitchen.

"Who is the head of house?" he demanded.
"Myself, Sir," I replied.
"Come here!" he ordered.

II

Standing on the threshold, he pointed to the whole front of the house with its white shutters and said to me, "We need this house." He appeared very young and wore the symbol of the medical corps on his shoulder.

"But my mother is ill," I said.

"In bed?"

"Yes."

He was suspicious that I had told the truth.

"Let's go see."

The rather large bedrooms seemed to suit him. He stopped close to my mother's bed and looked at her. I could see that he understood that her illness was serious.

"This will be Madame's room, but I am taking all the others. I am awaiting the wounded," he said.

"Are there many?"

"Yes! The battle at Carentan was hard."

"The town was taken?"

In this questioning I had tried to express the confidence and at the same time the doubt that Germany was to impose on the world. This false attitude served my purpose as the young man seemed to lose his stiffness. With a tired gesture, he smoothed the fatigue off his face, and he took off his helmet. He did not answer my question but lightly shrugged his shoulders. Thus I realized that the neighboring town was liberated.

Then I asked as if we had never spoken of anything else, "Do you need all the rooms?"

"Yes."

"It's late, and I have refugees here—women, girls, and someone has to be with my mother."

"I know."

He seemed to ponder. Soon he consented to leave us a room. Then a Red Cross car arrived, and another doctor got out with nurses and a wounded man who dragged himself to the door. Paying no attention to him, the Health Service personnel carried leather cases and medical equipment into the kitchen. The motor had been left running, and the car started.

The first doctor beckoned to the soldier to sit down. A bullet had gone through his chest, and he was having difficulty breathing;. His skin was greenish and sticky like that of a dying man. Night had fallen. Someone lit a candle and began the first bandaging in this poor light while over our heads the shells again shrieked toward their landing farther up the road. Blood had made a somber track on the young man's back. The doctor was rolling up bandages. The car came back soon. Silently, nurses took heavy stretchers holding gray masses out of the van. At last the war became a reality. We had its proof and result. Its contagious ferocity was affecting us, but since these were Germans we were ashamed to feel any pity—oh, sad thoughts of war! Our friends also must have losses, deaths, and wounded about to die who bled like those men. A doctor asked for towels and sheets. The dying were stretched out everywhere on mattresses and our beds. Then more wounded men arrived. And at the same time in the darkness, the house was filling up with soldiers busy lighting the fire, unpacking canned food, Marseille soap, sugar and cognac. Doctors were crushing empty vials of vaccine under their boots. Hospital odors were spreading. Then, overtaking the other noise, some blind shells exploded in the vicinity. You could feel in the aftershock glass and iron falling on the gravel.

In the morning the Red Cross car began to take the heavy stretchers away to other centers. New wounded arrived in narrow Russian or Polish forage wagons pulled by Mongolians. They were covered with green branches, but blood was dripping under the leaves. Flies were surrounding them in the sunshine. It was only about nine o'clock when they had brought in the last of their sad cargo. Taking advantage of this moment of calm, the young doctor washed at the pump, shaved, brushed his uniform and shoes. Soon he was ready to receive more bleeding bodies. While waiting he smoked. With his blue gaze, he watched the formation of the planes in the sky, and as a pilot headed for the farm and righted himself above the large red cross that had been unfurled on the grass, he smiled with disdain.

I approached to try to get some news. "Tired?" I asked.

"No," the German answered gravely, "not tired but…"

"But?"

"The past days have been hard."

"Really?"

"Yes. We fought over toward Saint Mère-l'Église."

"Saint Mère-Église."

"Yes. And as for Saint-Côme-le-Mont and Carentan, we took some big losses."

"Lots of wounded, dead?"

"We don't count the dead. Eighty percent, maybe."

"And the Americans?"

"Very good soldiers with equally good weapons."

"And…tomorrow?" I looked him in the face, but I had gone too far.

He asked violently, "Tomorrow?"

I tried to slow down, adding naively, "Maybe tomorrow the battles will take place farther from here."

Without answering, he looked at me with flashing eyes, then went on, carefully articulating his words. "Maybe tomorrow you will be lib-er-ated?" He turned his back on me sniggering,

And then I went in because a shell had just exploded too closely, putting a flock of wood pigeons to flight.

Dusty Russian cars nearly out of gas were still turning into the courtyard. The drivers were calling to each other. Some were rummaging through the stables in search of a harness and halters. A donkey was looking at them from his pen. They ran and tried to grab him, but he kicked. I intervened as a matter of form. A German nurse, sent by the doctor, made it painfully clear that I was to let things alone. Happily, my mare was in a more distant field. The village's other horses had already been taken. At this moment two German soldiers were robbing the hen house. Through an open window in a bedroom I saw two others forcing the doors of a wardrobe. So I came back to the room where our friends were gathered and where my mother had her bed brought down from upstairs. It was necessary to wait. And so the day passed, a tumultuous, agonizing yet less bad day than the following one would be.

The shells were falling so close that we couldn't sleep. They would come in fours or fives, and each time we felt that they were in the courtyard, on us, because we did not yet know how the crushing, red gusts of very close explosions would be.

In the morning, the young doctor came to see us. He didn't seem to be in too bad a mood.

A woman asked him, "Are we in danger?"

"You ought to leave," he said.

"But we want to stay."

"In an hour our soldiers will be here and maybe they will kick you out. Good-bye."

We hadn't seen that some of the men were loading crates, running around in the bedrooms and bringing down the wounded. When their galloping around stopped and their Germanic or Mongolian voices fell silent, we went out. The sun was high. The courtyard was strewn with broken crates, dirty papers, and bandages and seemed empty and dead. Some cars and trucks appeared, but the farm's short entrance road seemed to protect us from being noticed by the enemy. Toward the east could be clearly heard the tenuous, clacking sounds of submachine guns. We said to ourselves, "They are coming!"

Cows heavy with milk were mooing in the distance.

III

Bloody linen and a bad odor made the kitchen nauseating.

We snacked on some biscuits in our common room. The clock calmly ticked away the time. A desire to sleep kept us quiet. It was noon. Shooting in the courtyard made us jump. It was only a small isolated group of soldiers killing our last hens to take them away. They had mean faces. One of them with a nasty look and weapon in front of him came in and asked for something to drink. I showed him the door to the cellar. Still others passed by, but the battle seemed to lose its fury. Would we be liberated without further damage?

I had hidden our mare in an isolated garden shed. About five o'clock American planes strafed the town road. German infantry were weaving through the fields. Hope kept us breathless by the bedroom windows. But night fell at last without bringing our liberators. Ever more frequent shells whistled above our heads. We could name the crossroads, villages, and roads where they fell. When they came too near we were quiet. Toward morning, neighbors with wan faces came to find out how we were doing. The dawning day seemed decisive to us.

The maid heated up our coffee. A few stray bullets cracked against our walls with a dull thud, and the shooting began again in the distance. The planes were already coming back, passing so low that you could

Les Routes Sans Oiseaux

hear a light whistling under their wings. We waited. The sun was already high in the sky.

Two Germans entered brusquely. "Head of household?"

Always the same question. I introduced myself, and they said only one word:

"Leave!"

"We are…"

"Everyone! Out in five minutes!"

We had to obey. Our suitcases were ready. We added a blanket, a loaf of bread, and a kilo of sugar. The mare was harnessed quickly, and we left in the presence of the two Germans who were waiting.

Our refugees had once again closed their travel bags. On the way we separated because they preferred to go across the fields, and, besides, my cart was too small for everyone. We tearfully shook hands.

"Good luck!" we said to one another.

We had to flee just when our allies were arriving right behind us. And we also had to abandon the house, its sunny courtyard and the livestock that seemed to bid us an unconscious farewell. My mother who was ill and so very emaciated cried bitter tears. The servant was lamenting over her family that she would not be able to see again. My little spaniel crouched under our legs.

"Let's go!" I called to everyone.

The wind blew on our feverish faces. The road was deserted here, but you could hear the battle escalating everywhere. The shooting seemed to come closer, and the artillery was starting up again. We had to think. It was necessary to leave. We had no choice, but above all we had to try to escape danger in order to return here as soon as possible. I know very well this country where I was born, where I hunted every corner and have many friends and family. The American surge was developing in the direction of Périers and Lessay, from east to west, cutting across the peninsula along the great marshes and heaths. We thought that we might be overlooked if we sought safety close to these marshes; and tomorrow we could return by the back roads. Everything seemed clear. Besides we had cousins over this way who were developing a large isolated estate that was far from the roads. The immense swampy grasslands of Gorges and Méautis bordered their land on three sides. The large machinery of modern warfare would not risk coming here to get bogged down.

In the village I turned boldly in that direction. Worried folks and women in tears were dragging their bundles out of their doors. At the intersection I had just met a car of German officers who had stopped as if to listen for new sounds in the sky. They were absorbed and unconcerned with the comings and goings of soldiers and civilians. We felt like an enormous storm was coming.

A young boy who worked at the farm came out of his house and asked my advice. Should he stay? I had no idea. And how could you give an opinion when the stakes were so great? I told him only where I was going. He could follow me if he wanted to. I let go of the reins of my mare, which, out of fear or impatience, was already white with sweat.

Les Routes Sans Oiseaux

Three or four pistol shots had just burst out ahead of us at the other end of the village. A dog barked; another bullet and the dog was silent. After passing the last house, I pulled once again on the bridle. A soldier with a smoking submachine gun at his side went back into this abandoned house, and it was then that I saw a man crouched against the mud wall of a chicken coop near a doghouse. With his bloody head on his shoulder and half-closed eyes he seemed to be sleeping. He was a poor stunted person that had been named Hercules in mockery. A welfare child, he had always lived with these farmers who had fled without him. Maybe he had tried to defend their possessions in their absence. Now, huddled against the foot of the wall, arms between his legs, he seemed unaware when we called to him. His murderer had shot him from the side, shattering his temple and the nape of his neck. The bullets had left white grazes and holes in the mud wall. Hercules' big yellow dog, lying down at the end of his chain, no longer moved. He, too, had been shot by the Germans.

Beyond this house the road goes down to the fields. Numerous soldiers were unrolling and attaching wires between the trees on the street. Farther away where the land rises abruptly, exhausted and unconcerned infantry soldiers were sleeping along the side of the road. They were in rags, unarmed and wore wooden shoes or bootees on their feet. They were survivors of Saint-Côme, and had fled through the marshes and could take no more. I know now that many had passed through Méautis the night before when they were in full retreat. At the same time new troops were arriving. Vehicles were lined up under the hedgerows. One cut across in front of us to get to an old road. Next came two cannon pulled by horses just like in the olden days. Everywhere there were telephone operators carrying drums on their backs and feverishly stretching wire. Several trucks surprised by a plane were smoldering in an orchard. The smoke carried a bitter odor of rubber that spread down the road. A hundred meters farther along we arrived at Féodal's house.

This chap was my father's friend who had been in the whole war of 1914-1918 in the worst places. Returning to his village, he never thought of getting married. The war was the great adventure of his life and had left him no desire to take on anything else whatever. Since his parents had died and had left him this house and a few assets, age crept slowly up on him. Once in a while he would still venture out with his carpenter's box on his back for a bit of diversion and day work, but only for folks he liked. With his brown hair, bright eyes, and mocking face, he sported a soldier's moustache and other military traits. Especially when he had been drinking, he would adopt a Parisian working-class way of speaking and an untidy, carefree style of dressing in an old non-commissioned officer's uniform with a worn belt buckle bearing the Germanic "Gott Mitt Uns" [God With Us] slogan. He remained young in spirit in spite of wrinkled cheeks, yellowed complexion, and graying temples. Always ready to be useful or drink a pint, he was the life of the party. He got his name Féodal—Feudal—during heated political discussions. He was

Les Routes Sans Oiseaux

proud of it and, although he scoffed at the idea of the word, he liked its sound.

He noticed us as he was standing at his door. In two strides he crossed the little courtyard that was separated from the road by bushes and a narrow gate.

"Where are you going?" he asked.

I explained our adventure to him.

"Come into my house for the time being," he said with authority. "Quickly."

He had taken the reins of my horse, and, as soon as our feet touched the ground, he cried out, "Get inside!" as he rapidly directed our cart toward the shed next to his thatched-roof house.

He came back behind us and hurried to his fire where tobacco leaves were drying in a pan.

"Sit down," he said.

"Well?" I asked.

"Hush! Let your mother rest. The trouble is going to begin again."

Then he told us, while watching his precious tobacco leaves, that about every half hour an American battery shelled the intersection that we were to cross three or four hundred meters farther on. And it was in the knick of time. It seemed to us that shells were hissing over the house closer than before. They exploded with a loud racket like noises in a resonant room. More hissing, violent landings, then heavy, buzzing silence.

"Maybe you can leave now," said Féodal.

From the door, I surveyed the shed, but my friend had thought of everything and had put a chain around the neck of my mare that was trying to rear.

"This is a dangerous place," I said, "François, come with us."

The lad was undecided. He had arrangements to make, so he said.

I told him about the murder of poor Hercules, adding, "Come, don't wait until they chase you out."

"No, not now, but see you soon," he finally uttered. He helped us get the cart out, and we got in.

"Well then, see you soon!" we said.

I beckoned him to release the bridle and got back on the road again, paying close attention to the battle and the outbursts of artillery. At the crossroads where we were going, there was damage. A cart with broken stretchers was stopped; its horse was dead. Then some meters from the crossroad, in an unfinished dugout under a hedgerow, sat a German officer in ceremonial headgear, holding his raised left hand in his right. His wrist had been blown off, leaving only a big, bloody stump hemorrhaging out of his sleeve. In the next dugout, a soldier seemed overcome with stomachache and was writhing on the ground. A little farther away, in the third hole, stood another soldier with his hair flying in the wind and sideburns framing a mean-looking, scheming face. He was spreading lard on a piece of bread with one of those long knives used to kill hogs on our farms. To the right and left in the fields, the trucks' wheels had crushed hay and wheat, torn up fences and strewn mooing cows on the roads. One of the cows followed her lost companions, then turned around and trotted back to a field where the white head of her dead calf lay. A few kilometers away on this road that leads to the great Gorges marshes, a narrow embanked passage descends to the right toward my cousins' farm. For a while, we went ahead on foot sheltered by the high banks. Then, as the path widened, we could see among the trees the long slate and thatched roofs of Vassanville.

IV

The manor house dated from the fifteenth century. Its buildings and dependencies formed about a half-hectare, four-sided enclosure. North of the courtyard stood the lofty, tuffrock house surrounded by narrow moats. Low walls guarded the stone bridge that led to the house's courtyard and entrance. The coat of arms of the former masters was hung high over the massive chimney in a large, sunny kitchen. Since the occupation, brass and pewter utensils had been removed from the oak shelves on the wall. The long table took up a whole side of the room. I will describe other details about the kitchen, house, and courtyard later for they were the witnesses of our anguish during difficult weeks.

My cousin, Henriette Arnaud, greeted us at her door. She was a young grandmother and recent widow, who managed her farming estate with the intention of leaving it to her youngest son. Her daughters had taken shelter here with her grandchildren who were running around everywhere. A farmer from the town had also taken refuge here for himself and all his family, along with several servants. We would be setting up a little, isolated colony in this out of the way place. Since all the bedrooms were taken, we were put in the large room on the first floor. Mattresses, chairs, and a little table were brought downstairs for us. Everyone wanted to help us settle in. "It will only be for a day or two," we said, hopefully.

Each person gave reasons for hope and told what he had seen. While I was shaving my overgrown beard, my cousins were uncorking an old bottle of apéritif. Seated casually on a bed or an arm of a chair, they drank to victory.

Through the open window a beautiful day welcomed us. A hen was leading her chicks into the sun. A puppy was playing, yapping around a child. In the kitchen, the women were setting the tables. What peace! But indeed the war was not far from us. Across the low country we heard its uproar. Shells dropped on my village and the road that we had taken. But here we felt that we were at a distance and sheltered from their landfalls. The battle would go back and forth in front of us without getting close to us. Our feeling of security was so strong that in spite of our sad thoughts we joined in the conversation with a sort of gaiety, though we did not forget the friends left behind and our homes. The Germans were pillaging our place to their hearts content, soiling and breaking up the old things that we loved. And our poor lost animals would prowl and sniff around the courtyard and stables. But here we were seated and served at long tables just like on a holiday. No enemy would come here to empty our bottles because they had to guard the fields by the roads and burrow under the 105mm howitzer attacks. As I described the scene at the last crossroads to the others, it seemed like something from another war.

However, Henriette asked, "Was that at la Croix-Piquard? So close to here?"

"Yes," I answered. "It was there, just an hour ago."

Someone pointed out that the shells seemed to be getting closer. Nobody answered. And since planes were passing over the farm, some got up to run to the door and wave handkerchiefs.

"This is dangerous." I cautioned them. "The Germans could see you."

"There aren't any Germans here."

"Yes, there are," replied Henriette. "Their patrols sometimes come this far. We must be reasonable." She looked worried even though she tried to hide it. She soon gave me a discreet sign, and I followed her into a small, rather dark room where her son, Pierre, came to join us.

When the door was closed, their cheerful masks disappeared. In a low voice, Pierre said, "Mama is imagining things."

Then, with a resolute tone of voice, Henriette confided her worries to me. American paratroopers had landed nearby, too far from their lines, and were waiting for their army's thrust. Naturally they had no food.

"What would you have done in my place?" asked Henriette.

Pierre flared up. "It goes without saying!"

I thought about him. If the encampment were discovered, they would take hostages and the son...

"I recommend great caution," I ventured.

The paratroopers were not staying at the farm as they had set up quarters in a little woods that was too close to the house, in my opinion. Their only neighbors were marsh birds and ourselves.

I knew this small woods well. It was thick brushwood surrounding a few stunted oaks where the marsh water rose from autumn on.

"Let's go see them," suggested Pierre, as if my visit to this site could calm his mother. I followed the lad through the old paths. It was mild, and the distant battle seemed dead. The only noise was a small observation plane that sounded like a harmless, old motorbike engine. The scent of blond tobacco floated in the air around us. After a few steps under the trees, a hand stopped Pierre, and I heard the laugh of one of the lookout men who whistled in a special way.

Suddenly, a Canadian appeared and asked us in a country accent like that of the old French colonists, "How are things?"

A few steps farther and we were in front of the leader. He was a young, strapping soldier listening to a radio with a few comrades at the foot of a tree. He beckoned us to squat as he was doing, near the trunk of the tree. Then, letting go of his tiny radio, he spoke cheerfully. The Canadian interpreter told us that all

Les Routes Sans Oiseaux

was going well on the coast. The command thought that the American front should go beyond us very soon. The officer agreed with these words with a gesture and a smile of approval.

Pierre asked, "Do you still have enough meat?"

The Canadian took it upon himself to answer by shaking his head no, and my cousin announced that he would send two hams in the evening and that milk wouldn't be forgotten either. Before leaving we accepted cigarettes. The dozen big smiles all around us bespoke the joy and courage of these brave lads in their rolled-up sleeves, who were waiting their time to fight and die.

We went back toward the house, treading slowly on our soil that these men from America wanted to be free, this rich sod of my homeland on which armies from all corners of the world were going to confront each other. We walked in silence, thinking.

"And so?" Pierre asked me.

"So nothing. How many are there?"

He didn't know—maybe around thirty—obviously too many to consider hiding at the farm. We came to the fence of the last fields that opened on a secluded corner of the courtyard used for storage. During long months, harvest wagons and machinery used for making hay were kept there. It's a forgotten, little spot, obstructed by logs, old wheels, and choked with nettles. From there you could see the back of the house, its darker stones, smaller barred windows, dependencies, and a large marsh nearby. Standing on the edge of the water was a German watching us with his submachine gun on his back and his cap pulled down on his head.

V

A German officer and some other soldiers were studying the map by the door, and Henriette was graciously giving them directions. We got over our initial apprehension. We could assume the innocent attitude of passers-by because we saw that they were trying to find a road that was poorly shown on the map. The first German was still looking at the ducks on the edge of the water. Everything was all right. The small group got back on the road.

Henriette, who was a little flushed, smiled at us and said, "They were going to go over your way."

I felt my throat relaxing slowly, but this alarm that ended so well could have some aftermath. These Germans were looking for an old road that used to lead to Méautis by the narrow swamp below the farm. We had showed them another road at random, but they might come back in greater numbers and disperse in all directions. We were painfully aware of this. Then came along our friend, Féodal. He had a bundle on his back like a hobo and a walking stick cut from hedgerow. With a steady pace he crossed the courtyard and greeted the group in a natural way.

"I am arriving like a beggar," he said, knowing that he would be received with pleasure, but nonetheless there was a certain melancholy in his smile as he said that.

Les Routes Sans Oiseaux

We immediately questioned him, and he confirmed what everybody already knew—the Germans were retreating for the moment, but the arrival of reinforcements worried him somewhat.

"It also seems to me that they are beginning to dig themselves in, and that's a bad sign."

"They won't have time," I said.

Féodal had no answer to this.

During our short absence, our cousins had decided that day to dig a long, deep trench covered with thick planks where everyone could take refuge in case of danger. We went to the nearest hedgerow to choose a good location. And there we were, striding in the tall grass, when an almost silent shell exploded a few meters behind the embankment. Flat on the ground and gasping from the violence of the explosion, we inhaled the bitter smoke. Then another shell fell in the trees, followed by several more, driving splinters into the bark and branches and, farther away, landing on the roof of the shed.

A large bull that had come up to us out of curiosity knelt down with a muffled bellow, then lay in its own blood. We must have been very pale. Féodal picked up his walking stick, brushed off his knees and tried to laugh to reassure us, but we weren't listening. The distance that separated us from the house seemed enormous.

But back in the kitchen, the solid beams and the close joist gave us some feeling of reassurance and some security. Instinctively we visually measured the thickness of the walls that formed all around us a natural and solid shelter. We were discouraged. Féodal placed the jagged splinter of a shell on the table. Everyone weighed it in their hands and rubbed their fingers over its sharp edges. This piece of iron told us that war was coming upon us, that it was on our tracks, and that there was no longer anywhere to flee.

"And the bull..." said Pierre. He didn't finish his sentence, for laughter brusquely cut off his voice—a strange, jerky laugh that stopped short.

Nevertheless some peace enfolded the house again for it was suppertime, a happy break after our emotional experiences. Meals were always copious in the kitchen. We had even too much meat since the 105mm howitzer shells had become our providers in killing many of our animals. And we always had bread to eat, even in the worst of times. Sometimes only our appetite was lacking. But this first evening around the long table represented a moment of happiness in our misfortune. And while the June night was slowly falling, noise of heavy artillery remained steadily spread along former boundaries and let us dream of the rest that finally awaited us in our beds.

The following day at the same hour, we were chatting in front of the crumb-covered table when a woman came to say in a low voice that some trucks were coming into the courtyard. We watched out the windows and through the half-opened door as slowly, noiselessly, the trucks lined up next to the stables. Armed soldiers got out of the trucks, but they didn't seem to be paying any attention either to the house or us. A tall Prussian of subordinate rank inspected the

Les Routes Sans Oiseaux

stable, barns, and storerooms. With a kick, he opened doors then entered with a pistol in his hands. Two or three soldiers followed him with guns at the ready, like hunters behind a pointer. The group gathered slowly in the courtyard.

There were too many of us in that ground floor room to watch them. We knew that after the stables were inspected, the house would be next. Quickly we went to our darkened rooms, stretched out on our beds, and began an anguished time of waiting.

As night fell the shooting began again on the roads. Through the broken windows smashed the night before, the brutal sounds vibrated in every room of the old house that outwardly appeared to be sleeping. Once again the artillery was hunting out our hiding place. Bursts of shells came closer, then passed us by. But finally the thunder crashed in the courtyard where two or three shells had exploded together. Then, after seconds of waiting in the great silence, the stride of a boot defied the night. I was worried about the nearby paratroopers and also about Féodal who didn't come back from his foolish escapade. He had put himself at the disposition of the Canadian who wanted to make a little visit to the enemy's camp. My cousins had lent clothes to the soldier, and our two henchmen had left with a few grenades and daggers in their pockets.

We were to find out the next day that all went well and that, after going to the neighboring village, they had returned to the little woods without passing by the farm. But the waiting was interminable with the silent enemy marching under our windows. Then I wished that some new shells would riddle the cobblestones. But the artillery became quiet.

I woke up from light sleep under the glare of a flashlight. In the darkness, I could see the silhouettes of several Germans and Henriette. Henriette explained in a low voice that we were refugees. The beam of light passed over my mother's bed, and then Marie's since she was sharing our room, our sparse baggage, and the bright eyes of Mascotte, the little spaniel lying in the corner. Then the door closed, and the Germans went quietly upstairs. I could hear them as they inspected every room, even the attic. Finally they came back through the hall.

Henriette came cautiously back into our room. "They are not going away," she murmured.

"What did they say?" I asked.

"Nothing, not a word to me, but Pierre heard them exchange a few words in their language."

A soldier coming back into the kitchen bumped into a chair, then opened the buffet. Others relit the fire. At midnight the shells were still falling.

Day broke slowly under a threatening sky. Maybe we had gotten a few minutes sleep. The courtyard seemed deserted. A crow lit on the dung heap and waddled around. Roosters crowed.

VI

The large room where we had our beds is now destroyed, but I can still see it, and I think that I will never forget the details of the furnishings and floor

Les Routes Sans Oiseaux

plan. There was a bronze statue of Joan of Arc flanked by two sconces that reflected in the mirror over the dark marble fireplace. A high window with small panes and a narrow door overlooked the courtyard. Because of the blasts, I would close the inside shutters, and we were in darkness.

On the walls were portraits of departed members of the family, children with first-communion armlets, smiling portraits that presided not long ago over family feasts at long tables then covered with white cloths, all in the fragrance of cakes, fruit, and flowers. Sometimes shafts of light that came through bullet holes in the shutters played on the portraits in their polished oak frames. Through the cracks in the door I would often spy on the soldiers passing by in the courtyard. The broad view of stables, roofs, and cobblestones surrounding ponds and gates open on the fields were a link for me to the slightly damp smell of that prison-like room where we lived at the time.

There I was before daybreak hoping against all odds that the Germans had left in the night.

Sometimes the pigsty emerged from the shadows and full daylight bathed doors and windows without any frightening presence of the enemy. I breathed easier. I told myself that in the morning we were going to open the shutters and laugh and shout that we were free, that the enemy had retreated, that our allies were already marching noiselessly in the nearest fields. We were uneasy about breaking the great silence with our joyful cries, but break it we must to dissipate the anguish of this morning that was as dead and dark as hell.

However, at the peak of our excitement appeared the first German coming out of the trenches with a heavy step. He was dirty and slimy, ashen, his back tired from his gun, his hands in his pockets. The only thing I could do was to throw myself on my bed from where I heard other detestable voices coming toward the pump.

Sometimes the cadence of heavier marching brought me back to my observation post. I saw four men carrying an injured comrade, who, speechless and ghastly with closed eyes, let himself be tossed about on a makeshift litter. The soldiers hastily stretched him out inside the kitchen door to bandage him temporarily. With sleeves rolled up like butchers, they ran to wash their hands and came back to the wounded soldier, speaking to him in low voices. Then the ambulance or just a Red Cross sidecar arrived with a hanging stretcher where the man was laid out in the open air and exposed to falling shells.

These soldiers on morning shift were to receive provisions that were brought to them in unlikely wagons stolen from everywhere and drawn by run-down horses. In their bare hands, they accepted butter, bread, salami, and, above all, precious long strips of cartridges that they hung around their necks, full haversacks of grenades and replacements for Bren guns in yellow steel cases. Yet, some soldiers went back up to the farm for no other reason than to sit on the little wall in front of the door, letting the rising sun warm their shoulders and maybe to see civilians and feel less lost in this inferno. We imagined that after so many days of battle without planes or relief they must be discouraged. And this strengthened our hope, but we were not yet aware of the power of their discipline and fanaticism.

Sergeants got into the habit of eating with us at the kitchen table. Then the soldiers did the same thing, for in the doomed unit that occupied our sector, a certain camaraderie bonded men to leaders. And so it became prudent to offer them our places at table and to take our meals in our rooms. Sometimes artillery men recognizable by the muted noise of their high boots mingled with these infantry paratroopers and SS in motley overalls fastened at the knees, high shoes, and green helmets. This whole group came and went incessantly through the house, elbowed the servants, and treated us like intruders and maybe even spies. They sensed that there was plenty of food and drink here that would be good to loot.

Our presence became quickly intolerable to some of them, though others we would have to admit, were always good-natured. I remember that for us the worst enemy was a tall, Prussian feldwebel who pretended that he couldn't understand or pronounce a single word of French. We simply called him the "SOB." When he was there, no one came out. And now I realize that most of the time I saw him from the rear. By his side was always a small group of corporals and soldiers who laughed hard at his jokes. But when he crossed the courtyard their eyes followed him with hatred and anger. At that time our most fervent wish was for a 105mm howitzer burst of shots that came sometimes too late sometimes too early, killing only our last chickens and depriving us of the pleasure of seeing this evil-doing brute reduced to a pulp. Later on, he was to be the cause of our worst anguish and the tragedy of this house.

The good weather of the first days turned bad. It was cold, rainy, and the cloudy sky covered the battle with grayness. The mud-covered soldiers tore the tarpaulins off our carts for their shelter. At night when we had to get up under a more violent attack, it was so dark that taking a baby downstairs took time and we could hear the soles of shoes testing the stairs and the wicker cradle creaking. Other than the blinding lightning, there was no light outlining the windows. In the drafty kitchen, we huddled against the walls, recognizing each other by voice and considering the attack finished when the noise of a downpour broke the silence.

But I have just forgotten to note that on the last day of good weather a staff officer arrived staying only about a half-hour at the farm with his very young officers in rich uniforms, new vehicles, and busy telephone operators. The leader got out last and saluted my cousin with neither courtesy nor arrogance. He was about fifty years old, dressed simply, a bit shorter than average, hardy, had brown eyes and hair, and appeared to know our language. With his forage cap he was wearing a cape that hid his epaulets and non-commissioned officer's boots. He had ordered three of

Les Routes Sans Oiseaux

our most comfortable rooms for himself. While we were moving our bags and covers to sleep in the barn, he sat down on a bench in the kitchen where I saw him close his eyes in fatigue and rub his hand over his face as if trying to chase away tiredness and worry. Then a lieutenant came and stood at attention in front of him and said a few words. The superior got up immediately and went out and got into a car that rushed away. The other cars followed. The only one left belonged to the telephone operators who were hurriedly rolling up their red wires so that they could leave.

I was to see this person again under other circumstances. For now, we interpreted the leader's departure in a favorable light, considering it as the announcement of close and violent shelling and imagining an allied attack this same day. The truth may have been simpler, or maybe it was only a mistake on the map—unless our paratroopers had been seen in the vicinity which was a possibility. If the latter, then it was urgent to warn them, and they left in the night, managing to cross the flooded marshes. Their camp was discovered only the second day after their departure. But, guilty of rashness or haste, they had left eggshells and bones in the woods—traces that were extremely dangerous for us.

The "SOB" came into the kitchen that day bristling with anger. Two armed soldiers who asked for the lady of the house were with him. My cousin came quickly to ask me to accompany her, and when the feldwebel saw us he gave an evil smile. I immediately tried to speak a few words of poor German in order to explain that I was a relative taking refuge here and offering my services to help my cousin understand the questions that would be asked. But he pointed to an interpreter who seemed to want his turn to talk in a French that was about as good as my German. Above all we had to stop this overly eager man, to confuse him with muddled explanations, and to avoid any precise questions.

"Ya, ya," I said, going back into my gibberish.

My cousin fought from her side, talking about old folks and children who were sheltered here. That wasn't the question. But we wanted to gain time, to think and figure out what was on the "SOB's" mind. We had often thought of the danger we were exposing ourselves to, but the allied paratroopers' camp discovered by the "SOB" himself was just too much. Crimson faced and wild eyed, this non-commissioned officer suddenly burst out in violent cursing in such a brutal voice that his mad gesture of tearing his pistol out of his pocket did not add much to his threat other than making it more immediate. I can no longer remember my thoughts of that moment. I think I was as calm as someone standing at the edge of a precipice without the time to measure its depth. My cousin was motionless, speechless, and flushed with embarrassment. It soon seemed to me that the non-commissioned officer who was cursing us did not know what to do with his gun that he was not yet ready to use but could no longer put back in his pocket.

We had to make it easier for him because sooner than losing face, he would likely fire his pistol.

"Monsieur," I said to the interpreter, "there is a misunderstanding. I didn't know that such an important thing was in question, but if enemy paratroopers are here, that is indeed very serious."

The feldwebel listened to me attentively. I saw that he understood. A little later he slipped his pistol back in its holster.

"You gave food to these enemy paratroopers?" asked the interpreter.

I looked at Henriette who didn't flinch as she answered slowly, "I never saw any paratroopers."

The Germans got out the white eggshells and the bones and put them in front of us.

"I do not understand," she said again.

And so, precise, detailed, and overwhelming explanations were given to us. Fortunately for us numerous refugees from Carentan, gone several days ago to a distant location, had camped in a neighboring thatched cottage for a week and had received provisions at the farm. The "SOB" himself must have noticed them.

"I have given eggs, meat, and bread to lots of people for some time now," said Henriette.

"What people?"

"Oh, strangers. Hungry refugees from everywhere."

Nothing more was left but to release our bloodhounds on a path where they were going to be lost. The deserted house saved us.

"Maybe the folks over there saw something?" said Henriette innocently.

"Show the way," said the interpreter.

They found the same evidence that was in the woods. The "SOB" decided all at once to have us told that we were free, but as we left, the look on his face worried us.

We came back to the farm. In the interest of safety, it was decided that Pierre would leave the next day and go for shelter at the home of friends in a nearby village. I helped him to bury the silver and precious objects. To avoid being noticed by soldiers who were coming and going in the courtyard, we carried the objects in our pockets, made several trips, and took different paths to get to the old bakery. We had chosen this spot located in a little field at the end of the garden as a hiding place. We would be able to dig in its earthen floor, and the closed door shielded us from the outside. For digging we had only a rusty, old spade with a half-burned handle that had served for a long time on baking days to push ashes from the oven into the corner.

Soon we dug a rather deep hole on the edge of the ashes that would hide the traces of our work later on. Then, both of us sat down on the smooth kneading trough to catch our breath and rest a little. The light scent of charred wood and flour still pervaded this dark, cool room. Crickets were chirping. Under a darkened beam, worms had left sulfurous tracks. Silence, solitude. So much sweetness bound us to this place; without a word, with nothing more than a nod of the head or a momentary look, we were able to share that precious instant with each other. A pig running free in the field came and rubbed against the door, making us jump in surprise. We realized that it was risky to remain there like conspirators. Pierre glanced at our work and smiled in satisfaction. We looked all around and stared at the sky that could at any moment drop more shells.

On the way back we ran into Féodal who was looking for us. "Quickly," he exclaimed, "the "SOB" is there, and he is furious and almost out of control!"

Without too much trouble we slipped into the crowd of refugees—servants and kinfolk—that encircled the lady of the house who was dealing with the brute.

"I don't understand anything," said the poor woman, "speak French."

But, without listening, the feldwebel paced back and forth like a caged animal in the middle of the kitchen as the interpreter tried to explain. "The chief says that you must leave."

"For good?"

"No."

There was the problem. Go where? Why? The stupid soldier pointed to the stables and barns.

"Go to the stables?"

"Yes, yes."

The "SOB," his face red with anger, rubbed the butt of his pistol again, when, very opportunely, three men carried in a wounded soldier. We had not been aware of the latest artillery rounds; this soldier would remember it for a long time in his beloved Germany; that is, if he ever got the chance to see his homeland again. Both his legs had been torn to pieces, and he was bleeding heavily. When his comrades rolled up their sleeves and tried to bandage him, their arms immediately became red with blood.

The non-commissioned officer yelled, "Bring linen!"

Just as previously, my cousin brought the best she had. The wounded soldier, stretched out on the cobblestone of the kitchen floor, closed his eyes submissively. The "SOB" knelt at his side, took his dirty hand, and looked at him intensely as he would a beloved brother.

We had left the room in silence, but I was still present at the departure of the wounded soldier on the stretcher hung from the sidecar. His blond hair was shining in the sun, and the linen that bound his legs rapidly became stained with blood. He spoke in a low voice, and his superior immediately lit a cigarette and put it between his lips. The motorcycle turned slowly, then disappeared down he road.

The "SOB" officer entered the kitchen, and the interpreter's shrill voice called out in its sharpest tone, "Madame! Madame!"

It was after that when Henriette came to tell us that we all had to leave the house for an hour or two and go to the stables.

VII

We unconsciously huddled together on the cobblestones with our blankets and suitcases while the interpreter circled us like a sheep dog.

"You leave only in threes or fours," he barked.

Féodal had my mother's bag and naturally fell in with us. He was pale and had the same wild look that he had before the scuffles. Had the feldwebel standing on the threshold noticed this?

"Just a minute," the "SOB" said.

But another problem took the feldwebel's attention away. My cousin and her son were also carrying luggage. He gave an order and two soldiers rushed forward to seize the suitcases. The interpreter explained things. We moved away.

Some groups entered the storerooms in the pressing shed, and soldiers came to close the doors. I had, of course, taken the path to the old bakery. What was going to happen? We were lost in speculation.

Féodal was in a rage. "At any rate it is time to get this over with! I have had it with this SOB!"

"Be quiet, old friend," I cautioned.

We were followed like the others. Féodal took my mother's arm since she had trouble walking in the grassy field. We arrived at the abandoned hovel. Our guardians closed the door behind us and attached the outside chain, locking us in the building. Somehow or another we settled in the darkness and began to speak in low voices while listening to the noises outside—planes flying so low that the gust shook the old tiles. Then a few explosions in the distance. Pigs were still grunting around the bakery and rubbing against the cornerstones. This dark room that had become our prison seemed colder than before.

"What are they going to do to us?" asked my mother as she began to cry.

"Maybe they are just going to rob us or at least frisk our pockets," replied Féodal calmly.

We had nothing compromising on us, but we valued our money. Our friend jumped up on the dough trough to get to a crack that he noticed in the wall and signaled to us that this would be a good hiding place, so it was there that we hid most of our savings. Marie regretfully entrusted her nice bills, kept warm in her corset, into the dust and cobwebs.

"Farewell!" said Féodal gaily, alighting from his perch.

He could not have been closer to the truth. This building, damaged by an explosion the day before yesterday while my cousin's son-in-law was baking, would burst into flames some days later. Terrible new worries kept us from even thinking of coming back for our possessions.

Our guardians made a first round, then several bursts of 105mm howitzer shells exploded nearby. We looked uneasily at the dilapidated, old ceiling hanging low over our heads. Féodal rolled a cigarette and smoked without speaking. He had to relight the butt several times, puckering his lips under his moustache toward the flame of his lighter.

At last, after some time, our two infantrymen finally came back to unlatch the door, and smiling, said to us, "Go back now!"

It was after seven o'clock when we arrived back at the farm. Our friends were already in their rooms. Henriette came in and sat down with us. "Are you going to eat something?" she asked absent-mindedly.

She didn't ask what had happened to us. She seemed reflective in the room's dim light.

Féodal asked right away, "Is something wrong, Madame?"

She motioned for him to get closer. "Pierre is going to leave at dawn, and I fear for him."

"What, exactly?"

"I do not know. Everything! They searched the house after going through our suitcases."

"That was predictable."

"And nothing is out of order," said Henriette. "You could say that they were very careful."

"Did they steal anything?"

"No, they went everywhere, emptied our wardrobes and suitcases, and then put things back in place. There were only little indications, like a piece of fallen wool or an upside down embroidery. It's so alarming."

"Oh!"

"Yes! They found nothing," added Henriette. "Neither a pack of American cigarettes nor a weapon, but what about tomorrow?"

"We understand very well that tomorrow they might find what they want. But if the "SOB" intended to hide compromising things today, why would he not have found them right away?"

"Perhaps because he wants to surprise us if he gives us the order to empty furniture and pull back our bedding right in front of him."

Féodal got up. "In that case, we don't have a minute to lose," he said. "We had better check everything."

To assure ourselves that there was nothing compromising hidden in this old home with its many rooms, filled wardrobes and chests and dark corners, we divided the task. Féodal was in charge of the attic and all the old things left there. Each refugee was responsible for his room. Henriette and her son would do the rest. It was work that had to be done rapidly, in silence and almost in darkness. And we were not to forget either the back of a frame or bedsprings. After almost an hour Henriette and Féodal came to tell us that nothing had been found. Feeling a little calmer, we wished each other good night.

VIII

The feldwebel whom we called the "SOB" was there early in the morning and was very loud. The night had been hard. We had not even undressed for bed, and twice we had to jump up for artillery alarms that each lasted about an hour. Bumping into doors and furniture in the darkness, we made it to the kitchen where we always met for solidarity in times of great danger. An American attack flared in the direction of the road, and we were in for intense artillery preparation that we took calmly at first since it was not aimed at us. The foggy night air carried the sound well. The 105mm howitzers had never seemed so angry and distinct.

From the beginning we had tried to locate the fires that reddened the sky. We remained speechless confronted by this endless image of war, but then new flashes of lightning tore the night to pieces. First they spread like sparks from burning paper, and then their lightning razed the ground in bolts of fire while splendid lights deployed slowly in the clouds. On the crackling background of the furnace, powerful explosions came from on high. Then the attack became an enormous, rolling machine. We thought we heard a fantastic engine with huge wheels advancing slowly like a giant steam plough tilling bodies like clods of dirt. Its heavy movement shook the ground down to our very feet. These silent underground shocks that resounded beneath our heels and through the flagstone gave us an even greater supernatural impression than we had had from the lightning and strange noises. Widening the range, large-caliber shells exploded at random, sometimes close to us.

Against all this nothing would be able to defend us; the thickest walls would yield under their impact. A baby whined in his fragile cradle. Finally for a few minutes we were suffocated with silence; the immense machine had just stopped, and the sky was dead. There was no light at our windows. Then the firing began again everywhere, on villages, fields, and farms. It focused on us, hurling stones and splinters, breaking and destroying everything, and threatening to sweep away the house where we were huddled. It was so heavy, unjust, and cruel that our tears flowed.

The time shells especially frayed our nerves. Their evil power seemed so absolute that their targeted man would be crushed without hearing their thunder. In the midst of the racket, the big door opened and soldiers entered. You could see their stooped figures in the lightning flashes. They turned over a table and dishes and helped a drunken man to sit down. He was either vomiting up his alcohol or dying. In the brief flash of a cigarette lighter we saw emerging from a bloody uniform a face that was nothing more than a swollen wound with a gaping, foaming mouth. My cousins and my mother were horrified and wanted to go back to their rooms in the midst of the debris, and, for the first time, they sobbed at length. After the experience of that night the evil feldwebel returned to us.

At dawn we took account of the damage: the pigs killed in the courtyard, caved in roofs, a wide hole in the frame of a barn. We heard the "SOB" kick the garden gate open brutally, and his voice that at first seemed far away became suddenly violent and near. Soldiers were rushing to gather around him.

He came upon our little group with big steps, and holding in his hands a kind of white rag, a piece of curtain or lace, he bellowed, "What is this?"

We did not recognize it right away, but Henriette soon understood that it was a piece of old linen used as a scare crow on current bushes in this season.

"Yes," she answered, "it is used to scare away the birds in the garden."

"In the garden, ya, and the signal can be seen from a distance," said the interpreter.

"The signal?" Henriette tried to laugh, but the non-commissioned officer's scathing look made her turn pale.

How to explain the simple and ordinary truth to this brute? She struggled with this.

"You understand," she said, "the little birds..."

"The paratroopers, yes," the feldwebel answered, waving at the surrounding area with the piece of the cloth.

"No, Sir."

"No?" The German's sneering became ferocious.

The poor woman tried to fight back again. "I will explain to the commander."

"To the commander?" Ah! Yes, you speak to me. Now."

And coming close to Pierre whom two soldiers surrounded right away, the "SOB" victoriously put the rag under the lad's nose.

"For the paratroopers, right?"

We sensed that the German had already made up his mind and that things were going badly. Féodal jumped in first. In vehement German gibberish mixed with French, he tried to plead this lost cause. First he was rather calm as he tried to explain the innocent country custom of protecting our produce with whatever we had on hand.

He said, "Come with me, chief, I am going to show you on the spot."

The German spoke to his men and followed Féodal, and all the refugees went along, too. Here, by the bushes, was the proof.

"As you see, the birds..."

"Me understand," the chief smiled maliciously while looking beyond the fields at the nearby countryside occupied by our allies.

In a rage, Féodal tore away all the red and white rags and trampled them into the damp ground. When he came back to plant himself in front of our derisive enemy, soldiers surrounded him and began to search him. He threw his pipe and lighter at their feet.

Then he grabbed his army belt with a metal buckle that was a war souvenir and said, "*Gott mitt uns.* I took this at Verdun, and now I am giving it back to you." He stood there, his arms folded across his chest.

The non-commissioned officer, very red in the face, spit out only a few words. Our friend, Féodal was now a prisoner. He left right away under escort with Pierre. The young lad kissed his mother, waved to us and followed his captors. At the courtyard gate, Pierre turned for a final farewell, and then we saw him bow his head close to Féodal who was walking very erect.

IX

My memories of the days that followed are dim. They consist of nothing more than a series of anxieties and dashed hopes. American patrols sometimes came very near and then were pushed back. The shrill roll of their submachine guns came closer in the fields, and then the grenades and machine guns joined in, and the Germans who had run across the courtyard soon returned with their wounded. To punish us more, artillery sprayed the ground.

One day at noon a shell entered a bedroom that a woman had just left. She came down the steps shouting fire as the smoke was choking us. Other shells fell so close that they deafened us and forced us against the walls. We figured that the time to leave would be when the flames forced us out. Fire didn't break out then but caught the next day around midnight in the barns. All the crackling, heat, and red glow through our obstructed windows made us worry that our carts and wagons in the shed might burn. They were our sole means of transport if we received an official order to leave this place. We felt that our allies were near, but the threat of evacuation weighed heavy on us by the hour, for leaving would mean the end of what freedom we had. But our presence created difficulties for the Germans, and tension was rising by the day. This worry, along with anxiety for our two comrades taken captive, Féodal and Pierre, filled our thoughts.

At nightfall, I could hear Henriette's voice praying, while the enemy soldiers were at the table. Just as every day during peacetime, she knelt on the floor of her large kitchen with her daughters, sons-in-law, and servants, and began in a slow, clear voice, "Let us put ourselves in God's presence and worship him."

The soldiers would then be quiet. Even in the bedrooms and the rooms where we were huddled, the lulling of eternal phrases brought its gentleness. The litanies of the Blessed Mother unfolded their ardor in a slow crescendo, "Pray for us, pray for us…"

Then the repetition of the invocation suddenly ebbed into a slow rhythm in which the prayer seemed to die away. "Have pity on us, Lord."

At that point we heard the scrape of a chair being pushed back and footsteps. I believe that we were asleep when Henriette called to us from the door, "Get up, we must leave!"

A soldier came in with her and, after I asked him some questions, he could only repeat,

"You must leave!"

It was raining and we were to take only one suitcase and leave our means of transportation. What about the ill and the handicapped? The orderly shrugged his shoulders, knowing only one word, "Leave."

I shouted back to him, "Non!" In order to see his face, I grabbed his hand and turned the blinding flashlight toward him. I saw a face without malice, big blue eyes that were surprised at my boldness, and a hay-colored, unshaven beard.

"Monsieur knows nothing about it; he has his orders, and his men are here," said Henriette, conscious not only of the helplessness but also the revulsion that this man seemed to experience in the face of his task. "We must see the commander." she added.

The soldier didn't answer, and I guessed that this was what we had to do. Henriette repeated, "We want to see the commander."

"He is not here."

"We know the house where he is staying, and we know him personally. Tell that to your leader. We know him because he has already been here."

Les Routes Sans Oiseaux

This was maybe being too aggressive but it was the only excuse we had, and surely the only one that was likely to make the "SOB" who had given the order, hesitate. However, we had to act quickly and boldly. Without delay, we pushed the surprisingly obedient soldiers away, opened the door on the black, rainy, fiery night, and without any hesitation we quickly crossed the courtyard. Would they fire on us? We sensed that the corporal would not give that order, and furthermore we no longer had a choice since slowing down would be more dangerous than showing confidence.

"We must have courage!" exclaimed Henriette.

My hip was aching, but we went ahead. German shells were hissing over the farm at regular intervals. After the prolonged boom from their distant launching, they followed a long circuit, and as we did not hear their explosions in the east, we had the feeling that they were going to be lost in the distance. I have noted this strange impression on other occasions. In the rainy night, the moving whistling sounds seemed to us like the rapid flight of silent birds.

As we were crossing the fields, the heavy tread of a courier on our tracks stopped us and shouted, "Go back, Madame! Go back!"

He put on his most pleasant voice; we had won. But should we try to go farther right away? And for what?

"Return!" said the breathless man. "You do not leave yet."

It was a rainy night, and at any time the red flashes that we saw fading in the distance might explode over our heads.

Henriette said in a low voice, "We must go back." And so we returned to our quarters.

The "SOB" did not appear at the farm the following day. The corporal with the big wide eyes came to see us. He wanted to explain to us that he was happy at the outcome of events, very happy, in fact, as he had an elderly mother and young children in Germany. To me his eyes seemed tearful at that moment. Was he sincere? I think so. He was also a little simple-minded. He offered me a cigarette and talked about the war. He said that soon the Americans would be driven back into the sea. But he recognized their courage and the strength of their weapons.

"And so?"

"We have something else forthcoming, Monsieur, an electric cannon."

"Ah, yes."

"Americans, kaput! Tommies, kaput!"

He was killed some hours later. His vacant blue eyes never lost their look of utmost surprise.

The threat of being sent away was not eliminated. The evil chief was not likely to accept defeat, and orders could come from a higher authority. The problem of transportation would then be keenly felt because the farm had only two horses and a mule for five families and numerous servants. All the other draft animals had been stolen or killed. I had let my mare go in the marshes in the first days and hadn't seen her

Les Routes Sans Oiseaux

since. Moreover we were not allowed to go in that area. The Germans had taken half of my harnesses along with the tarpaulin of my wagon. I had hidden the rest under my bed, but what good would they do?

We felt that the firm ground supporting our habits, daily concerns, and our past was soon going to disappear and cast us into the unknown. We still sometimes thought about all that we had lost, our dear ones that we would see no more, our abandoned animals and our home, but already all these things were fading in memory. All that counted anymore were the noises of war, the attack, the enemy, the frightening worry at every instant of being taken hostage, and the dread of hearing about the death of those taken prisoner and not heard from since.

When it would be necessary to leave—for we sensed dimly that it would come—what would those unable to walk do? And how could we carry the food and linens necessary for the long days of our exodus?

We will take the hay wagons," said Henriette. "We will pile up wheat, containers of fat, bacon, covers, mattresses, sheets, and the sick folks and children will sit on top of everything."

Those were our precious belongings that one single explosion could destroy along with us.

This thought put our worries in perspective.

"We'll see!" we said to ourselves.

And so, with not much concern, four of us played cards at the foot of a bed, and during the game our oldest members reminisced about World War I. The game began with gaiety, and we let ourselves sink into a strange mirth while rolling cigarettes and having a drink. The need to laugh is perhaps the most curious sensation in such times. However, these moments did not last very long and were always replaced by new worries.

Soldiers were setting up an observation post on our roof where a fanatic was amusing himself by shooting his pistol into the kitchen. Though there was no real harm, an atmosphere of fear permeated the place. The threat of a brutal evacuation or the taking of new hostages took precedence over everything else.

Perhaps we did not fully realize the danger of those terrible hours and held on to a deep feeling that the danger would pass. I have distressing memories of those raw and rainy days. A handsome, purebred horse was tied to a heavy cart for a week. Maybe with nothing to eat or drink, without horseshoes, worn-out hooves, and limping from dragging logs used by the soldiers to cover their shelters; he had been abandoned in the courtyard under a shower of shells in the night. In the morning, his belly was exposed and his thighs mangled, but he was still breathing and attached to the overturned wagon. The rain spread his blood around him. I can see once again soldiers with their exhausted faces at the cruel hour of dawn, making wooden crosses with branches. I see the wounded and the dead. I see Henriette's eyes shining feverishly with anxiety.

We asked for a meeting with the one that we believed to be the commander. Arriving near the house in the meadow, my cousin spoke first to a young Prussian in a fine uniform. This arrogant soldier squinted while looking at the fields or trees without even pretending to understand what we said to him.

"The commander came to my house," Henriette said boldly. "I would like to speak to him again."

"The commander?" jeered the officer.

However, he gave an order to a soldier standing at attention, who turned on his heel and motioned us to follow him into the courtyard. Then a non-commissioned officer came toward us, took orders, and had us follow him through a kitchen where there were soldiers in shirtsleeves and blue aprons. Next we entered a dark room with windows blocked by sacks of dirt. Two other lieutenants astride a bench were smoking cigars at a big table covered with gray cards. In the last dim room, an officer, whom we took for a commander, appeared to be waiting for us by the light of a lamp. He stepped up and once again we recognized his intelligent look and calm, courteous voice.

My cousin blushed and tears spurted from her eyes. She murmured just this, "Sir, I beg of you."

At that time it seemed to me that the officer stiffened slightly. I rapidly tried to explain the purpose of our visit, the futile grounds for arresting Pierre and my friend Féodal. I waited for a while under a stare that had become suspicious. At that moment, a neutral voice assured me that in full battle all safety measures had to be taken and that an investigation would be made. I tried to plead, but with a wave of his hand he replied, "I will consider it!" The officer bowed to my cousin, and there was nothing more to do but leave.

Was this man unaware of the fate of the hostages on this date, June 25th? I doubt it. But this matter remains obscure and always will.

I heard the noise of typewriters upstairs. Probably this was headquarters preparing a notice that all the residents of the region would receive in a few days. In fact, a typed page was later delivered to our house by an orderly. It announced in French and in German that we were to retreat to the south of the Lessay-Périers-Saint-Lô road by July 1 at the latest. The residents were authorized to depart with their property and even their herds. Beyond this time limit, the evacuation would be carried out in trucks, without baggage, and any civilian encountered in the forbidden area would be considered as a sniper.

X

The order arrived on a very confused evening. Combat had not been too hard that day, and the soldiers of the paratrooper and SS divisions, who with more liberty than the other regiments, had come in a larger number than usual to eat and drink at the farm. The "SOB" was seated like a comrade in their midst at table, and, for the first time in the campaign they were playing quick card games like baccarat. French money was piling up by the handful in front of them, and from the room where I was stretched out on my bed I could hear their laughter and excited voices over the distant roar of battle. Here they were, in a half burned down farm, so close to the front trenches—tombs that awaited them—amid worried civilians and the stench of death, yet the soldiers were laughing loudly and happily playing with Luck. Then suddenly a surly voice broke out in rage, and a riot followed to the noise of boots hurled around the room, broken wood, and shattered glass. The fight was violent and short, and then two shots were fired.

My cousin and our servant, both pale with fear, came into my room. "They are killing each other!"

I would have shouted bravo if the quarrels of these beasts were not so dangerous up close. Now the "SOB" was yelling orders and insults, and then the dead silence that followed was so threatening that when one of our cousins came to the door and spoke casually we pulled him inside and quickly told him to be quiet.

"Damn!" he exclaimed. "I don't give a damn! Read this!"

He handed us the evacuation order that he was to deliver to all of us, and it seemed that an enormous wall was going up in front of us and putting an end to our hope. We counted on our fingers that we still had three days to stay here. A lot could happen in that time.

Neighbors came the next day to find out about our decision. "What if we refuse to leave?" we asked each other.

But we could do nothing against this power. Some folks were already leaving. They did not want to risk their lives and feared as well the crowded roads of these last days. They took little with them—food, mattresses, and a few chickens in cages. Some, who no longer had their horses, left with wheelbarrows. According to the senseless order, we were allowed to take our flocks; however, everyone had already abandoned the cows and sheep that constituted their livelihood. Hearing this devastating news, we remained silent and confused. What day would we leave? We did not know. No doubt the very last day. Above all, we wanted to hold on to hope and wait for Pierre's return until the end. I don't think that any of us slept those last nights.

It was cold and rainy. The battle was becoming a constant artillery duel with long, successive German rallies into a bleak sky. The American 105mm howitzers arrived in a pack, followed by countless others pell-mell, without direction or restraint. Then it appeared that under all this firepower the Germans were forced back into their lairs and would be quiet for good. When their enemies seemed tired they would re-emerge from their silent holes and once again coldly calculate their shots. In the night, I tried to imagine their haunt. I brought back in my mind every corner of the surrounding area, trying to determine where they could be lurking. I visualized fields, paths, and a line of small tall pines on a slope. I was sure that it was there, but our careless allies were aiming lower and shooting everywhere, which seemed shortsighted and wasteful to us.

Without the energy for bodily care, we let our beards grow. On Thursday, June 29, one of our two mares was lightly wounded in the belly, so we brought the other mare and the mule into the sheepfold for better protection. Friday, June 30, we seriously began to prepare our departure. We brought down the grain,

Les Routes Sans Oiseaux

killed a pig, and plucked the fowl that we found frantic in the courtyard after the alarms. We hid linen in unlikely places, such as under a paving stone or a bundle of sticks. A matter of conscience weighed upon me. If I left with my cousins, I would be a burden on them; if I left without them, it would be sad and cowardly. And furthermore, without even a donkey, I didn't have a way to pull my wagon.

"We will all go together." said Henriette. But she sensed my uneasiness. After thinking about it for a while, she kindly offered me her mule if I wanted to leave on my own. For the reasons that I just mentioned, I accepted. Since I also had Marie and my sick mother, we decided that we would seek refuge with friends who lived just to the south of the Périers-Saint-Lô road—near the boundary that I wanted to stay close to while awaiting the allied break-through.

Our departure was first fixed for the next day, July 1, at the latest. Then in rereading the evacuation order and weighing all the words, we concluded that we would be able to wait for dawn on Sunday, July 2. Henriette and her people would leave the same day.

The soldiers would look at us slyly and ask, "Not leaving?"

But we paid no attention to them. It seemed to us that we were already out of danger since we were covered by their leader's order. We crossed the courtyard without even listening to them. A dead horse, lying in the courtyard, was enormous on the broken traces, and the cadavers of the bull and other animals killed in the first days made a terrible stench.

We looked for thongs, ropes, and boxes. Our wagons were going to be heavily laden. I could have taken so many things—there was still so much left to lose! But my wagon was small and had spongy springs. My little spaniel, Mascotte, followed on my heels everywhere, seeming to say: "Don't forget me!" A fine and affectionate little animal.

Coming back in the house, I jostled the soldiers in order to get through the kitchen and without so much as excusing myself, I just said, "Come with me, Mascotte."

I found Henriette in a pensive mood seated next to my mother. "I was just showing this old finery to my aunt. It hurts me to leave so many things…" With a faraway look she silently spread out on her knees a piece of yellowed lace. I could sense that she was thinking about her son.

The morning of our departure was gray and cold. We hadn't slept. Soldiers had walked continuously through the house and courtyard, and two long artillery alarms had kept us flat against a shaking wall for several hours. As soon as the shells became farther apart or more distant, the soldiers' footsteps and voices could be heard again here and there. What were they going to do in the hidden recesses and in the stables? At the first light of dawn, I understood the reasons for this activity. To celebrate, or maybe even hasten our departure since they found our slowness annoying, the Germans had pillaged what was left of our hen house, killed several pigs and sheep, and carried it all away. A few hogs that were spared from the slaughter were just wandering around snorting. Doors and dormer windows were gaping just like the blackened walls of the burned barn. Every kind of debris and animal cadavers added to the desolate atmosphere. My first step on the cobblestones resounded to the other end of the courtyard where a servant's footsteps could be heard on a threshold. "What a mess!" said the servant.

When I worried about the horses, he reassured me. Emboldened by the silence, I advanced slowly. A soldier was sleeping, seated on the ground with his back against the wall. The servant motioned to me that others were resting under our car in the shed. The pavement around the pump was red with blood, and torn trousers and a shirt trailed in its pool. More than pillage had occurred in the night. Marie came out to help us saddle the mule. We pushed the wagon silently to avoid disturbing the sleepers. It was damaged by shells, but the frame and wheels were still solid. The horse had only one shoe out of four.

"So, he will just trot slower," said the servant in a low voice. Why was he speaking in such a low voice now, I wondered.

Henriette came up to us and also murmured a few words to us while the wind stirred the dripping leaves. "You'll be the first to leave?" she asked.

"If you wish."

"Yes, because there are enough of us to load the wagons, and since you'll be taking the bridge road you have to go at dawn, before the first planes."

I had not thought of this detail or of the fact that the bridge might have been demolished.

"The bridge was still intact last evening," she informed me. "I made inquiries." She asked that I load a sack of wheat, bacon, a ham, brandy, and bread. "Some chickens, too, if there are any left," she added.

Marie wanted to catch one of the rabbits out of their cage and went into a stable full of hay, but a furious voice stopped her.

"Rauss!" a German voice shouted out.

"Why?" I asked.

The German drew his gun, and we had to pull back without understanding why. Did he know the reason for his anger? All of a sudden he seemed to think about it and went after the rabbits. He caught one.

"Is this what you want?" he asked.

"Yes, Sir, thank you."

Then he beckoned me to follow him to the stable where he showed me two stretched out bodies.

"That one is dead!" he said.

The man didn't even have his eyes closed, and the other, who was turned to the wall, was still struggling to breathe.

"This one is going to die, too, and he is my friend…"

The only thing I could do before leaving was to bow my head.

Henriette was waiting with a shawl around her shoulders. The morning was bitter and cold. I realized that she had lost weight. I told her the story of the two dying men, and for the first time, I saw hatred in her eyes.

"So much the better," she said. Was it really Henriette talking that way?

Her sons-in-law, daughters, and the refugees and servants came to help us, to say farewell and shake hands. My mother painfully lifted herself up on the covers and suitcases with my little dog between her legs. Marie took her place on a sack, and I went inside one last time to see the tall mirror, Joan of Arc on her pedestal, the portraits on the walls, and the lampshade —all these fragile things that were still untouched.

Henriette came up to speak privately to me. "If you should get word of Pierre before I do…" Her voice trailed off with a soft sob. She planned to get to the west coast, and she gave me the names of several places where she might be contacted.

"Good-bye, Henriette, have courage," I said.

Strong as she was, she began to cry. Mother wept hopelessly as well. When I shook hands with my friends, I saw their lips quiver with sadness at our departure.

"Good-bye! Good-bye!" I couldn't say anything else. The mule turned his head to see me mount and seemed to understand that I was his new master, and so he quietly trotted off. Our friends waved us good-bye, and I wanted to call out, "Farewell! Farewell, my friends! Leave quickly because this calm is not going to last." But I could not utter a word. With a feeble gesture, I pointed to the sky and was on my way.

The air was brisk in this open cart, and the tires didn't make any noise. The only sound was a rusty spring that seemed to moan as we moved away.

Silence. In this morning hour, the smell of deceased flesh was interrupted by the fresh scent of the fields. No more birds; no living, familiar noises; no more whippoorwill calls, wagons, mowers, or pens for gentle cattle to rub against. Just disturbed earth, flattened hay, and a dead cow all swollen with outstretched limbs and glass-like eyes. Slashed, yellow branches were hanging everywhere in the green trees. Other branches had fallen across the narrow road, and I had to stop and clear them twice. Marie helped to clear the way. We all wanted to be as far away as possible from this fearful silence.

Back on the road again, I made the mule trot, and to cheer us up a bit I asked his name. Marie did not know, and my mother just shrugged her shoulders. So I decided that he would be called Pompon.

A German car sounded the horn behind us and passed in a hurry. These were the first uniforms and living beings that we had seen in almost two kilometers. We went through a little village and were astonished to see open, abandoned houses. We knew that the evacuation order had expired at midnight and expected to find people ready to go, yet these inhabitants had already left. In the well-tended gardens that were beginning to produce early vegetables and in the courtyards, little chicks were peeping, and rabbits and a cat were running around. Doghouses were empty. In the kitchens the clocks were still ticking. Bottles and glasses were left on one table. Were we going to see someone watching us from a doorway? No. The smokeless, noiseless air was filled with loneliness.

Les Routes Sans Oiseaux

A drizzling rain dampened our clothes, hands, and faces. I walked down the slope toward the marshes. Gray foliage of poplars appeared over the roofs of a farm. And behind us the American artillery was starting up at a distance. You cannot imagine how quickly the noise of battle dies out in the silent desert of the back lines. We felt that we were already out of danger in this place. I stopped the wagon to see where the shells were landing, and it seemed to me that they were aiming for my cousins' farm or maybe a bit behind it.

"Maybe we could park a little to the rear," I whispered.

Our friends would be busy loading their things in the courtyard at this hour. We felt remorse at being here, but at the same time we were relieved. If the bridge were destroyed, we would have to go back a long distance. The road whose shoulders were hidden by low-hanging poplar branches kept going downhill. Some trees had been cut in two and uprooted by bombs that left black craters in the chalky earth. But the dislocated bridge still held on its pier. The German car had passed through, so we could venture between the twisted railings. The marsh's endless extent of rushes lay in front of us. Pompon picked up his quiet trot. It started to rain more heavily, and my mother became pale and disoriented from the cold air and the movement of the cart that rocked like a boat. As I wrapped her in a coat I could feel her icy tears against my cheek. At each step, at each turn of the road, our house and our people were farther away. They could not know the sadness in our souls at this hour of solitude.

Surprisingly, a few remaining swallows flew by. The noise of artillery was loud and close on the low, marshy land and diminished sharply as the road rose in the high lands.

I stopped at a village with an iron-works. In one of the rooms we heard footsteps that we thought must be the blacksmith. Right away I remembered him, and I called out familiarly as I would to a customer or friend, "René! Is it you?"

I saw a black hat with an upturned brim and braided border—one of those hats that the country folk keep forever to wear to funerals—and then the face of a stranger in a gray pullover.

"René Lalande?" I inquired.

"Nein!"

At that moment, the stranger's comrade dropped a heavy drawer, and in the hubbub the black hat disappeared.

"Let's go, Pompon!" I called quickly to the mule.

A Red Cross station was set up in a nearby school. The car that had passed us was parked there, but under the shelter and behind the tall classroom windows there was no one. No beds, no wounded, not a living soul. Was the enemy army so disorganized? Such a lack of effective forces was probably due to the impossible path through the marshes that we had to take to Périers. And this dirt road narrowed even more on the way out of the village. Like everywhere else, we passed by lonely wide-open doors, abandoned gardens, and empty courtyards. Then we entered a sparse area on the edge of the marshes. As the land became poorer, the hamlets were farther apart, and the farms were less well kept with moldy thatched or ugly metal roofs. There was a gray, autumnal atmosphere that you would not expect in summer. Under a clump of tall trees abandoned by the crows, the drizzle glazed the piles of bricks and gray stones of the disintegrated Saint-Germain chateau. This fine rain of our coastal regions heightened the sadness of the ruins. But soon the rain stopped and once again all we could hear was the pace of the mule and the moan of the rusty springs.

XI

The little village where we were going was called Feugères. It is a pleasant market town at the edge of the first hills toward the South. The lower part of the town is similar to our region with its broad meadows, thick hedges, and swamps. The rest of the village blends in with the wide horizon of the Avranchin and the Mortainais. The sloped fields lead into a large stand of tall oaks. This region of the Manche is a country of sudden changes in landscape. Before arriving at the first trout streams, we had to go for several kilometers along brackish waters and winding, shady roads. Then we went through other villages before finally reaching Périers where we were expecting to find a few acquaintances.

The town sits at the crossroads of two main thoroughfares, Carentan-Coutances and Saint-Lô-

Lessay. The church steeple stands out as a landmark from where we were, a good distance away.

A large newly repointed house with white shutters and a wrought iron gate enclosing a gravel courtyard told us that the town was near. The house was deserted, and the sheds were empty. All around, lost animals were wandering through unfenced fields. I whipped the mule with no concern for his pain because we were in such a hurry to see and talk to folks.

"We have reached the first houses," said Mother.

They had not been too damaged except for several roofs and windowpanes. When you go into a small town, the first houses that you see are rural in appearance. They look like country homes in their furnishings and wide-open fireplaces. I stopped in front of an open door and called out. We expected to hear a footstep or see a neighbor on the threshold. Surely not everyone could have left.

"There must be someone,' said Mother.

A calendar was askew on the wall. A curtain was missing. A crucifix with palms was hanging on an unplastered wall of a little room.

My mother whispered in a broken voice, "No one is here."

I called out once more. "Is anyone here?" And when there was no answer, in a low voice I added, "Let's go."

The donkey trotted to the main street where we saw the first devastation.

Since that day, we have seen far too many ruins, too many gutted houses exposing beams and chimneys.

Les Routes Sans Oiseaux

We have seen too much broken plaster, collapsed frames, ruins still giving off dust, and heaps of debris that had been beautiful buildings and villas, now all reduced to tombs. The spectacle of death numbs any hope of finding a prosperous street with stores and cafés. This unexpected view of the ruins in Périers corresponded to the despair in our soul and the growing anguish of our trip. I believe that in the future when people speak to me about the destruction of war, the first thing that will come to mind is this village of the Manche in the silence of that eerie morning.

The ruins blocked the whole street and square. We were reaching the heart of the disaster. The steeple was still standing over the nave of the collapsed church, but it was so cracked and full of holes that it was a miracle that it was still there.

Where we stopped by heaps of rubble, there was a strong stench. Even our nervous donkey snorted and refused to go on. The only thing we could do was to turn around and look for a path out of this dead town. We started walking along walls that were still standing and came upon a sheep dog lying down with his head on his paws. On his neck he had a horrible wound that was covered with worms.

The odor was so strong that I attempted to cover up the truth by saying, "That must be what we smelled."

Mother shook her head as if to say no, but at the same time made an effort to whisper, "Maybe."

Coming back we took the Carentan road. Behind the stone calvary monument I knew a path across a prairie that should lead us to Périers' south exit. A sidecar slipped in the mud and was sputtering but managed to pull itself out. We were buffeted on the soft earth, and on the Saint-Lô road the exit became difficult. We had to take detours, follow a path in the ruins of a school, then take a street as horrible as the one on which we arrived. But we turned our backs on the ruins. We saw an open country road in the distance. Some houses had no roofs; others seemed intact. Gradually the houses had more space between and were surrounded by gardens. A man stopped at a gate on the edge of the road to look at us. We called and motioned to him for fear that he would take off. He put down at his feet a heavy wicker basket that he was carrying and got out his handkerchief to wipe his brow. I noticed right then that the sun had broken through and that we were hot.

The man was wearing a cap, an old gray suit, and hobnailed shoes. He had dirty hands, a soiled shirt, and a beard of several days' growth. He was waiting in a subdued way next to his basket filled with bottles.

"Monsieur, are you alone here?" I asked.

My question seemed funny to him, and he smiled. "I think so," he answered, "and moreover I am leaving."

He asked where we came from and where the Americans were. He also told us that many refugees had passed through during the preceding days, but that today we were the first.

"And maybe the last," said I, "for we have been walking for several hours in a desert. You are the first traveler that we have encountered."

Les Routes Sans Oiseaux

We understand better what goes on in the human heart when times are difficult. The stranger placed his basket on the running board of the wagon and said casually, "I will go with you for a stretch of the road."

He told us that he had taken refuge with his family at a farm in the area. Périers had had many deaths, and entire families had been buried in the ruins. The bombing took place in daylight, and Saint-Lô and Coutances had suffered the same fate.

"Why?" asked the man. "Why?"

We proceeded on the road that went straight ahead, rising and falling with the undulations of the prairies. A bomb had dug a crater on a stone bridge. At this spot the road was so narrow and dangerous that the traveler held his basket in his arms. Besides, he had arrived at his destination.

"Good-bye!" he said. "Good luck."

Other bombs had churned the earth in a field, but a white farmhouse with a new slate roof seemed unharmed in the distance. A servant was washing milk cans at the edge of a watering place. Cows were resting in the shade of a chestnut tree that flanked the courtyard gate. The man went off toward the house.

Alone again, I let the mule trot ahead. A German car passed us at full speed. A soldier was crouched in the back seat looking for planes in the sky, although no threatening noise could be heard. A truck passed us just as fast as the car had a few minutes later. Then the road was deserted once again. I parked the wagon near a greenish-yellow, scum-covered stream. We needed to eat and rest a little. Frogs stopped croaking. Toward the front the muted rolling of cannon was heard taking place far, far away. But on this road, we were thinking about all the parishes and villages whose names were etched in our hearts.

XII

In Feugères, the bells were ringing for Mass under a beautiful, sunny sky. Clothed in Sunday dresses, ladies and country girls hurried toward the church holding their prayer books. This respect of the social order so close to the disorder of the war seemed to have a surprising majesty.

We had not encountered anyone since Périers because the main road crosses few villages. Beyond an isolated intersection and near a little inn with closed shutters, two German army Fords had burned a few days before. We had taken a narrower path on the right leaving behind the wild country of the Baux, a poor area with a few scattered marshes but dry in summertime with Scottish broom, stands of little oak, and sad cries of crickets and birds. The Feugères road took off on a gentle slope toward the little village where we arrived in time for Mass, for it was Sunday which we had forgotten.

Just like many other local folks, the blacksmith was leaving his house to go to Mass. In spite of his nice clothing, he was willing to look at our mule's worn-out hooves. He was heavy, ruddy, and a bit bothered by asthma. His Sunday clothes smelled musty, but he was freshly shaved and wore a starched collar that annoyed him a lot.

"Come tomorrow morning and I will shoe your mule," he said with kindness.

He had guessed that I was going no farther. However, I tried to insist, but I could see in his surprised look how much my haste and worry seemed abnormal and even inappropriate. We were leaving another world. Here, in this place, the habitual routine had not yet been broken. The blacksmith told us that our friends were fine, but that their house, like all the rest in Feugères, was already full of people.

Then the good man had added, "If there is no more room there, come back here, and we will work things out."

Without seeming to worry about the German horns and the many soldiers that occupied the town, folks stopped as we were passing by and chatted among themselves.

"More refugees," they were saying.

In this context, the word "refugees" didn't have its conventional meaning. It seemed to take on a new and sadder, even shocking resonance.

Marie's face got red as we went on, and she finally exclaimed, "Maybe their turn will come!"

Behind the church there was a chateau with turrets, much like a villa, with a picturesque park, a tiny river, lawns, an old pine tree, and well-tended paths. On the porch, a young man sat in a lounge chair, reading a paper and smoking. He was wearing a short sleeved shirt, green breeches, and boots, and appeared unconcerned at the present situation.

Then the road became narrow. Little hazelnut branches caressed our faces. We were again in the middle of the fields. Soon the little mule stopped in front of white gates that enclosed a sunny, flat area where the path continued through the grass with no hedges or shade. On the right, in the distance, my friends' house lay peaceful, all white bathed in light by stark contrast to the hard glare of the slate roof. The small pool surrounded by reeds was resplendent in the greenery. A little farther along on the left a clump of tall trees hid an even more impressive house. The horizon was lost in the blinding sun.

A lady and gentleman coming out of the house noticed us and immediately went back in to announce our arrival. Our friends appeared on the threshold, and everyone looked at us. Suddenly we heard André's joyful voice, "Here they are!" He ran to meet us with his wife following him while rearranging her apron.

They cried out joyfully, "We have been watching and waiting for you every day!"

The warmth of their greeting brought tears to our eyes. We were no longer refugee wanderers and were meeting faithful friends again. Our laughter was bittersweet.

They had many questions. Where were we coming from? What had happened at our place? They knew all the details about the big battle. The debarkation took place without incident on our coasts and now seemed impossible to stop. The German response seemed slow and awkward.

"Come in quickly! You seem tired," said our friends. They were trying to put on a good face in order not to give in to pity.

The kitchen where they had us enter had the look of peace time. A young girl and some elderly women whom I did not know were seated all around. I noticed that our friends did not take our suitcases upstairs. Then I recalled the blacksmith's hesitation. So that we might speak more openly, I guided André toward the garden.

"You have no room for us?" I asked.

He seemed embarrassed and admitted that the only remaining room in the house was really uncomfortable. Oh, you good folks, who were still living under the rules of etiquette of the past! The little room of which André spoke had its window right over the garden. This corner of the ground floor was under repair at the time of the debarkation and had been abandoned by the masons. Its moist layers of plaster smelled of mortar. Since the flooring had been removed, the room was below ground level. André seemed crestfallen and racked his brains to find another solution. There were beds in all the floored rooms, but my friend did not realize that some straw on planks in a sheltered place far from the artillery would provide us a good enough place to sleep.

A half an hour later we were settled in. Our beds had to be placed facing the window which could be dangerous, but the area seemed calm. We had a closet and a chair, and our suitcases would serve as table and seats. The large garden that lay under our window was peaceful with its cabbages wilting in the sun and sparrows chirping in the branches.

I went over to the shaded pump in shirtsleeves and a towel on my shoulder and pumped some water. From the courtyard I could hear the voices of folks returning from Mass. Soon we were seated at our meal.

Merchants from Carentan were with us. The fate of their town was worrying them. But we had no exact information. We thought that the area was destroyed. The other refugees were humble country people who had arrived in a wagon and seemed timid. They were a large family including children, daughters, sons-in-law, and betrothed. They seemed ill at ease and did not respond to our pleasantries—this was after all a happy Sunday lunch. I found and shared in this place the unexpected and unexplainable gaiety that we had sometimes felt at Henriette's farm. Here, just as at my cousin's, we had two tables. The girls, Marie, and the boys who were willing were helping to serve and pour cider. Through the large, open door we could see fields of hay.

Soldiers went by on screeching, old bicycles on their way to the next farm. No one paid any attention to them, which surprised me. André insisted that this troop was nothing to worry about.

For two weeks, mobile canteens and offices of an SS company that had fought at Méautis—our place—and at Saint George-de-Bohon now held the edge of the Marchésieux marshes, next to Feugères, and were

Les Routes Sans Oiseaux

quartered here. Provisions were sent from here each day to the front lines, but the trip was dangerous because of the planes. The SS had already lost several trucks. Those who went on this mission returned in fewer numbers or disabled. Observers also noticed that for several days the number of containers of provisions was reduced. Therefore the number of mouths to be fed was decreasing, too.

When folks gave us the details, they spoke of the war as if it were a distant thing. They knew very few members of this SS company and were not frightened of them. As if to reinforce their confidence, one of those soldiers came in. He was graying, about forty-five years old, and he walked across the kitchen bareheaded with papers in his hands. Without looking at our plates, he went between the tables excusing himself in a low voice, "Pardon, pardon." He closed the door to the vestibule noiselessly.

"He's the interpreter," André told me.

In turn, another soldier came and went from the offices in the same reserved way. He was younger and had rank. Before going through our group, he had taken his cigar from his lips and he, too, murmured a polite word. I could not get over it. The folks around me told me that these SS must not be the real ones or Hitler fanatics. They were speaking our language and saw to it that their leaders did not annoy the civilians too much.

Besides, at the farm there was only one sergeant in charge of offices and liaison. The others were in the trenches. Sometimes lightly wounded soldiers would spend several days in the kitchen, but no one requisitioned beds for them, and they slept on the straw with their comrades.

We were in conversation at coffee time when two infantrymen with dirty faces and torn uniforms arrived in search of paratroopers. Relaxed folks seated at the table seemed to surprise them at first. Frowning with ill will, they looked us all over.

So André asked bluntly, "What do you want?"

Without answering, the two soldiers stepped over a bench and shoving aside a good old country mailman and his wife, sat down at the middle of a table. They talked to each other and then began to laugh. They ate some sugar cubes left on a saucer. One of them noticed a carafe of Calvados on the table. He stood up, jostled the guests again, and took the bottle away. Smiling at his comrade, he murmured: "Cognac."

"This is too much," said André, getting up.

The soldiers were frowning again, and the one who was drinking out of the bottle of Calvados threw the carafe on the table and took out his pistol.

"Monsieur, come here," he ordered André.

André, his face very pale, came over, and the soldiers started to smile again with an evil glint in their eyes. Without paying any attention to André who was awaiting their orders, they kept on drinking, sighing, and wiping their mouths., Finally, playing around with their weapons, they just said: "Food!" Then they took off their green caps in order to get more comfortable.

André still wanted to argue, but his wife, placing her hand on his arm, answered at just the right moment, "You will be served immediately, Messieurs."

Everyone stood up to leave the soldiers to their food. My friend led me out to the garden, and I admitted that I felt like laughing.

"I'm going to tell the others," he said.

When the German sergeant came down into the kitchen, the two soldiers were eating with relish. He addressed them without any brutality, and they scarcely turned their heads. They answered a few words with their mouths full, and the sergeant came toward us.

"Monsieur," he said, "it's the war." He saluted us ceremoniously and then went back up to his office and closed the door.

The two soldiers took off a little later without any more fuss. As for us, we thought that their attitude was typical, but the tranquillity of those around us was beginning to crumble.

"We are bringing you bad luck," my mother ventured.

Perhaps it was true.

XIII

We went to bed with a feeling of relaxation and deep happiness in our little room by the garden. At last, we were going to be able to sleep without fear, sirens, the uproar of shells, or the dread of being thrown out in the night.

We had sheets and blankets, and our rather hard beds seemed heavenly. My little dog made herself a nest in a corner and rolled over with a sigh. The setting sun was casting its last rays through our window as sleep overtook us.

I had hidden the harnesses under our suitcases with a distrust that the surrounding calmness could not dispel. Just a few days later, I would have good reason to congratulate myself for it, as the enemy's actions that we had known elsewhere would now take over this beautiful country. But the news that I heard that evening left me indifferent for a while to all the little worries that we were to suffer and prevented me at first from going to sleep.

I thought I heard someone knock at our door. Mascotte gave a muffled growl in her corner, and I got up in a bad mood.

"Who's there?"

All the residents of this household must have been resting in their rooms since it was almost night.

"I beg your pardon, I will speak with you tomorrow," said a calm voice with a country accent.

Curiosity made me open the door, and the man who was there went on in a low voice. "It's not such good news, you did not have to get up. I came at this time to be alone with you."

I recognized the father of this large family, a man already advanced in years but in good health with a fair and honest face.

"I would like to talk to you about your young cousin, Arnaud," he whispered.

I asked him to wait for me, and a few minutes later both of us were in the middle of the garden in the shade of a clipped spruce where in spite of the late hour there were still a few lonely bumblebees. In the evening freshness, the tree smelled of warm resin and greenery. The sky illuminated the garden, but night had already invaded the surrounding woods. I could hear the trucks rolling in the distance on dark roads. For a few moments the man did not know how to begin his story, so I reminded him of the name that he had pronounced.

"Yes," he said, "I saw your cousin. Before being run out of my house, I was mobilized for a few days by the Germans to transport ammunition to the front line in my car, over toward Carentan at Rouges-Terres. It was dangerous, but we were under gun threat and could not refuse. That is how I met your young relative and a man from your village, also a prisoner, who was about fifty, slightly gray, with a moustache and a dark jacket..."

"His name?"

"I do not know his name as I was only able to speak to them once and then only a few words in passing as they were under guard. There was a third prisoner with them whom I had never seen in our area. He was a short hunchback who dragged his leg."

"I do not know him."

"Me neither. The three of them were under some apple trees where there was an ammunition depot. The youngest, your cousin, seemed worried. He was thirsty. The others said nothing, but the one that you know was biting his nails in anger. When I came back from my labor two hours later, there were just the two of them standing in the same place. Your cousin had disappeared. I never saw him again, and no one could give me any information about him, not even the two other prisoners that I could no longer approach because each was guarded by a sentry with a bayonet fixed on his gun. To me they seemed paler than before, and from a distance they gave me a friendly little wave. A little later, I saw them go off in front of their sentries equipped with shovels and pickaxes. They were told to dig in the shelter of an elm hedge in the lower part of the field. It could have been eight o'clock in the evening, as that was the time that they gave us a little rest before the night's labor, the worst of all. The sun was setting behind the trees and shade covered the ground, but the prisoners were taking off their jackets all the same because the sentries were hurrying them, and they were hot. A chief had come up behind them with a pistol in his hand. The earth was already piled on the grass; in the hole, I could not see anything but the workers' white shirts. Once in a while, the German sergeant would step away, but then he would come right back. From the fence, I watched him pacing back and forth. Then I hid behind a bush. I felt something suspicious and terrible in this work.

"A plane passed over very low, almost grazing the trees, and the Germans threw themselves on the ground, but the prisoners remained standing, and the plane did not fire on them. The sentries got back up; the chief brushed off his elbows and knees; the little hunchback and your friend went back to their digging. Suddenly, I saw the soldiers aim rapidly at their backs. I could hear the sergeant's angry voice in the breeze, even against the noise of the constantly rolling convoys on the little country road and the distant uproar of the artillery and machine-guns. With fear choking me, I bolted up when I saw the soldiers taking aim. And then, Monsieur, in the same instant that they fired all I could see were the two white shirts above the soil. The Boches leaned over, guns ready. They aimed again. The shouts I wanted to cry out stuck in my throat. It seemed that the assassins took forever in releasing their second volley. At last, without firing, they slowly put their arms back in their sling. The chief came down into the hole and like the others leaned over. Two pistol shots did not make much noise. The German came back up. Then the two soldiers took the tools from the dead and began to fill the hole."

XIV

We were thinking about our kinfolk and Henriette, who were no doubt saddened from fear and foreboding doom on their exodus. Seated on our beds in our tiny room, we spent long hours silently watching the constant flight of sparrows that had not yet fled the country. We would listen to the noises of this big house filled with people talking and the sound of German boots overhead. Footsteps would come and go resolutely like those of a man in deep thought. And one small question kept coming back. "Had Pierre Arnaud been able to escape?"

At mealtime the noise, conversation, and activity helped us to forget our worries for a few moments. Folks from our town came to see us. They arrived one rainy morning and crowded any way they could into our little room. It was humid, and water was streaming in the garden. I told our neighbors about Féodal's death. They didn't quite seem to realize the real horror of the situation. They spoke to me about our village. They had learned that the houses were partially destroyed. During the pauses in the conversation, we could still hear the rain dripping on the leaves outside our window.

I spread out a map on a bed. Our place of refuge was at the center of the straight line from Lessay-Périers to Saint-Lô, a front rigidly set by the German command as a last retreat. Therefore the allied surge on the sides might be able to surround us. We all thought about the possible maneuvers on the west provided by the Lessay waste lands—these huge deserted spaces of hard soil that were intersected by good roads. But the enemy could be attacked here, and once more we would be in the heat of action. Shells from the sea had fallen in a field five hundred meters from the farm. I had heard nothing, but our visitors had been suddenly awakened in the night, even though the landing points had been farther off. They agreed with us that the calm could not last. Every time the clouds opened we could see planes, and troops passed by on the roads every night.

The days now seemed longer and more monotonous to us. When we were tired of playing war games together, we amused the children by making Sta, the pretty sheep dog of the house, jump. She was a wonderful and extraordinarily intelligent dog that really enjoyed our games. And if we wanted to stop her jumping and fetching, she would come up and give us a pat and a look that seemed to say: "Come on and play some more." To invite us to toss the ball again, she would retrieve it and place it at our feet. But soon I would leave Sta to her antics surrounded by laughing children, and I would come back to the quiet little room and find my mother in her corner.

Some refugees tried to make themselves useful in the garden by weeding shallots and hoeing beans. I would hear them talking of this and that, farm work and weather, and I envied them their tranquillity, though I couldn't bring myself to take on these fruitless tasks.

One evening I was present at the departure of provisions for the front lines. The little truck—a commercial blue Renault stolen from some civilian to replace vehicles demolished by planes—had been waiting in the shed since six o'clock. By the sun it was now eight. The return of good weather with a few white clouds in a periwinkle sky tempted the bombers that were prowling constantly overhead in groups of four or eight, watching the roads and unleashing their bombs on bridges in the distance. You could see them dive one after the other and then rise back up with a shrieking sound. Heavy smoke rose. A few seconds later, the explosion rocked the house.

The Germans would watch these maneuvers and then quickly return to the darkness of their shed when the planes passed too close. They had attached green branches to the tarp and hood of their van. One of them would take the wheel from time to time, start the motor and then get out slamming the door. The cook was there in a dirty white smock with two aides that were as slovenly and idle as he was. There was also a spectator, a wounded soldier, who seemed pleased to have his arm bound up in a scarf. Finally, the three men on fatigue duty assigned to the risky task seemed worried. They were the ones who watched and listened to the sky most. All of a sudden, they made their decision. The containers of soup were raised into the van, the engine started, and the vehicle made a big turn and then quickly headed toward the meadows. The corporal who always accompanied the interpreter was standing on the running board and made a little salute in passing. He watched the planes and remained ready to give the alarm to lurch the truck under a hedge. They disappeared without incident.

Then the cook came up and commented, "Very dangerous, just like the front."

"Yes?"

"Ya, like the front."

The cook looked like a good guy. He wanted to offer us a cigarette and without holding out his little, green cardboard pack that contained three or four, he took one in his dirty hands and gave it to us, repeating:

"Oh, ya, dangerous!"

Just then a silent plane flew very low over the house and our heads and continued its descent right in front of us. You could hear the rustling air from the wings.

Les Routes Sans Oiseaux

Was it going to land? Over there at the edge of the trees, it kept on lowering. The hedges almost hid it. And all of a sudden, its big machine gun spat out while the engine raised the plane back up with a joyful roar. Climbing abruptly, then tipping its wing, the determined plane fired another long burst of shots. Black smoke rose in the greenery. The cook had taken off, and I joined him in shelter. He no longer had his smiling face, and his lips were trembling.

"Terrible disaster," he said.

The little truck did not come back.

XV

The jalopy that replaced the missing truck was a strange contraption that belonged to a vendor of metal and rabbit skins. The tarpaulin had been attached by pieces of tin hammered on the hoops, and the spare wheel was tied to the radiator with strings. You could not see the make of the old car under its chipped gray and green paint and old-fashioned windshield. Through a narrow door that would not close, you could see horsehair coming out of the seats. The engine sputtered as if making fun of its occupants, those proud soldiers of the Führer. But the soldiers had long since gotten over these humiliating inconveniences, and furthermore this heap was better and lasted longer than the peasants' slower ones. Did the American pilots take pity on this heap? They did not destroy it.

I had learned from the cook that the corporal was the only survivor in the last supply team, but that he would probably be permanently blind. Now the only one crossing the kitchen was the serious and worldly looking soldier who seemed out of place here. He passed through almost every evening with a frozen expression and a far away look, religiously carrying in his hands watches or wallets covered with mud and blood. The unit had been severely tested in the Marchésieux sector. Like many others, it had been holding on for weeks without relief, reinforcements, or planes; but soon, tomorrow maybe, it would be overtaken.

This burning hope kept André, his wife, and I, by the meadow gate for a long time in the evening. Everyone was asleep, and we spoke in a low voice while listening to the distant noises of the night. My friend identified by sound the half-tracks and trucks which were continuously rolling on the roads. For what purpose, we could not tell.

Was it the arrival of new supplies? All kinds of rumors were circulating, and our crystal set was out. The traffic ahead was sometimes getting heavier behind the castle's tall trees on the east. It seemed as though cars were turning in front of the castle stairway. We could hear voices and see yellow lights blinking for a second under the trees. They were timid lights, hardly visible under the ones that were blazing on the horizon. Nocturnal battles always took place under dazzling lights. We would fall silent in those moments. Far away, the sky was red or mauve way up above the dark trees. Showers of sparks seemed to be projected from a wheel toward the clouds where they were falling in an

Les Routes Sans Oiseaux

endless motion. That machine of superhuman dimensions was making a rolling noise interrupted sometimes by violent explosions.

We were so absorbed by this sight that we did not notice the interpreter who was right next to us one night, as we said, "They can't keep holding on in this hell."

The well-behaved interpreter coughed discretely in order not to embarrass us. Then, when he saw that we had recognized him, he came up to us and said in a most natural way, "Tomorrow it will be my turn to go over there."

"You?"

"Yes, me. Everyone must go over there to die."

And looking at the illuminated hand on his watch, he added brusquely, "Now it's time to say good night."

He extended his hand to us in an unusual manner. So that meant that very few men would remain to man the office and the provisions of this unit. And the cook was killed the next day while trying to milk a cow in a neighboring field. One of the few shells that fell in this area blew his head off and at the same time ripped apart the unfortunate animal. This is the way a company gets obliterated in the combat zone.

The Germans who were staying at the castle were coming more often to ask for milk and butter. The lady of the house no longer dared to refuse. Two Wehrmacht paratroopers, furnished with a light covered cart and a lame horse, wanted to carry off a pig, and, while we were starting to put up an argument, they shot the animal, loaded it in the vehicle, and left without saluting.

It started to rain again. On the evening of Thursday, 13 July, we were waiting for dinner in the kitchen while watching a light rain fall on ripe hay that would be left uncut. A small German army car stopped in front of the door. A heavy-looking feldwebel, with his cap pulled back like a young career officer and a very long and full cloak dragging down to his ankles, entered the kitchen. He made a face, asked for the chief—that is the master of the house—and unfolded a map.

He had a pointed nose, receding brow, rosy cheeks, gold teeth, and a receding chin covered by the collar of his coat. He had a twitch in one of his pale eyes like a smoker bothered by a cigarette. Stressing each word, the man pointed to a place on the map, "Is this La Grande Maison de Feugères?"

"This is not the place," said André.

The German frowned, looked at my friend distrustfully, and answered by pressing his dirty fingernail on the paper. "It's here."

He was wearing a yellow metal wedding rain.

"No," said André again, explaining that you could make a mistake on the map with a simple line, but La Grande Maison de Feugères was the registered name of the castle and not of his house.

The feldwebel shook his head and repeated what he had said, and André said no again, but the German became angry and red with rage.

"I am in command here!" he said.

André let it be known with a gesture of helplessness that he would no longer argue about it.

"Me want to see the rooms," said the German.

"But I have many refugees, whole families, and sick people."

"No care! Me want to see the rooms."

This brute came by us with his hands in his pockets and went upstairs. We could hear his heavy footsteps wandering through the rooms on the second floor, and then he came clumsily down the stairs.

He acted as though he owned the place when he entered the kitchen and gestured. "This one, too," he said, pointing to the kitchen.

"All of these people have not eaten," said André.

"I'll wait." replied the non-commissioned officer as he dragged a chair to the threshold and sat down to light up a cigar. He must have briefly explained the situation to the driver because the soldier started laughing, then went to park his car.

We knew what was coming.

"They are running us out?"

"Yes," said André, "but I'll explain to you while we are eating. We have only a little time." But how could we talk in the presence of this enemy who knew our language?

The awaited explanations from the soldier were given to us in dialect. They were simple. Headquarter officers would be coming here to spend the night. The officer in charge of quarters was taking the second floor, and we were going to have to pack off and sleep in the stables. This was not too bad. The first thing was to take up the mattresses and covers from the rooms. We were hurrying to finish our meal when the insolent feldwebel who was sprawled on his chair got up brusquely to stride across the entrance hall. He made a few wild gestures, called out a welcome, and then a little striped khaki car just like the first one stopped abruptly in front of him amidst shouts of glee. There were three or four young officers with beautiful white stripes on their caps, who hurried toward our door while others followed in another car that we could not see.

They were all wearing the same long, dark green raincoats and were laughing gustily. They clapped each other on the shoulder as though grateful to be together after a perilous journey. Eager soldiers mixed in with them while unloading their suitcases and bags. Crowded in the very narrow doorway, this troop blocked the last rays of daylight from our table while they looked us over. We felt very vulnerable in their presence. Their guttural language and the odor of leather and wet wool pervaded the room. Some of the women got up. But we had to stay awhile out of self-respect. Somebody took a bit more bread, another some cider. One of the young officers came up smiling with a switch between his fingers.

"Very good." he said with a heavy accent, pointing to our food. "This cannot be wartime!"

Looking a bit silly, we tried to laugh, but the big feldwebel didn't like jokes. He interrupted his superior to explain certain necessities, and then said to us, "All the civilians here are going to work in the shelters this evening. When they have finished they will go off to sleep. We need shovels and pickaxes. Now move!"

I remember the confusion that followed. We all tried to avoid the task, and André claimed that he didn't have a single tool left. Some of us didn't understand. Shelters? But where? Why?

The feldwebel's voice thundered brutally and then there was silence. Nowhere in this world are there such larynxes or men capable of such fury. This German scared us with his flashing eyes and foaming mouth. He could break and smash us under his boots.

Within a minute we were lined up in the garden listening to his orders. And to add to our confusion, shells were whistling over our heads, about to explode some hundreds of meters away, a sound that we recognized. A second burst of shots followed, slightly to the left of the first, then a third to the right. Did this brute that was commanding us know that the fire would begin this evening? Anyway the effect was surprising because the ferocious feldwebel suddenly seemed to shrink and lose his voice, as well as his mind.

He started to order us in German while clinging to the walls. "Los, los..."

He quickly showed us the places that he must have spotted while he was inspecting the rooms in daylight. Now it was almost night and the bursts of shells were all the more serious though still several hundred meters away. The smell of powder wafted in the humid air. Under the unending hissing the feldwebel no longer knew what to do and had to rely on our good judgment.

"Here, against the wall, shelter for the commander," he said. "Do you understand? Billets and boards to cover...and over there, make it larger and cover it also for four officers. Over there..."

He stopped with a bewildered look to gaze at the sky, and his heavy cheekbones under his cap now seemed to us as big as a fist.

I have praised sufficiently the innate courage of the German soldier in order to describe the non-commissioned officer's panic without being accused of bias. As soon as some dirt had been removed, he jumped in our hole, interfering with our work and getting his legs hit with shovels. If we had grabbed him by the scruff of his neck to throw him at our feet, he probably would not have reacted. He seemed crushed by stupor and fear. And even though the shooting had stopped, he remained stunned and speechless. One hour later when the work was finished, he went around like a robot looking at or rather testing each hole. Then he dismissed us saying good night.

XVI

I was sleeping deeply when the brutal and dreaded voices awakened me around midnight. My mother asked me softly if I had heard the noise. Her voice suggested that she had been awake for a long time. Marie, too, seemed wide-awake. They must have heard what was going on from the beginning and shared their impressions and fears with each other. The officers and soldiers had first made a big disturbance and after the evening's heavy shelling had gone to bed. But now we did not know what was going on over our heads. One angry German was giving orders and pacing in long strides. We could hear a faintly begging feminine voice trying to be heard in the avalanche of threats, and then a calmer masculine voice, André's. A child began to cry. Finally, a door opened and these mingled voices and sobs seemed very close. André and his family came down the dark stairway step by step, dragging heavy bundles. I lit a candle.

Our friend came in. "So there we are!" he said simply.

We had already understood what was going on. The soldiers were chasing these folks out of their makeshift beds in some little abandoned room so that they could take their place.

The young woman had trouble holding back her anger and tears. "Brutes, animals, dirty Boches!" she murmured.

And there we were, trying to keep her quiet when the great thundering noise of several shells tore into the night:

"The shells are falling nearby."

"Oh, yes, a kilometer away!"

"Do you think that maybe they can see our light?"

The young woman dried her tears, handed her child to Marie who made a place for him by her, and stretched out fully dressed close to my mother. Meanwhile André sat down on my bed to talk at greater ease.

The soldiers occupied the kitchen. A damp, run-down old sitting room with propped-up beams over the garden could serve as refuge. We decided that we would begin the work of cleaning and arranging it in the morning. I felt like having a cigarette. The heat in that overly small room was becoming unbearable. I blew out the candle so that I could open the window.

A pale moon was rising in the east. Its light spread gradually in the still sky where a few clouds were scattered, but our window remained in the shade for a long time. In front of us the garden and fields brightened softly. Except for a vague rumble in the distance, all was silent. You could hear a drop of water fall or a leaf stir.

We were leaning on our elbows on the windowsill when suddenly we heard footsteps on the soft earth. Armed soldiers in helmets were coming from the end of the garden. We were in the dark, and the moonlight and calm of the night reminded me of lying in wait for foxes near their holes in an April hunt. Faced with these plundering enemies, and thinking of Pierre and his poor companion, made me yearn to grip a rifle and take aim. Instinctively I lowered my head while grabbing the windowsill. The good dog, Sta, growled softly next to us under the door of the shed, where she was penned every evening. Her master quieted her with a gentle whistle. The Germans were coming up slowly looking on all sides. They approached the rabbit pen from which they took several rabbits that they killed with the back of their hands. They tied the animals together with a string. This was hard work, and both of them crouched on the path with their guns on the ground. At last one of them took the brace of rabbits, and they went back the same way they had come.

Toward morning you could hear tanks and trucks rolling on a road. We were exhausted. We believed that the SS were going to run us out of this house, but a kind of numbness overcame us because we were so sleepy.

To the contrary, the Germans seemed to have decided to treat us with perfect indifference and to act simply as though we were not there. Their cook made his coffee on the stove and prepared sandwiches as soon as it was light. He had put two tables together to make a large one. All around it he placed chairs and benches. With a towel on his shoulder—in fact, one of the house towels—he laid out plates of sliced bread, bowls, cups, jams, salami, canned milk, and a kilo of sugar. He greeted me like a café waiter and right away filled up a cup that he handed me. I accepted his excellent brew.

"Real coffee?" I asked.

The cook smiled with satisfaction. "Ya!"

He lighted a cigar and for my information motioned for me to look in two large cases. There were canned goods of all sorts: sardines, asparagus, ham, chocolate, butter, candles, and cognac. He selected an unopened bottle that he uncorked to take a swig, then casually handed it to me. Automatically I wiped the rim of the bottle before drinking.

"Very good!" I said. This cognac, like all the other bottles, was of superior quality.

"You found all of this at Carentan? Ca-ren-tan?" I asked.

"No," said the cook.

"Saint-Lô?"

"No, no. Many kilometers."

"Ah! You come from afar? Berlin?"

"Berlin, no. Our division, Das Reich." (He stuck out his chest, and I understood that this was something important.) "In France, it is..."

"Yes..."

"Toulouse."

"Ah! Toulouse. Very good. You come from Toulouse. Many kilometers. It takes many days on the road."

"Many days, ya." And this thought made him quite sullen. Then he added in a dreamy tone of voice, "Many days and many battles."

Maybe I should not have been asking so many questions. I already knew that the Das Reich Division, which seemed to be a sizable unit, was coming from the south of France as relief. This was bad news, but I put on a delighted look.

"Artillery, no doubt? Lots of horses?"

"Nich horses, Monsieur. Big auto artillery. Prima artillery."

I assumed an expression of admiration. Tractor-drawn artillery, think of that! "Much artillery?" I asked in an innocent manner.

"Oh! Ya, Monsieur, many cannon."

He took another swig of cognac without worrying about the early hour. The sun was coming through the window.

"Normandy, prima!" said the German in with a sigh of satisfaction. "Tommies caput!"

Our hostess was eager to use her stove, but the cook was adamant. Pointing to the pans that were heating, he merely replied, "Water for the chiefs, Madame." He said it with such a tone of voice that persisting would be an insult.

"But afterward?" asked the young woman.

"After? Lunch for the brass, Madame. And after that, dinner."

The cook began to laugh, but resuming his courtesy, he grabbed a coffee pot. "Coffee, Madame…?"

"No, thank you."

A soldier came in carrying some plucked chickens.

"Those are my chickens," said André's wife.

"Yes, Madame," answered the cook, and added with great dignity, "We always pay."

"Of course."

XVII

The conceited cook informed me that he was like a comrade to these impressive officers. That is the word he used. I concluded that in fact this well-fed boy had only himself to congratulate for his position and the relationship he had with the brass.

I have not yet mentioned his fleshy face and shiny cheeks nor his corpulent body that was stuffed into the belt of his new trousers. He was the type of heavy southerner, with carefully pushed-back black hair, bushy eyebrows, and coarse hair in his ears, on his chest, and on his fat arms. His deep-set Prussian eyes could hardly be seen between his bloated cheeks and brow.

But a Das Reich Division Headquarters cook must remain vigilant, even in trying times. Next to a large stove where mess is simmering, the cook's eyes bubble with happiness and sometimes with derision at these contemptible French. Then, upon the arrival of a superior, his Prussian gaze flames joyfully. He does not click his heels but brings them together and extends his arm: "Heil Hitler!" he calls out with a throaty laugh. "Heil Hitler! This is a beautiful day, commander! Two or three chickens from these detestable French are simmering in our pots.".

The superior responded to the cook with the same laughter and came over to shake hands with him and to get a light for his expensive cigar. Then turning around and taking a few puffs, he laughed loudly in order to assert the master's right to laugh and to demonstrate a good soldier's duty in war.

All the officers in the great Das Reich Division had walking sticks—walking sticks of all styles—thin, shiny wands, thick, carved clubs, some with silver tips, others with mahogany pommels. They were a collection of trophies, a fad that was in keeping with the soldiers' hearty laughter and the casual way they wore their caps. We seemed quite humble, poor and weak among these men in their baggy pants and handsome

Les Routes Sans Oiseaux

gray flannel shirts decorated with braid and golden stars that outshone their stripes. These arrogant boys amused themselves by shoving us in the doorways and insolently staring at the women, while the commander was enamored with the farm servant. He was always blocking her way with a fervent avowal of love and calling her "my dear, my love, my treasure." Without understanding a word, his comrades guffawed at his funny impassioned face. The poor girl blushed because she did not know if it would be wise to show her displeasure, and often she smiled shamefully as if asking for pity.

Then the officer would take out his walking stick-sword in a tragic manner and with a different tone of voice would pretend to plunge the sword through her body. She would escape with a cry, and the lover would go after her, begging all over again, "Come back, my dear!"

The soldiers would collapse in laughter on the benches and clap each other on the shoulder watching this inimitable scene. The servant in her wooden shoes, big apron, and hair askew would run away from the crazy advances of a powdered commander wearing the iron-cross and so many other medals. Here in the midst of battle, these young officers were spending their time in such games! Their superior was also very young. He did not look like your typical German. While he was not very tall, he was slender in form with fine features, dark eyes, artistic hands, and seemed quite elegant even in shirtsleeves and low infantry boots, another fad that only he was pursuing. His vulgar buffoonery, grimaces, and laughter surprised us as much as his impeccable French and his presence in such company. However, this civilized man, who was neither spiteful nor malicious, accepted all the coarseness and probably all the crimes of his subordinates. He presented an insoluble problem in our minds.

The other officers were easier to figure out. There was one young, fat lieutenant, a real caricature of a Boche officer. Walking around in his tall boots that he struck with his cane at every step, he wiggled his backside like a turkey. His neck was stiffened, his cap lowered, and his fat, sallow cheeks were streaked with red scars. He would undress the women with his pale stare that seemed to say, "I could take you!" Then he would lower his eyes and smile dreamily.

There was a young, very tall lieutenant, a stupid looking giant. He carried in his hand a long switch of freshly cut ash, apparently the longest that he could find. His bones were really of abnormal proportions especially the length of his thighbones. I visually measured his endless thighs. And if I have forgotten this man's features, it's because I saw him more as a skeleton.

There were also several young lieutenants or captains, and a company surgeon who seemed strangely silent. He seemed to put himself above the games and never laughed. With his boots propped on the windowsill opening on the meadow, he spent hours sitting motionless and listening to the war. His dreamy eyes liked to follow a butterfly. He was pale and heavy-set, fair, and wore his cap in the ivy-league style like his comrades, but he had higher rank so all the other caps would bow to his every morning.

One day I saw him bandage a wounded man. The man came with a bare torso into the kitchen and made the fascist salute before sitting down on a bench. The doctor stood up. His assistant came to his side to unfold the medical kit and bandages. When the doctor had examined the soldier's superficial wound, a wide tear in his back, the doctor raised his hands to his chest like a gloved surgeon and once the silver thread was ready, he began to stitch. Skin on the back is very tough. He had trouble inserting the needle. The soldier was sweating but remained still. Then, the assistant wiped the blood that had run down with a rag, powdered the wound, and applied the bandage. There was no blood on the doctor's hands. The wounded soldier stood, saluted once more, and was on his way. Without returning the salute or even checking the instruments laid out on the medical kit, the company surgeon lit a cigarette, deeply inhaled the first puff and came back to the window to sit down. The smoke flowed slowly from his lips.

And then there was a master sergeant who was a bit out of place in this world. He was a frightened and fawning non-commissioned officer, in a canvas jacket as green as a tarpaulin. And lastly, there was another cowardly brute that had not yet revealed all the twists of his soul.

XVIII

He always tried to look important, and, when shells were not falling, was always seeking an opportunity to talk with the commander. This officer often played with Sta by the door, amusing himself by throwing the ball over the white fence so that the nervous animal would throw herself over the tips of the bars and fall softly on the ground as she went to retrieve the ball.

Then the officer would clap his hands. "Sta, my beauty! Here is a lump of sugar." And Sta seemed to be his friend and let herself be petted.

They still tolerated our presence at meals at the big table in the kitchen, provided that we did not stay too long. The other refugees asked us for news about the farm and the soldiers, while the feldwebel, playing with his new friend by the door, looked at us suspiciously. One evening we were having dinner when this non-commissioned officer arrived, dragging a calf that he had just caught in the field. The animal was resisting, but the German was heavy and strong, and the poor calf balked and leapt in vain. He could do nothing but look at us with his big eyes. The officers made a circle around the poor calf, laughing loudly. They took their canes and struck the sides of the struggling animal, still laughing. Then the feldwebel had a bright idea. To torment these civilian enemies, he crouched down, grabbed the animal by the front legs, and straightened himself up. The calf was standing on his hind legs. Dragging the calf like a wheelbarrow, he came among

Les Routes Sans Oiseaux

us with slow and regal steps. Some one of us was about to cry out.

"Be quiet!" said André, adding just this: "Let's eat!"

Everyone looked down at his plate, even those who had their back turned to the scene were elbowed from behind. We remained motionless and silent. The German came toward the door. While standing on the threshold he became furious. Brusquely throwing the animal to the ground, he pinned the calf down, then with a demented gesture he seized his dagger and eviscerated it. With its intestines in a pool of blood, the calf cried out in agony and then seemed to give in to death and put its head down on the stone. The executioner got up with his bloody hands. The commander stood up and said something in a low voice. Two soldiers dragged the animal out on the cobblestones. That was the end of that terrible scene.

Evening was coming.

Two very close shots awakened us during the night. I had just heard Sta bark. Now, all was silent. I heard footsteps going away in the distance.

André arrived shortly. "Open up!" he said.

He appeared overcome. From the old sitting room that served as his bedroom, he had followed the whole drama. Someone had wanted to open Sta's door. The dog gave an alarm. The door was yanked off its hinges, and then there were the two shots.

"They killed her," he said, "because they still needed blood, but killing Sta is serious—much more serious and vile."

He was speaking loudly and gesturing in the dark. I told him that this noise could be dangerous.

"You are right," he agreed. We continued to whisper our indignation to each other. It was as if a person had been slain in our presence in the night. We could only imagine the animal's silent agony.

My friend exclaimed hotly, "The savages!"

"Be quiet," said my mother. "It is still only a poor animal."

"I want to speak to the commander immediately! I am going to see him!" said André.

"The commander? You never know. What can he do about his soldiers? Maybe he himself fears their fury? Tomorrow we will bury Sta like a faithful friend."

The next day all the refugees in the barn decided to leave.

XIX

They agreed to go to Brittany where a Périers merchant had family. The covered cart would carry baggage and, more importantly, the older people who could no longer walk.

The man who told me about Féodal's death came to bid me farewell at our departure. Did he know other details that he wanted to share with me? Did he fear so greatly the Teutonic cruelty that we were confronting? His eyes were so full of tears and his lips so trembling that he could no longer speak.

"That's it," he murmured.

I followed him a part of the way. He led his horse by the bridle in front of the caravan. The children had loaded heavy packs on their beautiful vacation bicycles that they pushed dutifully along the shoulder of the road. The adults followed behind. The wind was blowing hard on the sun-bathed grass. German artillery fired so close that the horse jumped at each shot. I had not gone out for several days, and the open air, artillery noise, and shells in the distance with their long trajectory over our heads, reminded me of other stages of our journey. Would our turn to leave this place be tomorrow maybe? At the fence by the meadow I stopped and shook more hands. Women were crying. The cart started up noiselessly in the dust on the little road, and when I turned around I saw a last handkerchief waving from the terrace. Then, when my friends realized who it was, they waited quietly for me to come back.

Now we were alone as we were in the last days at Vassanville. A family from Cherbourg was occupying the large room on the first floor, but they never had anything to do with us. They prepared their meals and stayed in their quarters. André, his wife, and I agreed to go and knock at their door. A young woman who was translating American tracts printed in German got up from the round table. She was very flushed, and her mother and little sisters were also distressed.

"You frightened us," they said.

But then they laughed and offered us seats. The news from the American tracts seemed excellent. The allies let the Germans know that Cherbourg was surrounded, that the front was more than a hundred kilometers long, and that a big tank battle was in progress on the Caen plain with aviation involved. Photos also showed us prisoners on a road and a street in Bayeux with intact windows. From this peaceful room where we were reading the translations, we could see German soldiers crossing the field and at the same time hear our windows shake at every shot. We were still at war. To help us forget this sadness, our neighbors offered us a glass of port that was souvenir of happier times. But here we were in the midst of battle, surrounded by enemies. There was a violin on the bed. The young woman took it up and began playing the *Hindu Song* softly. I was surprised to find myself close to tears.

The women were worried. The young girl put her violin down and told us that shells had fallen in the village that morning. The teacher's little daughter had lost a leg. André decided to go and find out what was going on. We were living too close to these headquarter brutes and no longer knew anything that was happening in the countryside.

This was how he learned that the mayor had left somewhat in a hurry, and that the Germans had forced several families out of their homes. At the house it was important to save immediately anything that could be hidden or buried and to keep watch over the horses and my mule.

The weather was beautiful. At the window of our little room overlooking the garden, I listened to the distant drone of allied planes. They were shooting at the enemy hidden in the hedges, and their fire was coming closer and closer to the house. The planes flew on easily following the sparks of foolish debauchery of burned ammunition on the ground. The multitude of enemy soldiers cowering in the grass, and especially their awkward way of revealing themselves without any hope of bringing down even one allied plane, surprised us. Leaning out our window, we watched light bombers advancing right over our heads. The infantry was firing around us, but the planes were probably looking for something else, maybe the location of artillery. Wings and fuselages were sparkling in the blue sky under the tranquil high, white clouds. The line of their formation headed abruptly toward the ground, and the deafening noise of heavy machine guns burst forth. Bombs and big shells were falling everywhere in the garden, and the planes made a horrifying noise as they descended. Thick, dirty smoke rose up after each explosion as the bombs hit the ground. The first blast shook us with the deafening noise of breaking windows and suffocated us with dense smoke. A second and third shock followed, and the windowpanes tumbled out. We remained motionless and numbed.

The commander and the surgeon, who had come downstairs at full speed, passed in front of us; then the long-legged giant and the feldwebel bent over by fear followed, hurriedly huddling against the walls. It occurred to us that we might be in danger. My mother remained crouched in her chair in the corner. The whir of motors kept on. The infantry almost stopped. And two more bombs fell. Their noise seemed stronger and heavier, but only one piece of glass fell out of a dormer window and broke on a gutter before falling on the path.

Once again I looked at the sky where six allied planes were flying away in perfect formation. In a little while the officers came out of their holes. These fine lieutenants, now all rumpled and covered with dirt, had to go by us again, this time under our derisive look. They filed by quickly except the commander who stopped and wanted to talk while brushing off his knees.

"You get very dirty in wartime," he said.

He was annoyed by my smile. However, I thought that he was calmer than I was because I could feel my fingers shaking. I lit a cigarette.

The commander also smiled and said, "It is a fine thing to appear to be very brave; but in combat you should never be brave for nothing. In the first place, you have to endure. After this war, I may have rheumatism, but you are likely to be dead."

Content with what he had said, he left.

XX

In these notes rapidly written during our exodus, the first dive-bombing that we had witnessed up close was Sunday, July 16. The headquarters staff had been at the farm for only two days; however, it seemed like more than a week to me. Some days are laden with too many memories.

Les Routes Sans Oiseaux

After the afternoon alert the doctor had gone back to his favorite seat in front of the kitchen window with his boots on the sill. He was smoking a cigar. He had to disturb himself again though because a superior officer, whom I recognized right away as the one Henriette and I had spoken to, got out of a simple sidecar at the door. In spite of the good weather, he was still wearing his cape and cap with no stripes. The cook stood at attention. The doctor stood and clicked his heels, and, since the others were in their rooms, he opened the door to the stairway to let his superior enter.

"I know that man," I said to the cook, who had a smug look on his face.

"The general?"

"Yes, of course. I have spoken to him several times."

I figured from the cook's expression that being recognized by a general could be useful and would help me to get some information about my young cousin. So I decided to wait. Besides the visit was rather short. Soon the upstairs door opened, and we could hear voices and the noise of boots coming down. The general came first. He walked across the kitchen rapidly. I was in his way, and our eyes met. Did he know that one of my friends had been executed? Did he even remember my face? He hesitated briefly and went on his way. I had wasted my time. When he got outside, the first thing he looked at was the sky. The motorcycle driver was already starting his engine. No planes. The general exchanged a few words.

Standing on the steps bareheaded in a loose flannel shirt, the young commander remained motionless and very erect for awhile, his arm stretched out to give the Nazi salute. At that very moment, I was struck by the thought that the splendid, theatrical side of a vile regime would fall into the realm of dangerous legends. The German defeat was achieved. I felt it, and I saw it once again in this motorcycle fleeing under the menacing sky, and even in the sudden burst of pride of this overly long and dramatic salute. But I also sensed that these men would remain forever slaves to their dreams of grandeur and power.

He came back slowly and asked curiously. "You seem to know the general?"

"A bit," I answered vaguely. "I met him at a farm."

"Well, now we want to drink a liqueur."

The cook hurried as ordered, and soon the commander emptied his glass and said, "Prosit!"

With that he left. And suddenly, without any reason I began to have doubts about the victory of which I was so sure just a few minutes before. It is true that all around us there was continual firing. The Das Reich Division made a lot of noise. And the firing of 155mm howitzers, just hundreds of meters away jolted my nerves a bit.

We heard them pouring out all their rage at dusk, and we jumped at every piercing detonation. We finished our supper at the table that was now too big. Night had nearly fallen. This sad Sunday was ending in suffocating anguish.

Les Routes Sans Oiseaux

That was when they brought in the wounded child. A long cart in the shape of an oblong box covered with black, so typical in Normandy, carried him. Led by a man holding the reins, it drew up slowly to the steps, stopped, and a woman on her knees inside leaned over to see the house.

The man came to our doorstep, greeted us, and paused with an uneasy look. He said at last, "I am looking for a German doctor. My child is wounded."

For several hours the man had been walking on the roads from a neighboring village. The battle was raging on his farm with American shells falling continuously. A blast had struck his child.

"He is conscious," said the father, "but stomach wounds are serious."

The table was cleared rapidly, and the child was lifted onto it with the greatest care. He was a little boy between eight and ten years old. He did not complain, but he had that very bad color that I had seen so many times.

The doctor directed his attention immediately to the boy, and then removed the temporary bandage that was under the boy's school smock and pants. You could hardly see the wound in the evening dimness. There was a small hole in the lower abdomen that was not even bleeding. The lady of the house brought a candle.

Although he was a doctor with the brutal SS and working in a dim light on the kitchen table, he examined the wound with care and infinite kindness. With a worried expression, he kept looking at the boy's face. At last he stood erect again and spoke in German to his commander who had joined our circle and who did not reply right away.

The 155mm howitzers were making their racket. Perhaps the commander had not understood. We waited. The boy's anxious mother was still holding the linen from the bandage that she had made.

Finally, the officer said gravely, "The doctor believes that the child should be operated on at once."

On his order, a soldier rushed out and in a few minutes a car was there. The boy had turned his head like a sick person who is very hot. The candle had dropped hot wax on one of his hands.

"The mother may accompany her child," the doctor said.

This departure seemed unreal. The father didn't even kiss his family. He felt awkward and embarrassed to be there, not knowing what to do.

"You may return home," the commander said to him.

He glanced at the doctor, who motioned that the father could leave. Then, without saying a word or thinking further, the man took a few steps toward André's wife, who was still holding the candle. He told her his name, the name of his village, and added in a supplicating tone of voice, "Please, Madame, try to let me know…"

"Yes," she answered, "yes, I will try to find out and let you know."

The father tipped his hat and went back home with death hovering.

The American artillery seemed to have decided to end it all. The bursts crackled under the red glow that tinged the sky and sparks flew up in sulfur fumes under the dark woods.

The cart draped in black still had to go at a walking pace on its dark road, lost like an ant on the ground. And the artillery quieted from time to time as if watching its journey through the night.

XXI

Some nights the battles taking place east of us at Rémilly would get closer and move so quickly toward the south that my friend would get up in haste and whisper to us, "Are you sleeping?"

He would open our window, and then we could hear the firing of howitzers and tanks more clearly. The flashes of battle were spreading to the right well beyond the Rémilly front.

André was shaking with emotion. "They are coming on the Mesnil-Vigot road!" he exclaimed. "At that pace we can be cut off in an hour."

In the brief periods of silence, you could hear the feeble clack of automatic weapons. But we had been disappointed so many times that we remained skeptical, allowing ourselves to shiver slightly as though cold had overtaken us. We spoke in hushed voices.

When the bursts became more violent, André whispered again, "Good God! They have broken through!"

But this was not true, and like a curtain falling on a finished act, night and silence recaptured the sky.

The German batteries had withdrawn from the farm since the dive-bomb attack. We could no longer identify the dominating noise of a close howitzer that frightened us more than the others with its piercing howl like a strike of an enormous bronze drum.

On Monday, July 17, our brilliant general staff had slipped away. Within just a few minutes, soldiers had quickly rolled up the red telephone lines, leaving a long end hanging from a window. Accompanied by the doctor, the commander had been the last to come down from his room. He was wearing his tight-fitting coat, cap and high boots, and was carrying his maps under his arm. He had crossed the garden and gone to the end of the meadow where a waiting car started its engine. The cook, who had only one case to carry since the others had been taken away in the night with all the baggage, threw two heavy bundles in the pond. They were two unopened boxes of delicious orange jam that we retrieved a little later. Then on the cook's signal, the last little car stopped to pick him up, and he, too, left without a word.

Would they come back? Probably not. We believed that this rather shameful running away signified retreat.

The allied attacks toward the south could therefore end up surrounding us.

From its new positions above Feugères the German artillery had come back into the battle, and there was a constant firing of shells going this way or that over the

Les Routes Sans Oiseaux

valley. We sometimes naively wondered why they did not bump into each other, but their distant shrieking did not bother us much. While the German 105mm howitzers were reducing to a pulp the first lines on the east, the Americans had considerably lengthened the range of their big weapons. Time after time, the planes were attacking all around us but avoiding our meadow, so that we were unworried spectators of this battle, and more and more we got the impression that it had nothing to do with us. A strange feeling...

We observed the movement of troops on all the surrounding roads that seemed to signal a retreat. Our hopes became stronger. Then an inhabitant of the village came to tell us that munitions were arriving from everywhere, and we fell suddenly into darkest gloom.

Fortunately, our neighbors shared good news with us—photos of the taking of Cherbourg. The largest photo in the tract showed the Napoléon Square where two lines of enemy prisoners marched past under American escort. The famous statue of the emperor on horseback was in its place, and you could see houses and roofs that were undamaged. Civilians were watching the parade of the vanquished. At the head was the German general who had surrendered the square, a big man of tall stature wearing a full cloak, with a hairless, surly face, and his sheep dog by his side. The tract said that the division that received the order to defend Cherbourg to the end had capitulated. Our neighbors were from Cherbourg. On the order of German authorities, they had left their home several months ago to settle here. They could not hold back the tears when they looked at this photo of their liberated city.

"Over there, victory has already come!" they cried with joy.

It started to rain again, bringing an autumn-like temperature. One morning in the still, misty air, we heard the very close noise of machine guns and rifles. Shells and bombs fell in the village. There were victims. And some families decided to leave. Our Cherbourg neighbors came to us to say that they wanted to leave the countryside at all cost. They were determined to go by foot with a bundle on their backs. André found transportation for them that would leave at daybreak, and in the evening they came to say goodbye. They stayed quite a while with us as night fell over the meadow. We watched fires lighting up the horizon and had trouble breaking the silence. Listening to the distant battle, it seemed to us that our big house was becoming the center of a dead country.

The next morning three soldiers from the first unit came back from the front. Others came and went through the fields all the time. Still others came with a cart to carry away a calf or pig that they slaughtered with a bullet, without asking. But in their tattered uniforms, they all had the troubled and surly look of worried troops, for whom a civilian is nothing more than an annoying bystander in the way.

These three, quite to the contrary, came up to us like unsuspecting, dead-tired men arriving at a halting-place for a rest that they have been dreaming of for a long time. They looked wild with their wide-open eyes and their weeks'-old beard. They were walking painfully with their helmets on their belts, dragging their guns, and headed toward the courtyard where they hoped to find their old kitchen buddies. They made a feeble try at a salute and a smile.

"You are in the unit that had its kitchen here?" asked André.

"Yes, Sir."

André shook his head. "They've already been gone several days."

The soldier who had stopped called back his comrades and came toward us. He asked, "Gone?"

For him, this was mind-boggling news, and our explanations seemed to strike him with great misfortune. He translated quickly, and his comrades threw their weapons down on the ground in one single gesture, and then immediately in the same rage sent their belts and helmets rolling on the stones.

"For weeks we've been in the trenches. Our unit is destroyed," they said in their language. "We have no more leaders, no more comrades, only the three of us. With neither food nor sleep, we have still fought for many days. Where have the kitchens and office gone?"

I did not know and told them so.

André's wife came up and suggested, "They must be at Le Lorey."

"Lorey?"

"Yes, a little village toward the back of the front, Le Lorey, twelve kilometers away."

This distance, after so much fatigue, was beyond their strength.

"We would like to sleep," said the soldier who spoke French, and upon saying these words, he closed his eyes.

"There is some straw," said André.

He showed them where to go, but when he came back he told us that the soldiers wanted something to eat. His wife sent milk and a crust of bread out to them.

Some hours later, they knocked at the door. "We thank you, Madame and Messieurs," they said. "We are going to Lorey. Goodbye."

The next morning they were to return under a heavy rain. They entered, and little pools formed around them.

"And so? Your comrades? The war?"

Somewhat beaten by the storm, they did not answer and remained standing with their arms away from their bodies so that their steaming raincoats made of striped tent canvas would drain.

They were out of breath and in a sweat and had the same feverish eyes and unshaven faces as the first time. "We were told, 'The order is to fight until death.'"

"And now?"

"Now we must go back over there without rest or food…"

"Take off your wet clothes and sit down," said André's wife. The soldiers bowed their heads and sighed at this invitation, and then without a word put their weapons in a corner. We had understood each other at a glance. These men were only looking for a good reason to get out of the infernal circle where they were caught, and it was important for us to turn them away from battle.

"Go hide your coats and weapons in the attic where you slept while I set the table," said André's wife.

They lost no time obeying, and the lady of the house smiled and finally whispered, "These boys won't see any more war."

XXII

The group's interpreter used his knife and fork with ease, but the other two did not bother. They filled their mouths, even with their fingers. While they were stuffing themselves, the interpreter used all of his knowledge as a civilized person to eat as fast as possible without appearing famished. Thus he seemed to resume an old habit and even took the time to chat, searching for words to express himself correctly or to translate faithfully what we said to his comrades. The latter would stop with their mouths full and looked at us with tears in their eyes. They had an ingenuous look that you often find in the common people. The youngest was a pale, blond boy who appeared threatened by tuberculosis, and the other, a stocky, hairy brunet with a low forehead and the eyes of a child. He must have been close to thirty but had such a naive expression that I questioned him a bit. He took an old notebook and photograph out of his pocket. I recognized him immediately, in front of a little chalet covered with snow. He was wearing a black frock coat, a high hat, and wooden shoes with pointed tips. He was laughing, showing his beautiful set of teeth as he accepted a bouquet of holly that a little girl with long hair and a checked dress handed him. A smiling, heavy young woman with her hair in a bun and her sleeves rolled-up to the elbow was at the door of the château. In the snow there was a shoveled path and pines farther away.

"Your wife? Your daughter?" I asked.

"Ya." he answered.

He had stood up in order to see this photo of his little girl, wife, and home over my shoulder. He took back the little photo to look at it again and said a few words in a despairing tone of voice. The photograph did not tell me how he made a living.

"It is true," said the interpreter—and I am recording his comments without noting mistakes in language—you do not know that where we come from, Tyrolean Austria, the chimney sweeps wear this costume. And Christmas is a day of celebration for them. They visit the homes, and people give them gifts of money and liqueur.

"Are all three of you from this beautiful country?"

"Yes. My wife is back there, too, and this young man, who is a workman in the town, has his girlfriend there as well."

"And you, you work?"

"In a hotel."

Since we were speaking in confidence, I pointed directly to the collar of their uniforms and asked,

"Austria is your chancellor's country, so it is not surprising that there are so many SS in the army."

"The Germans need so many SS now that they are forcing them into the army."

From his pocket he pulled a ribbon that should have been on his sleeve. The ribbon bore the name of his unit, Hitler's name.

"Adolph Hitler!" he said with a scornful laugh. And he threw the ribbon into the fire.

When the meal was over, the three soldiers got out their wallets to pay, but my friends shook their heads saying they would not accept money. They wanted something else.

"Keep your money," said André. "This evening we will bring you your meal in the attic. Sleep well."

That is how three Austrian soldiers were hidden at the farm up until the last day.

Along with the SS some anti-paratrooper units, frightening fanatics that we had known from before, were spreading out behind the front. They made off with everything under the threat of their machine guns. Two of them came to the shed and picked out the cart they wanted. Since mine was too small and had no tarpaulin, they took André's. We knew that others might come along, so it was of utmost importance to hide what was left. We pushed all the other carts under an old woodshed and piled bundles of firewood all around. My mule was penned in the cellar behind a barrel. And we remained on the lookout, anxious about everything in this depressing atmosphere.

André had decided to stay in the mildewed, old sitting room with all his baggage. In the night, we would hear the wind softly open a door then slam it shut. The German artillery fired often because the allies were attacking toward the south after hellish preparations. The deserters had spoken to us with terror about the American firepower. They said that if fresh troops did not arrive in large numbers, the front would soon collapse.

The bulk of the battle might very well spare us. In the event that the house was destroyed, we had formed a project to strengthen for our use the trench that had been dug for the officers.

Saturday morning, July 22, the village policeman came to deliver a copy of the order posted in the village. We were to leave this very day under threat of brutal expulsion and seizure of all our possessions. Soldiers had run shouting through the fields the night before to take away herds of cows. The exodus was continuing.

We spent a part of the morning discussing the choice of a place of refuge. Upon leaving their house, our friends felt that they had lost everything and did not want to be caught in battle again. They wanted to go to Maine-et-Loire right away where they had acquaintances. As for us, we wanted to try one more time to get away, and since the center of the department had not worked out for us, we were determined to try our luck on the coast. Marie had cousins at Muneville-sur-Mer, halfway between Coutances and Granville,

Les Routes Sans Oiseaux

and that is where we would go. For today, the first stage of our departure, we did not have to separate.

Our friends were aware of an isolated farm in a remote corner of Feugères, in the Bournon hills, where we could perhaps hide until the long-awaited breakthrough toward the south that could succeed at any time. I had had to abandon that very dream when I left my house. I would accept, however, a last try—this one more dangerous—since we were going to violate the German order. Our departure was set for noon. We had to repack our things, get the carts and wagons out again, and kill a hog so as to take along fresh meat.

Georgians and Mongolians arrived in Feugères during the night. Their bandit appearance heightened our worry because these squint-eyed soldiers, whose mission was to organize the last defenses, seemed above all to want to start looting. They came to the house and watched us prepare for our departure without saying a word and then began lazily to dig holes on the edge of the meadow.

When the mule was harnessed in the shed by the woodpile, we loaded up our mattress, covers, suitcases, and grain. Then we attached a round basket full of bottles and food on the axle and, in true gypsy fashion, had two rabbits in a sack. We also had a great variety of things hanging on all sides—a grill, stew pan, toiletry kit, pitcher, a big, yellow enamel basin, and some plates, knives, and forks in an old basket. When all of that was ready for departure, our friends had not even begun loading their wagon and were squabbling amicably over what they should take.

Everything seemed useful and valuable for the long trip, but trunks and baskets fill rapidly. Noon was long past, and we were hungry, so we decided to eat there in our corner of the shed.

Why has this memory remained so clear, clearer than so many others in my mind? I cannot say. I can still see us sitting on the logs there in the shed. It was cloudy and cold, and my mother was coughing. I had opened a can of sardines, an old French brand in a red can with black and gold letters, that I had saved since the beginning of the war for a time of need. I had saved it along with a pack of candles in a blue box, a pound of chocolate, and a bar of soap. We had some butter in a cup, and on our bread we put our shining little fish that we no longer felt like eating. It started to drizzle so lightly that we did not realize it until we saw moisture on the square stones that supported the posts of the shed. My little spaniel was watching our every slow move. All was peaceful on the front. Strange voices were coming from behind the farm's long buildings. Then it rained harder, and water came into our shelter. But we were going to be able to leave. André and his wife came to see us. They were worried. "We have not finished," they said.

It was decided that we would be the first to leave. We had lifted ourselves up on the heavily laden wagon. The tight springs rocked us and whined imperceptibly in all this silence on the wet fields after the storm. The large and serene house faded in the distance. Every now and then the little mule would stop to graze on a bit of foliage in the hedgerow. For days now he had only hay to eat in his prison, and his black coat was already losing its luster. Then he would gently get back on his route under a cloudy sky where you could not tell what time it was. His hooves made a muffled sound in the empty air, and he would turn his head and look at the wide-open gates to vacant fields.

In the village, folks had gathered on some thresholds while doors remained open revealing disorderly interiors. I recognized some refugees from my area who came to shake hands with us.

"We will not leave until tomorrow," they objected.

And I replied: "We're not going very far. See you tomorrow."

In a courtyard, an elderly man was busy tying large parcels on a wheelbarrow. Farther along, a townsman, who was carrying a beautiful cane with a silver tip, was looking at us. Tomorrow he would be walking on the road. I felt his envy and despair as he watched us go by. The fragile, old man in an alpaca jacket and straw hat was alone here among country folks who had their own worries and could hardly care about him. He didn't know where he would go. This poor soul was lost.

The road was smooth with a long ascent that we soon left to continue climbing on a dirt path under lovely oaks. The little mule stopped, ears up, and snorting. In the midst of this astonishing peace, the horrible odor of cadavers reached us. And it was not that of animals. A strange emotion took hold of us.

"Let's go! Giddy-up!" I called to the mule.

At the first bend, there they were by the side of the road at the entrance to a field, three soldiers in their boots, lying under some branches. One of them was wearing his helmet and was lying on his stomach with his arms spread. The two others were on their backs, their faces toward the sky. Their faces were green, the dark green color of bile, and through their rigid lips you could see teeth in dark mouths and a spiritless light under their eyelids. The stench spread far. Why were they there, all swollen and unburied just as on a battleground? The folks that I asked when we arrived at the farm did not know. They said that the bodies had been there for three days and that the local soldiers paid no attention.

I learned that contrary to André's calculations, the farmers in his village were also going to leave, but that the order was general and too precise for them to be able to steal away. The town crier had explained himself badly—we had until the following day to leave. So we decided to turn back. We left this gray farm with its red tiles tucked away on a hill under tall walnut trees. We had seen refugees in stables and sheds ready, as we were, for the great departure. We went back down to tell our friends that they had time. Tomorrow seemed like a long wait. We were happy to return to our refuge. I made the mule avoid the dead soldiers and we passed quickly by them, but the odor followed us until finally it disappeared on the road as we continued in haste. The little old man in the village was still there and stared in amazement when he saw us coming back so gaily. There were no wagons ready for departure in the meadow.

Our friends came to meet us as we shouted out, "We are not leaving! We do not have to leave until tomorrow!"

XXIII

Maybe we would have done better to stay in the Bournon hills as the valley was hit that last night. I was happy to come back to the house from the shed when the shooting started. This was the first time that shells had fallen on the farm, and the slate roof seemed very flimsy to me. The old sitting room with windows protected by sacks of dirt was a secure shelter. The uproar lasted until morning. The village had surely suffered, but at dawn I found that our possessions had been spared. The shafts of the wagons were still intact, and the horses were resting peacefully. Only the mule had broken his tether but he was calmly grazing on his fodder. The worst blast had broken the corners off the east gable.

Early fog indicated that it would be a hot day on the roads. All was ready for departure. And since we had to leave this house, why miss the good early hours? In the distance we could hear submachine guns, a strange awakening in the fields.

Soon after, we left the farm. That day seems as long as the blazing hot road in my memory. The hours went by in a blur. First we arrived in the village. The shells had left their mark. The schoolyard gate was twisted. There were holes in the slate roofs, and the church steeple had nearly collapsed.

A silent restlessness reigned in the morning mist. Folks were moving around, loading their wagons, and dragging out mattresses and boxes. But all of this was in complete silence. A long convoy of refugees came out of an adjacent street, their carts and wagons making a heavy noise. Strips of canvas or old curtains hid the contents of featherbeds, soiled bolster pillows, old black painted trunks with handles, and sacks of grain hidden at the bottom. Hanging from the racks were all kinds of utensils—a frying pan, a trivet, and a surrender flag made from a white napkin at the end of a stick.

A little girl held a small dog in her arms, and her brother carried a birdcage. Other groups were ahead on the road—women leading a cow, others pushing a wheelbarrow. An older woman shook her head and turned her back to the road from her queenly seat atop a wagon. We followed along. The old lady's eyes seemed to be staring at us without seeing us.

We again encountered the terrible odor on the little road that we took the night before. The little mule turned his head and pulled to go faster but had to keep to the slow pace of those ahead. Military cars loaded with seemingly laughing soldiers roared by. At the first village a non-commissioned officer came out of a house. Bareheaded, with an open collar, leather seat, leggings unbuttoned over his socks, and dragging his feet in old sandals, he moved to the side of the road to take some pictures. No one turned their head, but they looked at what he was doing from the corners of their eyes. The officer had a red face and was smoking a cigar. His thin, blond hair hardly covered his pink skull. Farther along, the refugees passed knowing looks from one wagon to another.

We were in a bad way—dirty, poor, unshaven, and in rags. Our wives were wearing scarves on their tangled hair, dresses like gypsies, and dusty shoes. The children's eyes were big and tragic looking. Our elderly and sick were silent. We were defeated and uprooted, but we still had hope—hope and hatred in our hearts.

At the first intersection our silent procession became crowded. Other convoys arrived, stopped, and mixed with ours, causing a confusion that was made all the worse by passing military cars honking their horns impatiently. Like a herd, the crowd would squeeze over to the side of the road. The stream of traffic stopped in front of a café that used to sell gas. One of the wagons could not move. Its driver, who was from our area, extended his hand. He was not surprised to find us there. When he did not ask about our health or our turn of fortune, but only looked at us in a bewildered way, we sensed that something terrible has happened to him.

"This is what happened to us last night," he uttered.

Suddenly his face wrinkles and his eyelids redden as he pointed to his wagon. A body was stretched out in a sheet on a mattress. His youngest son had been killed that morning before dawn, in the stable where they were all sleeping. The man was going to bury his son farther on down the way in a church along the road.

There behind us was the mother with a kind of veil over her head. She had been slightly wounded, but was able to follow along. The procession got back under way.

"We're heading toward Belval," said our neighbor. "After that we do not know. We do not know what to do or where to go."

André, who has understood the tragedy from a distance, came over to our wagon and asked, "A dead body?"

"Yes."

He remained silent for a moment, looking down, with his hand on our mudguard. Then he went on, "Don't you see, we have to get far away from here and leave all this," And pointing to all the misery around us—our misery—he added, "Come with us to the end."

"We will go to the coast," I said.

André offered his hand before going back to his folks.

Men pushed the wheels of heavily laden wagons up hill. Sometimes they stopped and quickly hunted for rocks to wedge under the wheels. A horse no longer seemed able to go on in spite of the whip and handle striking his sweaty flanks.

"Giddy up! Let's go!"

The horse stood motionless with pink nostrils and foam on his bit. Suddenly, he tensed his muscles, gripped the road with his hooves, and the wagon load started moving slowly.

Farther along, a poor, skinny old donkey was suffering with deformed, worn-out hooves, but the master had no pity for the animal. A passer-by helped to beat him because it was hard to do to it for a long time. At each step the stick fell upon the donkey who seemed to accept this whipping as a necessity to go on.

Some men were harnessed to a wagon. They could no longer pull on their leather strap. Sweating and flushed, they were shaking under the heavy effort, and when they saw us go by some seem surprised to see me seated with the women. They could not know that I was suffering from my bad hip.

At last we arrived at the top. On our left, green hills stretched out before us, and we commanded a view over a beautiful horizon. Men running in the fields. A glider wandered like a buzzard in the blue sky. Here and there, smoke was rising like brush fires in the off season—farms and villages on fire. Brief points of light pierced the sky and immediately little black balloons—time shells—drifted down. The muffled noise reached us a while afterwards.

The road soon descended again. We could see the whole procession of wagons, and then André's wagon took a turn. He waved and smiled at us as his wife bade us farewell. Other carts followed them—folks from their village and also friends that we did not know waved to us in a more reserved way. They left our road, and we already felt some regret, but it was too late as our fate pushed us on—toward a good or bad destiny, we did not know.

The dead little boy was borne away, resting on the precious belongings that evoked his home.

XXIV

In order to find a little shade and to get out of the convoy dust, and to eat, I pushed our wagon onto a forbidden road—Verboten! We were not taking up much space under the slope. Officers in their cars, however, gave us dirty looks as they passed. But they must have understood that we were a part of the multitude coming behind us, and they continued on their way.

Seated on the grass, we got out some food but we were only very thirsty. We tried to nibble a cookie that stuck in our mouths like thick glue. After some cider, I swallowed half a cup of Calvados, and we talked about this stage of our trip. Marie told us that her cousin, to whose home we were going, was married, and that she had been working in the same house for a long time. Before the war they saw each other often, almost every year.

"But since then?" I asked.

"She has written to me one time."

All in all, not much. We were going there on a chance.

As my little mule grazed, my little spaniel looked at us without understanding why we are running all over the place when it would be so good to be home.

All the houses on the way appeared abandoned. The refugees entered these houses to rest or take things that they needed. I could say to pillage, but the word really did not convey the idea. The devastating war that followed us on our heel and the respect that we should

Les Routes Sans Oiseaux

have felt toward others' possessions, and even the intrinsic value of an object, depended on the situation. However, even in a group of good folks there are always some greedy people and thieves who satisfy their secret instinct in the absence of police. They were the furtive ones that tried to avoid being seen. They traveled alone or in little groups, always letting the larger part of the convoy pass or walk ahead. When stopped near a doorway, they might pretend to be inflating a bicycle tire or fastening a horseshoe. They incarnated distrust and depravity.

Bombs had fallen at an intersection. Their craters had disturbed the brown earth, torn the trees to pieces, and made roofs hang precariously over cracked walls. Men, birds, and animals had all fled.

Belval began with an impossible descent that was as narrow and cut up as a forest path. A heavy cart pitched in front of us, right under the mule's nose. A baby carriage with big, old-fashioned wheels rocked on the top. The shaft grazed the ruts in the road, chickens clucked fretful in their cage, and the horse yielded prudently under the load with hesitating steps while the driver talked to him in a low voice and held him steady with the reins. The road turned and descended more precipitously at every step.

Planes rose into view and began diving. In a moment, we saw bombs descend from under the wings, like fruit falling off the bough. As the plane neared, it seemed duller than it did high in the sky. The first one disappeared behind the trees on the slope, and the second and third dipped slowly. They veered slightly on our right in their howling dive. After each explosion that seemed to lift us up from the ground and throw us into a precipice, we waited nervously for the next one. It was a feeling of vertigo. Memory retains only insignificant details—the duller color of the plane and an oak tree with its light gray branches.

The heavy cart had turned over in front of us, and the mule had stumbled on his load. Farther on, a woman was crying in panic. I recall that my mother huddled against me and that Marie got off first. But there were no more planes. The engines went away, then seemed to come back, and then go off again, disappearing from sight. All this has lasted maybe thirty seconds. We do not know what had happened. Perhaps they were bombing the bridge at the bottom of this hill on the Soulle River.

"But did the bombs fall on the convoys on the road?" someone asks.

The man with the cart seemed rather calm. "I toppled over," he says.

We saw it very well. A horse's sidestep on the slope caused the accident, but the animal did not seem to be in too bad a plight in his harness on the ground. We, too, would have turned over if it had not been for this accident ahead of us. They told us that the mishap caused more fear than damage. A half over-turned cart had a few scratches.

We needed to help the man who was blocking the road. His whole family came up to us and gave us news. They had seen explosions near the deserted bridge. Their donkey was safe halfway up the hill at the entrance to a field. The released hens stayed underfoot rather than running around. While we were at work unbuckling the harnesses, the farm woman caught the hens one by one except for the last hen who, suddenly realizing the misfortune, took off in a hurry. The horse rose up and looked around in a dumbfounded way.

Now we had to unload the cart. A whole crowd of rescuers came over to help. I was able to get my wagon by, and there were enough folks here to put the other cart back on its wheels. At last we could be on our way again. They assured me that the bombs had not demolished the footbridge.

Where was my little dog? I did not see her anywhere. I whistled and called her, nothing…My mother was still shaking and begged me to leave. But I looked until I found little Mascotte hidden in the roots of a hollow oak. Her eyes shone in the darkness, and I had to tug at her collar to get her out of there. Her coat was rumpled and full of dust from the dead tree.

Down below, the road had turned into stagnant water. The whole convoy appeared to be blocked. Some men had uncorked big earthen bottles and were taking a slug. We were at the bottom of a narrow valley. A sluggish river ran through the middle of the fields. The bridge no longer had its breastwork. The bombs had made their hellish holes in the black earth and clay. You could see the craters made by the most recent explosions. They still seemed hot, wider, and deeper. In others, ground water from the porous soil had already infiltrated, making shining marshes like the bottoms of wells. Recent storms had polished the walls, but in those that had just opened up, the powder remained. The fields and the roads were covered with pieces of grass and dirt.

The mule snorted and, at his first steps on the bridge, he came to a halt. He listened to the sound of the water and then wisely decided to go ahead, raising his hooves high. A hen that someone has just caught in the distance let out a desperate cry. In front of us on a bare hillock, a lonely brown church with its steeple intact stood in silhouette, surrounded by a group of crosses. This brought to mind thoughts of the little, dead boy in his cart. This sanctuary was fitting for him. The dark steeple in an empty sky and the lonely surrounding wall evoked past centuries, centuries of calamity. I asked myself, *somber Belval, why does your name mean beautiful valley?*

We came to a short climb under a blazing sun. Time seemed off track, but I believed it to be evening by now. There were folks living in this part of the village, but I hesitated to ask my way because I wanted to see the route on the map and choose it carefully. I stopped in a shady spot. It was strange, but we were still thirsty. Since our bottles were empty, Marie suggested that we stop at the first house to buy some cider. She soon came back with a freshly drawn bottle and a ten-franc bill in her hand.

"The folks would not take any money," she said. "They expect to leave soon, too."

The cider was refreshing, and drinking like this in the shade of a tall tree caused our spirits to rise.

Mascotte jumped down to shake herself off and roll in the grass. We laughed at her tousled appearance, and soon we returned confidently back to the road where we were at last alone like ordinary travelers.

I kept the map on my knees to follow my itinerary because we had to take some difficult roads. It was Sunday. In the little courtyards of the thatched cottages or behind the boxwood in the gardens, men who had been to Mass in the morning were resting after a late country meal. Children were playing and stopped to look at the refugees as they passed by. Birds were singing in the hedges behind the bushes, and we looked all around to see them because for weeks we had not heard any birds.

After traveling a while through the peaceful orchards, we arrived at the big Hyenville road that was deserted among moors and wild hills. Three German infantrymen, singing in loud voices, passed us at high speed in a badly hitched trap that bounced behind the horse. Our mule did not feel like following. His slow, tired trot soon put us far behind the singing, drunk soldiers. The broom and heather plants and a frame of a burned car made a forlorn scene around us.

On the horizon planes appeared. I stopped the wagon, and from far off we again witnessed a bombing. We remained hesitant even when the planes were at a distance. Perhaps the Hyenville bridge had been knocked out. I looked at the map and concluded that it would be prudent not to go that far, but rather to detour southward. Soon we turned to the left, and after a few kilometers I chose little shortcuts again.

We passed through a village sheltered by enormous trees. The narrow road wound and divided. Troops were camping over there. The soldiers were freshly shaven and wore new shoes. Their trucks, camouflaged under branches, were probably waiting for the time of attack to try to push the allies back to the sea. The road became gradually more narrow, pebbly, and full of holes. It seemed to us as though it might disappear in the midst of little open fields. However, on the map, this little road continued and crossed a river. But a woman who was pulling her goat told us to go back and take other paths. After several changes of direction, the mule stopped. He was so tired that he would only continue under the threat of the whip. At last we arrived near a place that was simply called la France. I had not heard of this village.

Still hesitating, I ask, "Is this, uh, the la France road?"

It was. Before Quettreville we passed over our last bridge which was the most difficult, longest, and highest. The earth was torn up all around it. Bombs had ripped open the fields and the road, and the footbridge over the wide river appeared fragile. There were no guard rails on the right or left of the bridge to keep the wagon from falling into the water far below.

We unharnessed the mule. Bicyclists stopped to help us push the cart, but then we had to carry the mule to the other bank because he refused to take a step on the shaking planks so high above the water. A whip only made him rear. Petting him and words of encouragement did not work. And the cyclists advised us not to stay there because the planes came over often. What should we do? It was evening. The cart was waiting on the other side close to a wide crater. My mother was seated on a shaft. Then without any apparent reason, suddenly the mule decided to follow Marie. In the middle of the footbridge he stopped again, and then continued walking fearfully with tiny steps. On the other side, the harnesses were quickly attached, and we proceeded on our way again.

After the big market town of Quettreville, on the way to Granville, we went wearily toward the last little village that was to be our final destination. After about a quarter of an hour, a stone marker indicated that there were still three kilometers to go. We would still arrive before night; however, the house where we were going was farther than the village—at least another kilometer toward the sea. Finally we were there. The house was white and well cared for, with new slate roofs.

Marie's cousin came out, embarrassed not to have recognized her relative at first. "I am going to see the owner," she said.

He was smoking his last cigarette before going to bed. He scratched his head. "Yes," he said, "I will see."

He went inside. He was the mayor of this village and was going to do what he could. Nobody asked us to get down from our cart. That worried us a bit.

"Monsieur already has his refugee relatives here who are occupying all the bedrooms," said Marie's cousin.

Through a half-open window, we could see a dining room with a polished floor and beautiful chairs in place. This room must not be used often. A brisk breeze made the lace curtain flutter. The maid was going to close this window in a minute. The scent of a bouquet of roses filled the air. And my mother, who was overcome with fatigue, pointed with resignation to the room and smiled feebly.

The mayor returned and told us, "I have another little, empty house in the village. "I'll take my bike..."

We turned around, and my little mule took a while before he understood that we were not there yet.

XXV

People of modest condition, such as a grocer, barber, and family of workers joined us. This house, or more exactly, the room to which the mayor had given us the key, was bare. However, very soon our helpful neighbors found a box-spring mattress, some straw, a table, and two chairs. One of the neighbors brought in wood to start a fire in the damp hearth, and another took our mule into his meadow. The grocery lady asked what we needed for the night—perhaps milk, bread, a light? Soon a pleasant flame lit the fireplace, and we were able to bolt the door and hang a coat over the window. We were at home, at least for a while. And now, to sleep...

This dwelling opened onto the main road by only one door and one window. Upstairs it included two uninhabitable little bedrooms that we used for storage.

Les Routes Sans Oiseaux

It had a ground floor with holes that had been filled with bricks. The granite walls had badly deteriorated plaster but seemed sturdy. On the right side of the house there was a café that sold groceries, and on the left a bakery. We lived in the village center. The broad, curved national road shone by day at the level of our windowsill, and downward on the other side there was a large house with closed shutters.

During the days that followed our arrival, groups of refugees still passed on this road that was elevated and smooth as a canal. The carts were going slowly, and all carried white flags. Military cars with a lookout watching the sky crossed the village from time to time. Slamming on their brakes, they would stop rather close to us, and, in the silence that followed, we recognized the soft purring of planes while slow wagons of fragrant hay passed by. It was summer, the lovely season of harvest. The folks here were living in peace, symbolizing man's hope and innocence. In the noonday sun, melting tar mingled with the aroma of warm, freshly-baked bread from the oven next door, and we would sit and watch the sun set.

Once in a while I would stand chatting on the threshold. People tried to help us. The idea of leaving their homes did not occur to them. Mealtime was the only big activity of our day. It was easy to get milk, butter, eggs, and vegetables from the neighboring farms. The butcher was kept busy slaughtering. We were entitled to one hundred grams of bread a day, and with this, plus our own wheat, we would be able to get along for a long time. These things were our main concern.

My mother was very ill and suffered from depression that left her exhausted. I learned through our neighbors that a doctor from Saint-Lô, whom I knew very well, was also a refugee in the area. He came to see us. I had remembered him as an alert, young man, but the man I saw getting awkwardly off his bicycle at our door was almost old. Walking with difficulty, he smiled at our surprise. In his wrinkled face, only his eyes bespoke the vigor of his age and his faith in life. It was a miracle that he had regained his freedom from the prison where he had been incarcerated by the Germans for such a long time. After the guards had fled he had to remain in the depths of the prison until bombs demolished the ceiling and walls so he could get out. Among all the dead he was the only one who survived. Gravely wounded, he had dragged himself through the debris under a furious bombing and, through smoking ruins, had left the buried city.

He told us about the atrocious death of some very dear friends of ours. He had trouble getting the words out when he spoke of the horrors, and it took a lot of effort to get him to tell us the details of the destruction of his town. He preferred to talk about happier subjects. He pointed out, for example, that a farmer had lent him his suit and nice stiff shirt and that he had gotten his tie from a road worker and his socks from the village priest. And he was replenishing his wine cellar—someone had given him a liter of Calvados!

When he spoke to my mother, he chose words that would bring back her hope. His warmth and good humor were as effective as his remedies, and some days later my mother was again able to take a few steps in the house.

In the loneliest hours, I would go to see my little mule. I would lie down in the grass by him. The field was far away from the road, and the Germans would not be able to see me. And in the midst of this quiet countryside, I felt crushed by emptiness. The calm and void of the present brought me an unbearable uneasiness. It took me several days to understand that in an incredible way I missed the noise of battle, the guns, airplanes, and all that caused our anxiety of the last weeks.

On a cool Wednesday morning, July 26, the sky opened up with awesome sounds, and bomber squadrons flew over slowly from east to west. The white planes dazzled at impressive heights as they went toward the sea in formations of fourteen to twenty. Their migration lasted a long time. They had just gotten ready for Patton's great attack. When the last wave of planes stopped, an emptier than ever silence came upon us.

The bridge that we had gone over at some kilometers from this place sometimes underwent attacks from light planes. Then the folks would stand in the street and talk about the sight.

"Watch out! They are going to dive! They are releasing their bombs!"

The women would run back toward the house with their hands over their ears, and the explosions would shake us a bit. Then the groups of people would scatter in the village as the humming motors died in the distance.

From my bed at night, through the curtainless window, I could see silent German convoys, camouflaged by branches, passing in the moonlight. There were forage wagons and four-wheel carts. As soon as the steps of one team of horses faded away, another followed. Perched on their high seats, the drivers were holding their guns between their legs. Often a bareheaded infantryman would be walking behind with his hands on the light rails. Other detached soldiers went through the sleeping village all the time. They did not stop and never looked at the houses.

On July 28, about thirty wagons such as the ones that passed in the night stopped in front of our house at the beginning of the afternoon and stayed motionless more than an hour in the sunlight. Their drivers were taking a break and snoozing, and the horses were so tired that they did not have the strength to chase off the flies. Suddenly, on order, the convoy started back on course. The soldiers, as if seized by frenzy, got some of their teams to trot ahead by using the stick and whip. A minute later, a fighter plane's machine guns started to shoot, but the whole thing happened so fast that it is difficult to describe. The tracer bullets passed right under our noses like streaks of fire, and the shadow of the plane followed the road. The machine gun noise overpowered all others; then there was silence. The last wagon had stopped at the end of the village because its driver had collapsed at the wheel, and two poor bay horses, tied to the back of the cart without harness, were struggling. Farther away, a cart was aflame in a hail of bullets, and the roof of a shed caught on fire. All along the slope, horses and men lay on the road, and wagons were overturned. The planes had disappeared.

They carried a woman into her house. A young man sped away on an old bike. Then without slowing down a German motorcycle passed near the slaughter, riding along the shoulder of the road. The motorcycle seemed to be flying through the air and eating up the road until its sound eventually died away. The brutal bursts of other planes' engines assaulted our ears.

A little later autos, trucks, and light cars passed quickly by, fleeing from the front. On the lookout we followed their movement while we awaited the mysterious planes that would surge from the clouds or the leafy tops of the woods. In fact, the broken roll of machine guns burst forth, and soon gas, oil, tires, and shells of cars were in flame in the ditches. However, as soon as night came, German vehicles passed hurriedly in greater number, and their traffic became so thick that the road was a black stream of troops. Trucks, wagons harnessed to donkeys, mules and horses, stolen light carts, small cars, caterpillars, Russian or Polish service wagons pulled by ponies, and tanks, ambulances, motorcycles, English carts, cannon, or forage wagons— all of this machinery was going away, grazing our walls and sometimes stopping and obstructing our doors. In the moonlight, unexpected planes could annihilate these enormous columns and for that matter they could do the same to the whole village. We could be trapped in our house without exit and incinerated. I thought it would be wise to ask refuge at the grocery lady's, whose large café opened onto gardens in the rear. But during this unforgettable night, not one plane came over the village.

The quantity of equipment and the number of soldiers that left the sector between July 28 and 29 seemed colossal to me. These troops were to be recovered farther along, but at that particular moment the sudden absence of the allied aviation did astonish us. In all the noise of the convoys, we sometimes thought that we could hear the shrieks of allied bombers, but it was nothing—just a tank getting back on course or some other motor. The adjutants' voices bellowed out orders in the night, and the column shuffled, closed ranks, and miraculously opened a passage for the cars of high officers' who were asking directions. This crowd remained disciplined and remarkably flexible. Even in defeat, the Wehrmacht withdrew in an orderly manner.

Soon the moon set. The activity was still intense. The armored vehicles were knocking the corners off the steps of the thresholds and in front of the windows, like dark monsters, they cut their silhouettes on the starry night. At dawn's early light, the enormous column seemed to diffuse. When we got back to our house, the vehicles took up only one side of the road and bore toward the left where the two bay horses lay. The passing tanks had crushed their hooves.

The weather was beautiful. The allied aviators had not yet shown up. We stretched out on our beds. The harassing squadrons did not come back until the early morning, and they did not give us any peace for the rest of the day.

XXVI

Their whimsical whirring surrounded us in an up-and-down, nerve-racking movement—at times silently gliding high and at other times deliriously grazing the ground. Machine guns fired almost endlessly on the countryside or the village, and bombs fell all around. I decided to go to the closest farm to see if it would be possible to stay in a stable.

It was cool and clear outside. I could see a little bit of the sea gleaming on the horizon between the trees. The angry planes were still flying cautiously over the main road that was now deserted and obstructed only by dead bodies. Sometimes they would take pleasure in surprising a small group of soldiers here and there or a lost car trying to flee toward the coast by way of shady lanes or fields. These sky hunters had eyes as sharp as birds. You could see them suddenly tilt, while cutting their engines, to swoop down between the high trees and aim toward the ground. It would have been unwise to appear to be hiding, but after encountering several Mongolians, I thought it wise to get away from them as fast as possible because their presence would attract fire.

There were about twenty people in the cellar at the farm. A regular army lieutenant with long hair and an anxious face was looking at his map. He gave an order, and his men left behind him. They went along a high slope and soon disappeared.

From our vantage point, patrol planes flew like a swarm of bees ahead of advancing, silent, and hidden troops. Over toward Coutances and the center of the department, artillery rumbled. I went back to the house at noon without having made a decision.

The rest of the day passed without incident. Some refugees that I had known before the war came to see us. They told us all the details about the battle in their village. They spoke mostly of their losses, and when they left we felt relieved.

We needed silence to wait in quiet contemplation during this precious hour that seemed like a mirage. Peace settled in toward evening. In the tranquil air, you could hear a child's laugh, a civilian's footstep, and a cow mooing in a field. The moon rose high.

I clearly remember a fearful hissing sound of a crash accompanied by a bright light that awakened us during the night. A plane came down in flames. It crashed in a field two hundred feet away from us. The light of the fire illuminated the road. Folks got up to go look, and soon there were groups of curious people, women in nightgowns under their coats and even children watching. Unaware of the danger, these folks talked at length before going back to bed by the light of the dying embers. Soon there was nothing left in the calm night but the fading red coals. The road had become as deserted as the sky. When I woke up for the second time, some auto-tracks were slowly crossing the village in the mist of dawn. They were going toward Granville, just like the others had. Both worried and joyful voices could be heard from the windows.

In spite of the early hour, a man ran by and shouted excitedly along with the others that some Americans had just gone by. This man stayed in the middle of the road like a messenger. He loudly confirmed what he had seen and heard because these Americans had spoken to him. For those who still had their doubts, he showed a carton of ten packs of cigarettes the Americans had given him. He had just opened a pack and was deeply inhaling the smoke. In the briskness of the morning, we did not know whether he was shaking from the cold or his emotion, but his sincerity appeared obvious. I had never seen him before. He was about forty years old with a blotched red face, bare head, and open collar. He was wearing beach sandals and his feet were thin and white.

He saw me nearby and said, "Let's go have coffee!"

There were four of us going into the café that the grocery lady hurriedly opened, and then others arrived to whom we spread the news.

"I have trouble believing," said a stubborn fellow, "that several little cars could move forward without protection."

"Tell me I'm a liar!" answered our messiah.

This was out of the question, but one thing was sure—we did not see any other Americans. One impatient chap got up from the long table where we now numbered around twenty. We were emptying two bottles of rum that the grocery lady had hidden in 1940. He went to the door, listened for a long time, and then came back and sat down without a word.

"And so?"

"Nothing!"

The barefooted man in sandals replied, "They are scouts; wait awhile."

"Is it true?" asked my mother whose hands were trembling with excitement.

"It is true. It is certain."

"I want to see."

Everyone wanted to see. They came together in the street to talk about good reasons for hope, but two camps were already forming—the believers and the skeptics.

In the café, after the two bottles of rum had been consumed, the American cigarettes won the case. Even the sullen fellows agreed to celebrate with a drink. The stranger, however, felt that time was working against him.

"Where is he from?" folks were asking in low voices.

"We do not know."

While smoking, they watched him out of the corner of their eyes. He paid for drinks all around and kept on repeating, "That makes you feel really good, really good..."

This became monotonous. If the Americans did not come, this chap was likely to get out of here with a

Les Routes Sans Oiseaux

black eye. But all the time he was talking, he was listening to the noises from outside.

Suddenly he exclaimed, "There are the tanks! Do you hear them?"

We went outside to look, but it was only a little observation plane flying over the road. We could see the pilot in his seat. The whole crowd made friendly signs and waved their handkerchiefs. When he disappeared, we were still.

The stranger declared, "It will not be long. Wait."

We went back into the café to watch him more closely. When the tanks finally arrived, there were only a few latecomers outside who called out, "There they are! They are here!"

The tanks rolled in at a smart pace with their cannon lightly tilted toward the ground and a soldier standing on the raised gun-turret who was saluting the French. A small, open vehicle with a wide, low, and square hood—the first Jeep—escorted the column. From the tanks and Jeep, soldiers in olive-drab shirts, rolled-up sleeves, and hair blowing in the wind, were throwing sweets, cigarettes, chocolate, and cans of cookies and candy which rolled to our feet on the side of the road. At the passing of each tank, the same shouts of joy went up in unison and, on the gun-turret, the same soldier in olive-drab saluted with his hand raised to his forehead and a smile on his lips as if to say farewell. Sweets kept falling on the road, and the men, women, and children hastened to pick them up. The column was long. Jeeps passed around it. In the wind created by all the traffic, a soldier was holding a telephone to his ear talking just as he would in an office.

My mother looked at all this without waving. Marie raised her arm with an uneasy look, and I realized that the gestures I was making with my handkerchief seemed as if I were directing traffic.

Our happiness, gratitude, and relief were much too deep to be expressed in such a simple way. Other refugees ahead of us were stunned in the midst of the shouts and gesticulations by the other villagers. The end of their anguish left them immobile, smiling foolishly or raising their arms without conviction, or even letting others pick up the cigarettes thrown at their feet. Of course, later, we joined in the chorus, but the first minutes were far too emotional. We only felt like going into a corner and crying. When I chided my mother for not waving, she raised her hand one time at the soldiers and smiled through her tears.

Some Americans complained about the slightly cool welcome they received in Normandy and especially in the Manche. First of all, there was the incident of the troops that went through a bombed town. Did these men, who came as liberators and forced by war's hard law to destroy our towns, think that the survivors—family and friends—of the dead still warm under the ruins were going to cheer them? I hope that by now a better understanding has replaced their first disillusions.

The residents of martyred villages were not able to shout for joy or throw flowers that they could not find on scorched earth when the soldiers went by. Everywhere else, in the country and spared towns, they did receive a warm welcome. The soldiers should be aware of the fact that Normandy is not a country of frenzied, short-lived enthusiasm. A certain reserve always restrains us, and sometimes our strongest emotions that seem lost are in truth etched in the depth of our souls. Anglo-Saxons should be able understand this.

The soldiers perceived the French as importunate beggars because during the first days of fraternization and glory, children, women, and men came to the stopped tanks, as if begging for alms that were never refused. And to obtain these indulgences, they put on their most engaging smiles, with a glint of greed, and even covetousness in their eyes. It was an embarrassing sight, but remember, our friends, for how long we were deprived of the sweets that you were bringing us on your war machines! For the kids in the regions that you passed through, it was several weeks of Christmas. And we always recall the beautiful Christmases of our childhood.

Everyone got his stash of cigarettes and candy. You were so generous that we got used to the abundance. I never smoked so much in my life.

When we woke up in the morning, we would hear your tanks roll by, and the feeling of your presence was like the first rays of the sun. Soon we heard that you had reached Rennes. We were anxious to get on the road home, to go in the opposite direction of the armored tanks that were heading south night and day. But three armies led by Patton's Third Army were engulfed in the narrow Avranches inlet, and the road was temporarily closed to civilian traffic.

On Monday, 31 July, we wanted to try our luck. We harnessed the mule at dawn and loaded our things. Little Mascotte was leaping with joy. I believe she probably understood that we were going home. It just happened that a long convoy had stopped. It was better for our nervous little dog to get used to seeing that enormous machinery without the noise. The tank drivers waved to us in friendship and, because we were walking on the side of the road, tossed us a pack of cigarettes or some chewing gum that we caught like a thrown ball. The weather was gorgeous.

"Goodbye! Thank you!" we called.

The fields were covered with dew, and the farms seemed still asleep. When we arrived near the skeleton of an enemy car, passing became difficult, and our fragile wheels grazed the heavy tracks. Far ahead, the stench of a dead horse spoiled the fresh scent of morning. Our little mule balked, and from his gun-turret a joyful young soldier called out: "Hello! Hello!" He laughed at our plight and handed me a carton of Chesterfields as repayment for the trouble. Our wagon was a little damaged, but I was able to pass through. Soon the endless convoy got underway, and we looked for refuge at the entrance to a field. We were stuck there for more that an hour because the road was not wide enough for the Red Cross vans and Jeeps that were passing the tanks at full speed. Our trip ran the risk of taking a long time, so we thought it best to turn around and go back to whence we came.

Les Routes Sans Oiseaux

Bareheaded American soldiers without jackets were frisking prisoners in the village. With their hands on their heads, the Germans did as told under the threat of rifles. Farther along, civilians were bringing back Mongolians whose weapons they had taken. Other American soldiers strolled by the doors with heavy guns on their shoulders and helmets on their belts. Some went into the café and bought drinks for everyone. The messenger of the first day, the one in his sandals, recognized me and called me over to share in his moment of glory. He was still talking about his great adventure.

"Nobody believed it!" he said.

It seemed to me that the glowing Rosaceae spread over his face, his crimson forehead, and even the inside of his swollen eyelids that were filled with inebriated tears. He drank red and white wine, cognac, and Calvados, one after the other.

His plump wife with bright eyes came to the door to call him, "Achille! Please!"

"Just a minute, I am translating." answered Achilles the Great.

And, in fact, he was trying to translate his thoughts into a language that mixed German and English words. Brave Achilles, even if he knew nothing about the war other than the adventure of the final morning, he will talk about it for the rest of his life because it is the most pleasing part of the story to him.

Monotonous days passed, and I got into the habit of staying at the house. Tanks were still rolling by. We thought about our lost village, the friends we left on the road, and those who were dead—Féodal digging his hole and Pierre trying to flee under the bullets. We remembered the fires, the attacks, the shells, and the road—oh, the sad road. We were consumed by impatience to go back on that ill-fated road. Our great desire to leave would awaken us in the night, as would the noise of occasional bombs that detached planes dropped on the rear of the retreating armies.

Saturday, August 6, as soon as it was dawn, we decided to leave and to walk until evening, and, if necessary, to sleep no matter where rather than coming back a second time. Due to exceptional luck, we were able to cover the first kilometers rapidly. Our difficulties only began at a burned-out house where we had stopped Monday. Next, on the Quettreville square, two French police and a M.P. stopped us. We were forbidden to continue our journey, but they made us understand that we could take back roads at our own risk. We were used to that. We were going to return home.

XXVII

The road that I had chosen on the map avoided towns and even large villages. I will not linger on a description of this route that was often difficult with rugged ascents and descents winding through the hills of the region. The armored tanks had gone everywhere before taking only highways, and on scorched slopes you could see here and there reassuring signs saying "Road clear of mines" and "Mines cleared to the hedges." However, these roads were deserted, as folks were not yet leaving their hamlets. We would meet a cyclist or a few pedestrians who advised us on a detour to take, or a rare wagon of refugees like us who were venturing getting home. It was a strange thing that none of them wanted to talk. Each one went on absorbed by anxious thoughts and worries.

Toward midday, we stopped to rest for two hours in a little field of ferns where our exhausted little mule lay down to rest a bit. Soon afterward we again went gradually into the sad combat zone.

Ruins, mangled trees, destroyed fences, all covered with thick dust that stuck to everything—the grass, burnt leaves, and what was left of the walls. There were endless wires along every hedge and branch that the monstrous army which had ravaged the earth had forgotten under the dust.

We discovered all kinds of debris in the fields among the dead animals—scattered clothes, weapons, packages, frames of cars, and unexpected things such as a clock and a baby carriage.

We were suffocated by the odors of decaying cows and horses in the grass and stenches of human cadavers that were harsher and unlike others. The cows' spotted coats were flattened like bedside rugs in the trodden hay, and swarms of flies were buzzing around them. Other animals killed more recently were still swollen and stiff. Burned-out tanks were already rusting with lowered cannon.

Folks were returning, trying to recover their past life among the ruins under collapsed roofs. Their wagon was unharnessed in the courtyard, and their sweating horse was waiting motionless, its stomach cut by the saddle-girth. A man, woman, and children were walking in the house. Through the broken windows and doors, we could see them going from one room to another in the debris. The father came back on the threshold, raised himself up on a pile of boards and rubbish, and when he had gotten to the branches of a vine over the door he maintained his balance with one hand. His wife handed him a flag, a little calico tricolor flag on a blue staff. The father attached the staff firmly to the old vine while his family watched.

I said only this, in wonder, "A flag..."

The Périers-Carentan highway carried the convoys' confused noise afar. Black soldiers stretched the telephone lines over new telegraph poles for civilian use. Trucks were going back and forth constantly. One after the other, all the ruins in this street came into view. We knew every farm and every hamlet. The war had left its mark everywhere—blackened, collapsed walls, splintered trees, burned-out cars, and reeking cadavers.

"There's Legoupil's farm and Antoine Legrand's house," we pointed out.

We kept on going. There was not a roof left on the horizon. What was left of the walls was riddled with bullets. The stone cross at the entrance to our village was down. We turned on our path, and the noise of the convoys died away. Ruins! Smashed and burned ruins under the great silence of death.

Les Routes Sans Oiseaux

We looked in the distance. From the approach to our property, we first noticed the tall umbrella pine from which several branches were cut, but other trees were still standing. And we discovered that we could no longer remember from which angle it was possible to see our house.

"I have no more hope," said my mother. Our neighbors' home had been utterly destroyed like all the others. No one had come back to the village.

At the next turn, the same shout burst forth from all our lips, "The house!"

There she stood still firm and faithful. She was waiting for us. Perhaps even other miracles were going to occur. Our home was going to speak to us and tell us what she had endured all alone and what she had seen. But no, it was just a stone house, a poor thing defiled and murdered by men.

I had expected to see tall grass by the walls and all over the courtyard, and yet the ground was bare and trampled. "Everywhere my horse goes, grass will not grow any more," says the War.

We looked fearfully through the broken windows, and once again we lowered our voices. Before entering, we came back to the courtyard. Silence. We stood still like travelers in the middle of a desert. Listening. No more clucking hens in the courtyard. What ghosts would emerge from the silent house?

Suddenly a noise caused us to turn our heads, but it was only the poplar leaves whispering in the evening breeze. No more birds flitting and chirping among the branches.

PART THREE

Personal Recollections

1. La Meauffe by Madeleine Levannier
2. Medical Student by Jean Masselin
3. Pont Hebert by Yvonne Gautier
4. Conde-sur-Vire—la Platiniere by Bernard Chardine

[Nos. 1, 2, and 4 translated by Claudine Remy]

1
Story of La Meauffe, 1940 to 1944
By
Madeleine Levannier
[Translated by Claudine Remy]

The period 1940 to 1944 is still very much alive in the memories of many "Meauffois." It is the spring of 1940 when the first families of refugees arrive from the Somme. They live in the farms, but leave the villages when the Germans arrive. Only one remains to work in the quarries of La Meauffe.

In June 1940 a whole train of soldiers from the Red Cross remain for several days at La Meauffe station before the Germans arrive. Many of the soldiers find civilian clothing from the local inhabitants and try to find their way home.

Some English troops retreat directly toward Cherbourg, where they embark on the cruiser *Courbet*. German troops follow them with bundles of sticks with which to cross the English Channel. They are caught by a barrage of naval guns from the vicinity of Carentan.

Pierre Marrê, a young soldier from La Meauffe, participates in this action from the cruiser *Courbet* in the area of Saint-Vaast-la-Hougue.

The numbers of French soldiers taken prisoner at Cherbourg are marched in a column of a hundred, by Germans circling on bicycles, to Saint-Lô in one day.

Another young soldier from La Meauffe, marching in that column, escaped at the figure of St. Martin by jumping into a trench.

The Germans requisition the chateaux of St. Gilles of Vermanoir and the chateau of Fors, where M. Malgorne, director of the apple distillery of Germainerie, lives at the time. The arrival and installation of the occupiers creates a great uneasiness and a profound humiliation, especially for those who lived through the war of 1914-18.

In December 1941, a battery of German artillery moves into the chateaux of Vermanoir and St. Gilles. At the beginning of 1942, a permanent staff of German officers moves into the chateau of St. Gilles and will remain until the liberation.

From November 1943 to February 1944 a company of automobile repairmen remain at the distilleries of Lower Normandy. During this same period and until the liberation of the Mongolian troops in German uniforms near the distillery and the quarry of La Meauffe, they work in great secrecy. They do not dare speak to anyone. The work place is guarded day and night by German soldiers.

After the Normandy landing, the Americans will discover the work accomplished in the quarries. The Mongolians" have dug tunnels under the Aírel road for the storing of the V-1 and V-2, which would have been rapidly moved toward the north of the Cotentin Peninsula thanks to the nearby railway.

Second Part

A German staff coming from Saint-Lô will install itself in the chateaux of Vermanoir and St. Gilles from the end of November 1943 to February 1944. At the same time, a service of German gendarmerie will move into the girls school on rue Claies de Vire to assure the security of this staff. A service of civil police will stay at the chateau de Fors from February 1944 until the 8th of June 1944. The population resented this period of occupation and they resented the constant requisitions. They had less and less butter, milk, and meat. Their mistrust of the occupiers was more obscure than apparent.

The work of the prisoners sent to Germany was missed terribly. Many women proved their courage in doing the work usually reserved for men. For example, they organized to do the sowing and the harvesting. In 1942 and 1943 some young dissident men who had been hiding helped with the work in exchange for food.

The creamery of La Meauffe will continue to operate under regulations as a requisitioned factory. A part of the production will go to the occupation troops and the remainder for the population. To receive a camembert, one has to hand in the box from the previous one.

The distillery of Germainerie will continue to operate and 90 percent of the alcohol that is produced is sent to Puteaux, near Paris, for the manufacture of powder and motor fuel. The distillery, very well known to the Americans, will be machine-gunned several times by fighter bombers and notably, in 1943, it will be partly destroyed with its entire stock of alcohol. Happily, there are no victims among the workers, for the Germans had requisitioned them for work on the telephone lines and earth works.

Some of these men went to work in Germany. Half of the men from La Meauffe, with all the risks involved, managed to escape. During this difficult period, the director of the school of La Meauffe, with the assistance of young people and several adults, puts on some very successful theatrical performances at the Claudel cheese factory. The price of admission is the sale of goods and donations, all to go for the making up of parcels to send to the prisoners in Germany. This has the double advantage of providing an entertaining diversion and benefitting the prisoners.

As for the underground, it was mostly passive—rails on the railroads are destroyed, sleeper screws are damaged, electric lines cut.

In 1944, the Germans arrest Albert Houssin de la Raoulerie, accused of destroying electric lines. He was roughly treated in prison and, shortly after being released, he died.

The occupiers apprehended four children, also accused of cutting electric wires, Pierre Jacques, Yves Peyrat, Gerard Leroyer, and Marcel Eudes. They are sent to Saint-Lô to remain three months under the control of "public assistance."

Liberation, 6 June 1944.

A rumbling sound, intense, never leaving to the imagination, an intensive bombardment near the coast. No need to draw a picture. It is the landing in Normandy.

Allied planes attack the bridges of La Meauffe. The bridge over the Vire is struck by the first bombing on the 7th of June. The railway bridge will be damaged on the 8th. But the bridge of For will not be touched. In spite of efforts of fighter bombers and heavy bombers together, and despite the fact that several bombs explode all around, it will remain standing, well shaken, but still in place.

The church, the parsonage, and sixty houses of the commune are destroyed. Eight farms, the chateaux of For and Vermanoir are flattened, as well as the chateau of St. Gilles, only three hours after the departure of Rommel and his staff who had stopped there for the night.

On 10 June at the railway bridge of For, a platoon of American tanks makes its first appearance. It moves down to the church and, after attracting strong machine gun fire from the Germans, it returns to the Landes where it will be attacked again. The German front line starts at the church and crosses les Landes and continues to the côte des Buffets, cutting the commune in half. The two armies remain in those positions, face-to-face, for more than a month. Every day the Americans bombard the enemy lines more or less intensively while the Germans respond with five or six well-aimed shells.

10-12 July.
The American Army masses its troops obviously for an attack. It will take place on 13 and 14 July. About four o'clock in the morning after an intense preparation of machine-gun fire, the U.S. troops make their assault. They advance about one kilometer and dig in.

The second attack takes place on 14 July. There will be no more Germans on the firing line. They have evacuated toward Rampan, where the German army had put in a bridge over the Vire at the level of the church.

The Claudel creamery is destroyed by incendiaries, but the production of butter will not stop as machines and workers are moved into the cheese factory. Note that a month before its destruction, after the Germans had given an order to evacuate all civilians to the south of the town, M. Claudel had opened the doors of the creamery and invited the people to help themselves to the stocks that had been reserved for the Germans.

The Gesbert bakery was able to bake bread without interruption under the bombardment until the oven and the building were destroyed by bombs.

Two days after D-Day, one sees all around the town people getting together, worrying about what they should do. Instinctively, they choose their places of refuge. These have little to do with security. After the war, we discovered that many of these places actually were the most dangerous. They had for names: les Grandes Landes, la crêterie, le Carillon. It is undeniable that one goes toward a person in whom he has confidence more than to a certain place. This is why eighty people gathered at the Mathurin Le Meur house on les Grandes Landes and they had to be fed. Mathurin Le Meur agrees to take his wagon to the mill of M. Morel at Villiers-Fossard to seek flour. He is successful in bringing back a sack of flour, in spite of being fired on several times by German machine guns. The next day, Victoire Durand will bake bread.

At the beginning of July, a German airplane is forced down in the Grandes Landes. The pilot is slightly injured and he goes back to the German lines. Some days later, an American bomber, also in the Grandes Landes, is shot down by the Germans. He ejects, but his body is never found. In 1991, the family of the pilot comes to honor him at this place.

The commune is liberated. The people come home. Life begins again, but with mounting difficulties. In a corridor of two to three kilometers, nothing remains. The troops have passed through here and the looters also. On returning from their exodus, the inhabitants find only the ugliness of war. The commune has paid a heavy tribute to the war. Out of a population of 650 inhabitants, they have suffered seventeen killed and ten injured.

2
Jean Masselin, Medical Student
La Ferté-Macé
(Translated by Claudine Remy)

Our father, a former engineer at Schneider in Harfleur near Le Havre—allocated to the preparation of munitions at the end of the war of 1914-1918—was in May 1940 required by the army to set up a plant for the manufacture of grenades in a former textile mill, now empty, at Ferté Macé.

The rapid German advance in May-June 1940 did not allow this plan to be carried out. But the family retained a rented summer house. This is the same summer house where we would spend all our vacations near our mother while our father continued his industrial activities in Caen. Three rooms of this house were requisitioned by the German Army for an officer and two soldiers who were a part of the garrison occupying the sector of Bagnoles de Orne. The officer, twenty years old, was from Russia. He had been a member of the Hitler Youth and he had participated in the campaign in Poland in 1939-40. It was impossible to gain any conversation with the officer. He would give a brief salute on leaving in the morning and perhaps a salute when he returned in the evening. He usually came back late, probably having had dinner with other officers.

The two soldiers were reservists. One was a painter and the other a farmer. They were from the Hanover region. Obviously, they were not very enthusiastic about their situation. They were always looking for conversation, talking about letters they received from their families, showing pictures, listening to the radio with us at night for news from the BBC.

We always knew what their program of exercises would be for the next day—in the marshes of the area, in the woods of Bagnoles. When they could, they would bring us fruits and drinks. They always would inform us about the likely time of return of the officer, and they cautioned us to be careful about listening to the radio.

During the Russian campaign before the offensive against Sevastopol, they were transferred, but they did not wish to leave even though the coming operation appeared to be a dangerous one. One morning during their expressions of regret, I put a German helmet on my head and a rifle in my hand and suggested that I should go in their place.

One Sunday morning the German gendarmes were going on patrol, making a thorough search. When some of them entered the church during service, some of us were leaving quickly through the sacristy. This was the beginning of forced labor.

Our father would come back to Ferté-Macé on Saturday, and Monday morning would return to his professional activities. The connection was not good waiting at the station at Briouze, changing at Argentan for Caen. But when weather permitted, he did not hesitate to return to Caen by bicycle.

For a long time, we worried about the fatigue of our father. We could not understand all his moving about. After the liberation, we learned that he was cooperating with an engineer, Eugène Mestin, in making trips that would allow him an opportunity to observe the movement of German units.

In May 1944 when he had a few days of rest, we talked to him about the prospects of the next few weeks, persuaded that an intensification of air attacks at this period of the year would mean a military operation of huge proportions.

He confided to me that in his correspondence he would indicate the probable date of this operation in a letter mentioning the sending of a parcel. On my return to Paris in mid-May, I found a letter containing various bits of harmless news and this line: "The parcel that I promised will arrive for you between the 2nd and the 10th of June.

The future proved that he was not wrong.

LeDebarquement (D-Day), 6 June 1944

In the little chapel of the diocesan House of Students at 61 rue Madame in Paris, I was at the mass of Monsignor de la Serre, the resident priest. I was having very bad prayers. From a little radio inside we had learned, about 8 o'clock, that a landing had taken place at dawn in Normandy. I could only think of the risks of such an operation and of my parents, without forgetting the numerous family friends.

A quick trip through the streets of Paris, particularly in the area of le Madeleine, Avenue de l'Opera, boulevard des Italiens, reveals a reduction in traffic, but a reinforcement of military patrols around those arteries.

Late in the afternoon, a family friend telephoned me to say, "Alas! Caen – Falaise – Mondeville were liberated well before one o'clock!" [Actually, those places were not liberated until over a month later. – Ed.]

Friday 9 June – 5 a.m.

Noise of steps in the corridor, a knocking on the neighboring door, people shouting, more sounds of steps. Then silence.

I run down quickly to see the concierges. They are in their loge, crying. They tell me that the Gestapo has just come to get two friends who had just returned to their room the night before, after being away two or three days. They will be deported to Dachau, but will return, exhausted, after the liberation of the camps in May 45. What joy!

At this moment I cannot believe my incredible luck, because in the bottom of my cupboard there are some documents which, if discovered, would have assured my deportation.

The Mobile Surgical Group No. 1 of the French Red Cross
Giel, Orne, Mission of 16 June to 23 July 1944

Thursday, 15 June.

The S.A.E.S.R.P. (Section automobile d'évacuation et de secours de la région parisienne) calls and asks us to meet at the French Red Cross on rue de Berri, Paris, to learn of our mission on the Normandy front. Three ambulances must go to Alençon to carry a ton and a half of surgical supplies and equipment. Immediately we went to the depots to pick up our loads and agreed to rendezvous the next day, Friday the 16th, on Champs Elysée for departure.

Our presence on the avenue was quickly noticed by people who asked about our destination. Some of them wanted to give news and encouragement to their families in Normandy and they asked us to take letters to post offices relatively near the place of combat.

About 3 o'clock we departed by way of Versailles – St. Cyr l'Ecole. We encountered an aerial attack and saw rescue squads evacuating wounded people from the woods all around.

At Chartres, we stopped in Plaine de Beauce because of another air attack at that place. The passive defense, in the emergency, asked us to give them some first aid material. In view of our mission, and recognizing the situation, we let them have two or three cartons.

Before la Loupe, we encountered a German convoy in difficult conditions. It had been completely destroyed by machine guns and bombardment. Debris was all over the road for a distance of four kilometers. But we saw no officer or soldier. They must have been evacuated earlier.

At the edge of a woods, we look for a place to spend the night. A farmer tells us that a British fighter plane had crashed, but the pilot had been able to use his parachute and probably he was hiding somewhere, maybe in the Senonches Forest.

Friday, 16 June.

Departure before 9 a.m. The sky is overcast. We move slowly. All along the route, one of us will sit on the fender of the ambulance, straddling the headlight, watching the sky to avoid a surprise attack.

Stop at the prefecture of Alençon, at the end of the morning. The north exit of the town has just been bombed. About 11 o'clock, the Prefect invites us nine students to come to his office to give more details about our eventual mission – incorporation of the Red Cross surgical group for an indeterminate time, depending on the evolution of the military situation.

This group must rescue exclusively the civil French population who are victims of bombardment and combat, to work behind the German lines, moving as necessary to remain available to the civilian population.

The first destination will be Giel-Courteilles. Three of us will remain as volunteers with Michel Bailleul, future gynecologist-obstetrician in Alençon. The other six will return to Paris with two empty ambulances.

We shall have the benefit of refueling from the German tanker trucks left standing in the park of the prefecture.

About three to four o'clock, the convoy departs for the Forest of Ecouves. The flight of three "Lightnings" fighter planes obliges us to stop suddenly under the cover of the trees.

Arrival by late afternoon in Giel and unloading all the material in a building near the chapel.

Ground floor: First aid room and surgical equipment.

Operating room, including three operating tables, side by side.

1st floor: Two wards for civilian men and women, with forty beds each.

The surgeons will be available 24 hours a day as needed.

The externs (we shall be five) will be distributed as follows: One group of two for the morning, one group of two for the afternoon, one on duty all night (9 p.m. – 6 a.m.)

For the night shift, the externs had to learn to prepare baby bottles and to change diapers. We did our best.

Local nurses will be on duty from 6 a.m. to 8 p.m. assuming all kinds of tasks—dressing wounds, hygiene, surveillance, meal service.

It should be noted that we were short of dishes and flatware. Meals were served at two different times, allowing a half hour for cleaning tableware before the next shift.

One Sunday, the nurses were so tired that I offered to help with their work—the first plate in the middle of the morning, the last plate in the middle of the night. I shall never repeat that experience.

We would take our meals in the dining room of the orphanage at tables for eight—there were no reserved seats. We would talk about the problems of the day and the memories of past years.

Our meals were nourishing and the quality of the local products, such as milk, butter and cream, was enjoyable. Often we were surprised to see at each meal a liter of cream disappear at each table while some of the nurses talked about the cures of previous years at Vichy. And often we would finish our meal with singing "La Petite Nantaise" to maintain our morale.

Saturday 17 June.

About 5 a.m., a special motor noise, sounding like a V-1 woke us up. Our mission for this day will be to inform the different rescue centers of our presence at Giel, that our mission was primary care and post-operation observation for two or three days. The seriously wounded would be transferred to Le Mans-Mayenne, Tours, and Paris. The center of Banoles de l'Orne could be of no use because all the hotels were being occupied by services of the German Army.

Departure through Putanyes-Fromentel-Messei. We stop in front of the factories near the railroad station. On the way, we meet numerous workers of the Todt Organization marching to the east.

Pass through Flers [Dr. Masselin had his medical practice here from 1960 to 1985. –Ed.]. The results of a recent bombing, some of the buildings are still burning. The Place St. Jean is painful to behold. Last stops at the rescue squads in the country near St. George des Groseillers and Aubusson.

In the beginning of the afternoon, we go to Caen by way of Falaise. Going through the city is impossible after the recent bombing.

Fortunately, three German tanks were moving to the south and, in order to get around the city, made a breach through the hedgerow. A few minutes later, we were able to use the breach in the hedge and go on toward Thury-Harcourt. Two Spitfires fly overhead as our road climbs to Croisilles.

We will not be able to get into Caen, so we make contact with the emergency teams on the plateau of Fleury sur Orne near German anti-aircraft batteries that are firing at the planes flying over the town.

As if to impress us with a "calm before the storm" we noticed a man with a fishing pole on his shoulder, quietly walking back from the Orne. He was walking slowly as with a state of mind of one who was just returning from a fishing contest.

Return to Giel in late afternoon.

Beside the risks from the bombers, traveling on the roads was difficult because of debris of all kind, but above all, rolls of copper electric or telephone wire that would strike the legs or even the head of the man riding on the fender of the ambulance. We protected ourselves with improvised leggings and overcoats, but the face remained uncovered.

The painting of our ambulances was not appropriate: Four little red crosses of about twenty centimeters on each side of the vehicle. We spent Sunday in painting a big red cross on the top of each.

3
Pont-Hébert, Normandy Story, June-July, 1944
By Yvonne Gautier

On the arrival of the Germans in our village in June 1940, we hid in a field in the rue Les Fontaines. We were very frightened.

Our house at Pont-Hébert was at the hamlet Belle Lande, which had been in part requisitioned by Germans in 1942. We often had problems with these occupants.

My mother was seen by a civilian mocking a caricature of Hitler which was hung on a wall. She was asked to go to German Headquarters in Saint-Lô. But nothing came of it.

In the middle of the year 1943, our house was totally occupied by Germans and we were moved to an unoccupied house with no electricity owned by Mme. Clémence Piédagnel at La Fautelaye.

On June 6, 1944, my sister and I left Saint-Lô at 12 noon following the bombing of the Power Station at Agneaux and the train station at Saint-Lô. We walked from Saint-Lô to Pont-Hébert and met many German lorries full of troops going towards the coast.

On the night of June 6th-7th, we went to a quarry called La Vannerie from which we could see Saint-Lô on fire.

We had to leave Mme. Clémence Piédagnel's house because of a bomb falling close by. We then went to Mme. Piédagnel's mother, Mme. Horel, who lived on a farm called Ferme de la Houchardiére at Le Mesnil Durand, right in the country where we thought we would be safe. Alas!

It was quiet for approximately 15 days; then shells and American gliders were going by non-stop.

With my brothers, Roger and Michel, we walked to Saint-Lô along the river footpath. When we arrived level with the main school, we had to turn back because of unexploded bombs.

When we walked to Graignes to see the American paratroopers, nearing the village we came across German soldiers lying in the ditches. They told us to disappear, but we carried on and brought back some American cigarettes.

On the morning of July 9th, a large quantity of phosphorus shells fell on La Houchardiére farm; everything burnt. My 13 year old brother and Mr. Fauvel, who was an engineer at the Claudel Society, burnt to death. They were found holding each other as if to protect one another.

I was with my brother Michel in the barn. Everything was burning. Michel got out over the wall and luckily came back for me, as I couldn't get out.

The whole farm was almost burnt, but the fire stopped where the Saint Sacrement of Pont-Hébert church had been located.

My brother Roger was in a field adjacent to the farm. We thought he was missing. He hadn't heard the shells fall, which were silent but with a terrible result.

The farm la Houchardiére was so quiet, so calm, that we thought we were on vacation. There were some horses to keep us occupied, then my brothers and I were in our early 20's.

When having slept in a shelter, we went to La Bréhannerie where we spent the night in a barn on July 11th. We were badly shelled.

My father was hit in the lung by a shell and later died. Trees, apple trees, everything was flying around. I was hit in the eye, but my friend Désiré Mouchel said it was not serious.

We went down a narrow lane 200 yards from the river Vire. Here we dug a fox hole under a hedge. In this sunken road, we saw our father collapsed near the hedge. Mme. Lechevalier, André Lechevalier's mother, was also there and had part of her head blown off.

We hid in the fox hole. My mother was with Nelly, two years old, and my sister Reneé. I was with my brothers, Roger and Michel. We had placed the wounded and dead under some branches. Gilberte Gilbert was fatally wounded, but gave birth to a dead baby before dying. Gilberte Gilbert was André Lechevalier's wife.

We were on the west side of the river Vire. We could see from there the German soldiers on the other side of the Vire going to attack La Meauffe, to the north-east, but we didn't see them come back.

One day, we lit some sticks of dry wood and some logs (to warm milk for a child). It was at this time that our presence was seen by an L-4 Cub plane. It is after this smoke, which was visible, that we were shelled.

That was frightful. We thought we would die at any moment. We prayed and promised to go on a pilgrimage if our lives were saved.

All the cows had been killed, then we went to get some potatoes at the farm of Mr. Legourgeois, 200 yards away, but the German SS were there, and one spoke French and said to my mother to go to Paris. "You! Go to Paris," answered my mother. The American bullets cut off the branches all around us. With each shot, the German officer stooped because the GI's were 200 yards away. We came back to our shelter without potatoes.

When there was a lull, we decided, my brothers and I, to see what was going on on the northwest side. A German chaplain was in a tank away from all other traffic. This German was astonished to see us here. He thought that all civilians were evacuated. In French, he said that it was too late for us to leave this place, because on the front the fighting was very intense and we would not get away as they were well armed and numerous and very well equipped.

In the battle we heard some tanks just over us which shook the soil of our shelter where we were covered. The German tank or American tanks were in the sunken road. We were terribly frightened and screamed all day.

We stayed ten days with very little food, and unable to wash. In the following months as we washed, the dirt reappeared the following day.

The tanks and shells shook the earth so badly we were unable to move and stayed curled up in the earth. These were terrible hours and days as we were between the Germans and the Americans.

During a lull, we separated the dead, putting them behind a bush, as well as our father whose wound was infected.

We had in our area two firemen from Pont-Hébert with their uniforms and helmets. The firemen were Dufour and Dossier. They went to neighbors at Beaupré farm and The Five Chimneys, M. Hervieu's farm.

On July 19th, they went across the first lines of fire and described our presence and hideout to the American soldiers. The two firemen came back telling us to leave quickly and go to American lines because the allies would not fire. It was six o'clock in the morning.

We were led on foot across the fields, walking near the church at the hamlet Le Mesnil Durand. There was a German tank burning with the crew inside.

We crossed the fields of the farm La Vannerie, gate by gate. Then we found the lane to La Fautelaye that the Americans had mined. They told us it wasn't dangerous and led us across the mines. We were on the American front. At the cross roads La Rairie, we saw the first GI's sleeping in the ditch. We continued walking to the north to go directly to the farm Le Clos

Bessin, where there was a Red Cross Station in Mr. Legoupil's yard.

Here, a Canadian soldier came to tell me, "Don't walk without shoes! There is a pair of shoes in the neighboring house."

When we reached the crossroads at La Maison Blanche, there was a control, then we were enclosed in a little field at Mme. Madelaine's with no admittance to the road. There was a terrific amount of traffic.

In the evening, a U.S. truck took us to Les Fresnes at Montmartin-en-Graignes. There, some 155mm cannons shot toward Le Mesnil Durand. Here, too, we saw GI's come back from the front line to have a rest. It was forbidden to go on the road N° 174 because of traffic.

Five days later, we came back near our village in the district of Cavigny at le Château de la Mare. My two brothers volunteered to search for dead soldiers. They were very well paid for this work in the fields, the woods and the lanes. Later, they buried the dead cows. This entailed making six holes and placing dynamite to create a large enough hole to bury the carcasses.

The starting place for this work was Le Château de la Mare. It was while my brothers, Michel and Roger, were doing this job that Operation Cobra took place. July 25, bombs rained on the US troops, as well as on my brothers. The soldiers protected my brothers by pushing them to the ground. Needless to say, my brothers did not return to this very exposed sector.

I had stayed with other refugees at La Mare and peeled potatoes in the castle basement. There were some American women there who were not very nice to us and took away our rations.

On our return to our house at Belle Lande at Pont-Hébert, we found all our furniture gone, probably pillaged by some civilians.

May 31, 2000
Signé: Yvonne Gautier

4
Conde- sur-Vire, la Potinière
By
Bernard Chardine
(Translated by Claudine Remy)

6 June 1944.
Dawn

The bombing on the coast of Normandy was so strong that our beds were shaking. We immediately understood what was going on. My parents harnessed the horse to the cart to go to pick up my sister, Paulette, a boarding student at Bon Sauveur in Saint-Lô. They harbored some fears on the way, but thought they would be safe when they got back to Plotinière [a small farm village at the edge of Conde-sur-Vire. –Ed.]

About 10 o'clock

Attack on the munition wagons. We are not really in danger. Nevertheless, it is the beginning of bombardment and we are terrorized. Airplanes in formations of six are coming from the south about four times a day. Their target is our house. Paulette Chardine (age 13) and Christine Dedieu (age 10), when seeing the planes coming, would cry in fear and in play, "They strike, they strike."

Everyone would gather under the staircase. One saying remains clear: "Well, we said we were afraid of thunder!"

In the afternoon
The Misses Angèle and Genevieve Leperdriel (first cousins of Mme. André Chardine) arrive on their bicycles at la Plotinière. At this time their brother, Adrien, is a missionary in Oubangui Chari (now the Central African Republic). He was teaching school for the future Emperor Bocassa. When he was about 78 years old, his former student expelled him. The missionary father knew too much of the private life of Bocassa (he was a cannibal).

7 June, in the Morning.
Miss Genevieve Leperdriel is secretary of the Agriculture Syndicate on rue de la Mare in Saint-Lô. In the middle of the morning, she sees a document fall at her feet in the north courtyard of Plotinière. This was a document in her hand writing. It had come all the way from her place of work by the explosives and fires of the bombing of Saint- Lô.

12 June.
11:05 a.m.
The clock in the chateau de Torigni-sur-Vire stops. Several waves of airplanes drop about fifty bombs on the square at Champêtre with a sad balance sheet of thirty-two dead and numerous others wounded. About one o'clock the Douville family, who hold the mill and granary, arrive at Plotinière. Mr. Douville, seriously injured in the war of 1914-1918, is in despair. His only

son has just died, a victim of his duty in the passive defense.

In the Evening

There arrives from the cure of Torigny Dean Chaignon, Father Theault, and the chaplain of the hospice. They set up a chapel in the cow barn. They cover the walls with sheets. When circumstances permit, people of the surrounding villages assist at mass. The Misses Leperdriel serve as sacristies.

* * * * *

Raymond Pommier

Raymond Pommier has a patriotic spirit—glory earned in the war of 1914-1918. After the events of 1944, without hate of the poor soldiers who had lost in 1940, in conversation with them he sometimes would let escape the words, "We in 1914-18 won it; you, in 1939-40 lost it."

One day, R. Pommier and a small group was in the north courtyard of the Plotinière house where they saw a German who had tied his mare, Casine, to his automobile, moving toward the antiaircraft battery. The veteran of 1914-1918 was powerless in these events. I let you guess how insulting were his words. After having borrowed the mare to take away the automobile, Germans encamped at the farm village of le Bust kidnapped her. Hitched to a cart, she frequently was driven to Torigni-sur-Vire. The refugees watching would say, "That poor animal is just back from looting us."

Eventually, a park was set aside for all horses and cows found wandering in the region. We searched all the parks, but never did find three of our horses that had disappeared

2nd Fortnight of June.

Torigni-sur-Vire being bombed and burned, the bakery of le Plotinière is welcome. The villages, such as les Ebecquets, le Champ, la Danerie, receive a small ration of bread. Raymond Pommier is chief of the block of houses, with his sons and Marius, an employee. They leave early in the morning with the donkey, Rosette, to grind a hundredweight of grain at Mill of Vire.

One day the Germans seized their load on the road. The next day they decide that they would have five men, each with a back pack, walk by different routes. The trip was very hard. The following day, they returned to the donkey. Several days after liberation, they decorated Rosette, the donkey, for all the good service.

For meat, the refugee family Gornelle worked the butcher shop at the village of le Champ.

Last week of June

In the pasture, the Germans set up an antiaircraft battery in a building. They came to the farm to get food.

The only source of water is a pump at a well close to a duck pond. The quality of the water was questionable, but no one got sick. The diapers of Léone were washed there.

One day, several of us were around that pump when a German came toward us and asked, "Wash mess kit?"

We washed it with the same broom we used for everything else, thus dirty. We returned the utensils to him saying, "Mess kit clean, ya, ya, ya." These little jokes helped to maintain our morale.

* * * * *

One day the Germans came to expel us. The grandmothers went to bed and we told the Germans that it was impossible to move because the grandmothers were sick.

As we approached the front, we saw the Hardouin family with their harnessed horse and their donkey and M. Douville going toward Torigni-sur-Vire. M. Douville had been seriously wounded in the war of 1914-1918. During meals his place was at the head of the table with the respectable people. Having several barrels of flour, he was going to bake bread at Plotinière with the Lamoureux sons.

During the middle of lunch, a German arrived and ordered us to evacuate. The Aprigny family, a group of refugees from the region of St. Jean-des-Baissants, the Duchemin family (whose daughters came with Mme. Guillet), and Morel have already left.

They did not have the joy of assisting in the liberation of Plotinière. Could they have been happier elsewhere?

La Bataille du Bust: 28, 29-30 July

The Germans have a small number to face the American Army, but they have a favorable position. At this time, a multitude of shaded roads lead out from Conde-sur-Vire and cover the routes of supply.

At the beginning of the battle the resupply was by horse and wagon, followed by pack donkeys, and then men. This was a battle of the hedgerows. The village of le Bust was taken and retaken. The chicken dinner that the Germans had ordered Mme. Raoul to prepare for them was eaten by the Americans!

A field hospital was installed at the village of la Bélinère, on Rue aux Cochons. On the night of 30-31 July, once their formation chief was killed, the Germans took the road toward Torigni-sur-Vire. (It was George Bourges who had taken refuge in a barn who noticed this. There were some teams of horses and about thirty men.) Previously, their chief had come three times to La Couvanne to be treated.

"I have returned to kill these pigs!"

* * * * *

The soldiers continued the combat. They resumed the attack about one o'clock. On arrival at the farm of Edmond Leneveu we encountered three Americans with submachine guns at the ready position at the railroad overpass. Little Maurice ran back in joy announcing the news. He was far from thinking that he had helped the Americans liberate two hedges.

Why had it taken the American Army five hours to move a distance of 900 meters between la Couvanne and la Plotinière? Because from la Bélinère to la Couvanne the distance is three kilometers and the Americans had taken three days, suffering heavy losses. They were taking great precautions for the next village: la Plotinière.

About noon, George Bourges rang the bell of the church of Notre Dame to proclaim the message: *The land is free.*

31 July

The American infantry, marching in Indian file, passed through for several hours. We were at the foot of the avenue, offering glasses of cider...The Americans advise us that we are in a very dangerous zone because German airplanes come over every evening. But they respond very vaguely when we ask where is a safer place. It is true that the preceding evening we have seen flares dropped over the village of le Bust.

This evening, 31 July, German airplanes do not intervene.

PART FOUR

With an Infantry Battalion in Normandy (1944)

A Personal Narrative
by
James A. Huston

1
Hedgerows and Sunken Roads

The Battalion filed aboard an old freighter at Falmouth on the afternoon of July 3rd, headed for Normandy. The troops, by regimental order, had been dressed in long underwear and the oily, smelly, protective clothing (herringbone twill treated to protect against mustard gas); this had been done to insure warmth on the channel and to keep the woolens free of dirt and salt water so that they would be usable on the other side. That evening the men watched the vehicles hoisted aboard and secured in the hold, and then unrolled their blankets to sleep on the decks. They gathered in groups of five or ten around boxes of 10 in 1 rations to make their meals—some resorted to cooking strips of the canned bacon, laying it on dirty steam pipes of the ship. Bomb reflections against the southern sky and streams of colored tracers made a beautiful, if disquieting, display during the night as though it were a planned prelude to the celebration of the Fourth of July.

There was a constant stream of ships going both ways across the channel on that Independence Day. But Omaha Beach was the busy place. There, ships were anchored everywhere, with lighter and rafts and DUKW's or ducks (amphibious 2-1/2 ton trucks) carrying the cargoes to shore. Silver barrage balloons floated above the beach and C-47 transport planes took off from the air strip every few minutes. All this activity surely was a demonstration of the impotence of the Luftwaffe.

The Battalion did not get ashore until the evening of the 6th when the last members finally "hitch-hiked" in by hailing a Coast Guard cutter which carried them part way in and then transferring to a DUKW which took them up on the beach without even getting their feet wet.

As the Battalion marched up that hill, past knocked-out German guns, and later past a new American cemetery, everyone seemed to sense the deep debt which he owed to the men who had hit the beach to prepare the way.

That night, the Battalion mounted on trucks to move up to its initial bivouac area. A full moon was shining. Overhead, an occasional German plane set off a tremendous—and beautiful—antiaircraft barrage. The white moonlight lent a ghastly appearance to the crumbled stone houses of a destroyed village through which we passed. "It looks exactly like some of those old movies of the World War," someone observed.

Now the 35th, "Santa Fe," Division was being committed. But the regiment—the 134th—was being held out for the time being as corps reserve for Major General Charles H. Corlett's XIX Corps. Our two sister regiments, the 137th under Colonel Grant Layng, and the 320th under Colonel Bernard A. Byrne, were to make a limited attack in a zone to the left (east) of the Vire River between LaMeauffe and La Nicollerie. Our regiment now was moving up to go into an assembly area where it would be available for action on short notice. The Division was going in between the 30th ("Old Hickory") Division on the right and the 29th on the left.

Leading elements of the Third Battalion 134th Infantry Regiment, 35th Infantry Division, already were moving out in a thin column of files on each side of the narrow, muddy road in Normandy. A light drizzle was adding water to the mud and making its contribution to the general discomfort of the march. Members of the command group—the twelve to fifteen officers and men of the battalion staff who ordinarily accompanied the battalion commander—adjusted their equipment and fell into their place in the column.

"Thank God for Tennessee; thank God for Tennessee!" Big, tough Alfred Thomsen, lieutenant colonel, infantry, took a big step to avoid a puddle as he entered the road from the meadow gate; he planted his foot firmly in the mud and moved off with his battalion.

The battalion commander was alluding to the similarity which he sensed between the situation in which he now found himself and the marches which he had led through the mud of Tennessee during maneuvers. He was thankful that his battalion had had the experience of long and rugged training.

A small concrete marker along the road read –

ST LÔ
16 km

Colonel Thomsen noticed it as we marched by, and turning to me he said, "Saint Lô, Saint Lô, Sam hasn't that been captured yet?"

"No sir, that is supposed to be the key point that is giving them so much trouble."

The Battalion was moving along in easy strides, though sometimes the swing would be broken by detours around deep mud. Here was an infantry battalion at full strength on the march—about 800 men and 35 officers. Its three rifle companies—I, K, L—led off in order. Each of these had three rifle platoons (each with three 12-man squads, one BAR (Browning automatic rifle), and 11 M-1 (Garand) rifles in each) and one weapons platoon (a machine gun section of two guns and a mortar section with three 60mm mortars) plus headquarters personnel. Of the total strength of 6 officers and 187 men in each rifle company, 15 to 20 normally were back in the rear; this included the mess sergeant and cooks, the supply sergeant and artificer, and usually a few physically unfit who remained with the regimental train bivouac where all kitchens of the regiment were set up under the direction of the regimental S-4 (supply officer). The company clerk remained with the personnel section at division rear echelon headquarters.

Then there was the heavy weapons company – Company M. The greater portion of its eight officers and 152 men were riding with the weapons on the company's transportation—19 jeeps, fourteen ¼-ton trailers, and one ¾-ton maintenance truck. Those trailers carried the eight heavy machine guns for the two machine gun platoons (each platoon included two sections each of two squads), and the six 81mm mortars for the mortar platoon.

The fifth company was the battalion headquarters company. In addition to its company headquarters, it had a battalion headquarters section whose members assisted the officers of the battalion staff, a communications platoon, an ammunition and pioneer platoon which was prepared to handle ammunition and perform basic engineer work, and an antitank platoon. The antitank platoon had three 57mm antitank guns designed from the British six-pounder. For prime movers to tow the guns and carry the crews, the platoon had three 1½ ton trucks, 6 x 6 (six wheeled, six-wheel drive).

Lt. Reischel, battalion motor officer, was bringing up the battalion's transportation at the rear of the column. In addition to the heavy weapons company and antitank platoon vehicles, he had the two jeeps and trailers from each rifle company, two medical jeeps, nine jeeps from battalion headquarters, the 1½ ton A & P (Ammunition & Pioneer) truck carrying engineer tools and equipment, and two 2 ½ ton trucks, from the regimental train, carrying ammunition.

Members of the Third Battalion considered themselves part of the best battalion in the world, and they were glad of it.

Whatever the merits of that assertion, countless forces had interplayed in varying degrees to make the Third Battalion what it was at that moment. Every man who had in the past been a member of the battalion had left some noticeable or unnoticeable influence. And the turnover had been large since 1940; the Third Battalion already had a part in the war, for men whom it had trained had seen action with other outfits in the South Pacific and in the Aleutians, or had gone out to train new units.

Division commanders had left their imprint even down in the battalion; in the early days of training there had been Major General R.E. Truman, cousin of the Senator from Missouri who was to become President, and Major General William H. Simpson, later to command the Ninth Army in Europe. In California there had been Major General Maxwell Murray who had recently returned from Hawaii, and finally Major General Paul W. Baade who had taken over in California and taken the Division to Europe.

There was evidence in the Battalion of the great influence of persons who never had been members of the unit. Thus could be seen the hand of Lt. Col. Dean Coonley of Beatrice, Nebraska. Colonel Thomsen had served as executive officer (second in command and coordinator of the staff) of the First Battalion when Colonel Coonley was its commander, and many of the practices, procedures, and eccentricities which they had developed now appeared in the Third Battalion. Nor was this influence to diminish, for the addition in the future of other former members of the First Battalion actually strengthened this influence.

Colonel Miltonberger had made an imprint upon the Battalion which could have come only from a strong personality and a strong regimental commander. He felt keenly the position of the enlisted men—he had been in combat as an enlisted man during World War I. He always insisted on perfection in detail and discipline without compromise. The men always associated strictness and "spit and polish" with their Colonel "B.B."

The former battalion commanders—particularly Lt. Col. Utterback—had left their mark as well. But most important now was the influence of Colonel Thomsen, for in his hands the destiny of the battalion now lay. He had directed its training at Camp Rucker and Camp Butner, had led it on maneuvers in Tennessee and West Virginia, had supervised its preparation for overseas movement, and now he was marching with it down a road in Normandy—moving up to an assembly area prepared for combat.

The battalion passed more kilometer markers. The artillery, which had been a distant boom in the morning, now became louder and louder until a deafening blast indicated that some of the batteries were being left to the rear. Little red and white triangular signs on the hedgerows announced "mines cleared to hedges." Presently it arrived in its assembly area.

"By God, sir, I'm not sure how we are going to work our 81's and heavy machine guns through this hedgerow country." Lt. Ruby was standing under an apple tree addressing the battalion commander. "I think we may have to throw away the machine gun tripods and just set the guns up on top of the hedgerows. I think we'll try to have a mortar observer run this light wire for our sound-power phones right along with the leading companies; I'm afraid to depend on our 300 radios. I'm not sure how good they will carry in this country and there are lots of stories coming back from the 29th and 30th (Divisions) that the minute you start using them, you draw artillery right in on you; they claim the Krauts have the best radio locator equipment there is."

He turned to me and said, "Sam, see how they are working that when you go up and visit the 30th this afternoon."

When the Division had made its initial attack for a limited objective on July 11th, each of the battalions of the 134th had been permitted to send a limited number of officers—limited so that they would not interfere with the operations of the units—to observe the action. Word had come back that day that Colonel Layng and his party had ventured too far forward—a machine gun burst had hit nearly all of the party. It had wounded Col. Layng (Commander of the 137th Infantry) and killed Lt. Col. John N. Wilson, Commander of the 219th Field Artillery Battalion. It was on that same day that Major Warren C. Wood of the First Battalion remained overdue for several hours.

"I hear that Major Wood may beat us all to Berlin," someone had said. "They think that he may be a prisoner already." However, Major Wood had been safe, looking after Lt. Mullin of Company C who had been injured by a near shell burst.

That afternoon I called Bernie Haas, driver of the S-2 jeep, "Come on Bernie, crank her up, let's go see some more war."

"Yes sir, she's all ready."

We rolled out of the meadow onto a gravel road, then took a broken, dusty asphalt road across the Vire River and through a destroyed village. A turn down a narrow, muddy road—here Bernie had to shift to four-wheel drive—brought us presently to a battalion of the 30th Division. Coming upon a noncom at a mortar position, I asked where I might find the S-3 (operations officer).

"Sorry sir, but he was killed last night; shell got him in that foxhole right over there."

I tried to swallow, but my throat was completely dry. I asked some questions about the set-up of the mortar platoon and then walked over to an adjoining field to see some machine gun positions. There, in a corner of the hedgerows, we saw our first dead Yanks. Their bodies were covered with canvas, but their legs protruded; their neatly laced leggings and shoes made an incongruous, but bothersome imprint on the memory: that picture remained indelible—those neatly laced leggings and shoes. "Yeah," one of the soldiers said, "They got it last night; some get it every night."

I talked with some of the other soldiers lying in their foxholes—found out from Lt. Rub that this battalion used light machine gun mounts for its heavy machine guns—and was ready to go back. The chatter of machine guns over to the left did not make me regret this decision.

Back in our assembly area, all the companies were taking advantage of those few days' grace in order to prepare themselves better for the problems ahead. Although the Cornish countryside had been broken up into small fields by systems of hedgerows, and we knew then that the terrain of Normandy would have similar obstacles, we never had undertaken any special training for hedgerow combat; our thinking never had gone much beyond the stage of speculation. But now the problem was real. We could see that the defender was going to have some added advantages.

The hedgerows all were similar: banks of dirt, sometimes with stones in them, as much as four to six feet thick at the base and tapering gradually to a thickness of two or three feet. This embankment was four to five feet high and surmounted with shrubs or trees—frequently full-grown trees. The sides were covered with grass and shrubs. These earth and plant fences enclosed fields—usually meadows or orchards—of irregular shapes and size which seemed to average toward a rectangle about 100 yards long and 50 yards wide.

By digging down a deep foxhole—a covered hole—behind these hedgerows, the defender could make himself almost immune from all kinds of small arms or shell fire. But that was not his only, nor his greatest, advantage. He could have his guns zeroed in, put an observer up in a tree and wait. The attacker, on the other hand, usually could not see more than one hedgerow ahead and could almost never see any enemy activity, and when he discovered the enemy's presence by suddenly finding himself pinned down by enemy fire, he was too close to employ his own artillery.

At the same time, the enemy found that these hedgerows provided him with covered routes for supply and evacuation and withdrawal. There were numerous roads and lanes—always running between hedgerows—leading away in all directions. Frequently these would be considerably below the level of the adjacent fields, while the walls formed by the hedgerows would be just that much higher. Often the rows of trees would bend toward each other overhead and would thus completely conceal the route from air observation.

The rifle platoons practiced at attacking with their squads using their BAR's to spray the hedgerow running parallel to the front while a few men armed with grenades would work their way up the lateral hedgerows. Sometimes a squad would remain as the base of fire while a squad worked up the hedgerow on either side, or sometimes it would be smaller groups.

At any rate, they believed in themselves and were sure that, with proper support, they could overcome all the obstacles.

It was evident that tanks were going to have a difficult time moving across that kind of terrain—the hedgerows were too strong to force, and all the roads would be mined and under antitank gun protection. Lt. Charlie Hall and his Ammunition & Pioneer Platoon set to work to find out what kind of a charge it would take to blast a hole through with TNT. They found that it could be done, though it took a big explosion and sometimes a second try, but it looked like this was the solution.

Other final preparations included the disposal of excess baggage. All clothing and equipment that was not going to be used was put into duffle bags and these were all collected and placed in the custody of a regimental Service Company officer. All gas masks were collected and stored there. Whenever a piece of extra or superfluous equipment appeared, "Rocky"—Lt. Stoneburner, the Battalion S-4,—would call out "Send it back to the duffle-bag area!"

To the amusement of those who had chafed under the Colonel's strict "keep those chin-straps fastened" rule, instructions came down from First Army that all chin-straps should be put up over the back of the helmet and never worn fastened under the chin. This supposedly was to avert broken necks resulting from the sudden upward jerk of the helmet when the concussion of a near bomb or shell burst hit it. More annoying to the officers and the noncommissioned officers was the required identification markings—officers were to have a vertical white stripe on the back of the helmet and noncoms a horizontal stripe. In addition, officers had to wear their bars on the front of their helmets. Headnets dulled the shine considerably, but most leaders felt that they were to be asking for trouble from snipers. Most of them complied by putting on a strip of adhesive tape for the stripe and then taking care to smear it with mud; another bit of mud, or a leaf in the net, accomplished similar results for the bars.

Captain Abbot, the regimental adjutant came down to visit the battalion.

"You know, Colonel Thomsen, I heard of another captain up in the 30th who was killed by a sniper today; yes sir, got him right between the eyes; Tracy saw his helmet—said there was a hole in it right through his bars."

"Baloney," Colonel Thomsen answered. "If those would hit just a little off center once in a while I might believe some of them, but every time, it's right through the bars—right between the eyes. You can't tell me the Krauts are that good."

After hearing some of the stories which were drifting back on the sniper activity, some of the officers took their bars off their collars, put them underneath, and many of the noncoms tore off their chevrons. Some of them began looking around for different weapons. "Boy, I want something more than this little carbine up there with me," Bill Broderick, executive officer of Company L said, "give me an M-1 (Garand)." Several other officers followed suit; others picked up Tommy guns from someone in an armored outfit.

Actually, the carbine was not such an unsatisfactory weapon for an officer. It was easy to handle—only 35 ½ inches long and weighed only 5 ½ pounds—but had the necessary fire power (carried a magazine of fifteen rounds, fired semi-automatic (self-feeding), and had plenty of power (effective range, 300 yards; maximum range 2,200 yards; muzzle velocity, 2,000 feet per second—would easily penetrate the steel helmet). It was not intended that an officer should engage in a fire fight; his weapon was for his personal protection or other emergencies; if he were off firing at the enemy, it usually meant that his men were being neglected; his job was to run a platoon and direct the fire of many weapons.

The heavier (9 ½ pounds) and longer (43.6 inches) M-1 rifle was harder to handle. Its presence would make it more difficult for the officer to refer to his map, to use his compass and field glasses, to make notes, and to move about quickly. But in the hands of the rifleman, it was unexcelled. It too was a semi-automatic weapon, carrying eight-round clips. Firing the ordinary M-2 ball ammunition, it had a muzzle velocity of about 2,800 feet per second and a maximum range of approximately 3,500 yards.

We knew that the days of grace were running short. Up to this time, we had not heard any enemy fire in our area, but one morning before daylight we were awakened by a series of as yet strange, but not unfamiliar, noises. The sound, part shrieking, part whining, part whistling, would be at a relatively high pitch as it broke the silence and then as it descended to a lower tone it would stop altogether; after a momentary pause, a fairly distant explosion would make itself heard and then reverberate for added emphasis. And then would come another and another. But they were falling too far away to cause any real concern. Then from the direction of the front came the sharp staccato of machine gun fire. Yes, it was a German machine gun all right, just as it had been described back in England; it was firing too rapidly to be any weapon of ours. Sounded like somebody might have been catching a counterattack. But the noises of battle died away with the arrival of daylight.

We had been in this assembly area for four days now and there had been no official word at all on how long we could expect to remain. On the night of July 12th, Colonel Miltonberger went up to Division headquarters and, after a two-hour visit, called back to his command post at 10 p.m. that there was no change in our situation.

The 13th went by much the same as its predecessors; much the same, that is, until about 10:00 o'clock that night. Major Craig, the regimental S-3 (operations officer) called down to say that battalion commanders should be at the regimental CP at 2230 hours to receive an order; the Third Battalion should be prepared to move out at once.

The companies began breaking camp and soon the company commanders and members of the battalion staff were making their ways through the darkness to the corner of the orchard where the battalion CP tent—the blackout tent—was pitched. As they entered the tent, they invariably squinted with temporary blindness from the bright light of a gasoline lantern. Sgt. Drew, the sergeant major, ushered them in—watched the lantern—answered a few phone calls.

When Colonel Thomsen and Captain Carroll arrived back from regiment, they found everyone crowded into the tent ready to hear the battalion commander's order. He glanced about, and mumbling "I, K, L, M, Doc…1, 2," to himself, checked to see that everyone was present. The bright white light made everyone seem a little pale, but the personal features stood out. When the officers removed their helmets, it was evident that the channel clipper had reduced their hair to a similarity in which each could be distinguished only by the density and contour of his stubble and the extent to which natural coloration could penetrate the musty grayness of any dust remaining after the last wash.

The rifle company commanders were sitting on the dirt floor leaning against a canvas wall. There was Captain Joseph P. Hartung. He was an old army man—an old first sergeant. In spite of his strict discipline, he had a ready smile; he was a slow, deliberate thinker and talker, but he could make a decision and carry it through. He was of medium size, well built, ruddy of cheek, and practically bald of head. He commanded Company L.

Sitting beside Joe, one knee drawn up to support a notebook, was Company K's commander, Captain Richard D. Melcher of Nebraska. He laughed frequently, or flashed a quick grin as someone made wisecracks. Then he would assume an over-serious countenance. He was of more than average height, with a lean, wiry build. He spoke rapidly in short phrases; his voice soft and medium pitched. When he leaned over to make a note, his short hair could be seen to be dark brown—to match his eyes—and plentiful.

Of all the company commanders, the biggest in size and the oldest in age and in service was Captain James Lassiter of Massachusetts, commander of Company L. Another "old army" man who had seen years of service in the enlisted ranks, he was known throughout the regiment as the strictest disciplinarian in the business. But his own junior officers swore by him and openly called him the best company commander in the regiment. On the other hand, he was very mild mannered, did not go in for very much foolishness, and spoke with a soft, husky voice. His close-cropped sandy hair seemed to top an almost Prussian (sans the arrogance) military bearing and his spectacles seemed to add a bit of dignity.

Beside Jim Lassiter, the heavy weapons company commander, 1st Lt. Earl J. Ruby of Nebraska, was sitting on his helmet. He was the loudest—and the most prolific talker of the lot. He entered into everything with enthusiasm—he worked hard, played hard, laughed hard, swore hard; he had a keen sense of humor. His blond hair was clipped very short now. His blue eyes sparkled beneath dark eyebrows and seemed to carry a glint of laughter even when he was frowning, though they were capable of flashing anger when provoked. Slightly less than average in size, he was as "hard as nails" and took great pride in having a good heavy weapons company. Having been a typewriter man in civilian life, perhaps it was fitting that he should be commander of the machine gun company!

Captain O.H. Bruce, a young journalist from Maryland, was the Battalion S-1 and adjutant. Formerly a member of the 29th Division, he had won his bars at Fort Benning and a wonderfully even clipper job on his hair. He sat near the entrance beside Sgt. Drew inhaling slowly on a cigarette, blowing the smoke out carelessly from beneath his thin mustache as he waited to hear what the Colonel had to say. To the S-1 fell the myriad of details which always fall to the chief administrative officer; he was concerned particularly with personnel reports, casualties and replacements, morale, making reconnaissance for movement of the command post and supervising its set up, allotting space to the companies in bivouac and assembly areas. In addition, the adjutant was company commander of Battalion Headquarters Company; he was responsible for its administration, discipline and training, but not for its tactical employment (the antitank, communications and A & P platoon leaders worked directly under the Battalion commander, coordinating through S-3). Bruce had commanded Company I back at Camp Butner and during the overseas voyage, but now he was working into an ideal S-1.

Standing beside the Battalion commander, studying a folded map and holding an open notebook, was Captain Merle Ray Carroll, a reserve officer from the University of Illinois, Battalion S-3. He was well built and of average size. His brown hair would have been curly had it not been so short. As operations officer, he was the Battalion commander's principal assistant and always accompanied him wherever he went. He assisted the commander in making plans and prepared field orders for his approval; he had to keep up on the situation and have his operations sergeant plot it on the map; he had to supervise the communications and prepare operation maps and overlays; he would transmit orders and instructions for the Battalion commander to the company commanders and coordinate their execution. And he was not without duties when the battalion was not engaged in combat, for he was the training officer.

The S-4—the battalion's supply officer—was tall, straight, well built Lt. G.I.(!) Stoneburner—Stoneburner of Virginia. Rocky did not have the Chaplain's "What aboot it" in his speech, but he did have the "Lookchere" of Virginia's western counties. Technically assigned to Service Company, the battalion supply officer served two masters: the regimental S-4, who commanded the regimental supply section, and the Battalion commander, whose wishes he was trying to satisfy.

The chaplain stood at the doorway sticking his head in—stood there until someone cautioned him to watch the blackout and then he forced his way in. His slight build—sometimes carried with a tendency toward gangliness—did not suggest that he had been a cross country run champion only two or three years ago at the University of Richmond. He did not yet appear to be completely at home in a military uniform. He kept his helmet on his head, for he was conscious of his clipped brown hair. Dust and moisture had collected on his glasses and he was having some difficulty in seeing clearly. Alexander C. Walker was a Southern Baptist —with all of the "oot and aboot" of Eastern Virginia— who spoke softly but preached with a big voice. Chappie had been initiated into the Battalion carrying that 70-pound rucksack up and down the steep, rocky slopes on West Virginia maneuvers. That was enough to make anyone look like *Yank* magazine's "Sad Sack" —and he had.

Beneath the chaplain sat old Doc—Captain John Matthew, the Battalion surgeon. Doc was bald and wore horn-rimmed spectacles and did not have all of his original teeth, but he was an old football player: He played three years at Indiana and captained the Hoosier team in 1929. That he still retained some of his athletic prowess had been demonstrated in the volleyball games back in England.

Four other members of the "special" staff crowded along another wall of the tend: 1st Lt. Floyd Garner of Arizona, communication officer; 1st Lt. Charles D. Hall of South Carolina, ammunition and pioneer officer; 1st Lt. Eldephonse Reischel of Wisconsin, motor officer; and 2nd Lt. Clyde Payne of Nebraska, antitank officer. I remembered how little "Jack" Garner used to struggle with his rucksack in West Virginia; he used to bend down from the hips, let his arms hang loose and say with a sad expression, "Just an old pack mule; well I'll be in the old soldier's home before long; come out and see me sometime." Payne had been an enlisted man in the old Second Battalion and had been on the expedition to the Aleutians; he had returned to the States to go to Officer Candidate School. Elde Reischel was a short but sturdy German product. He was highly conscientious in supervising motor maintenance. To him fell the thankless assignment—"in addition to this other duties"—of graves registration officer; it would be his job to look after the dead.

Major Foster H. Weyand, executive officer, sat on a ration box in the corner whittling on a stick. The only successful hold-out from the channel clipper, his white and gray hair shone in the light. Occasionally, he would wrinkle his forehead and lift his blue eyes to regard Colonel Thomsen. Those two really made a pair. They loved to fume and argue; they used to sit and spat like a couple of old maids, though that comparison is unfortunate, for no two old maids would be able to toss about the language which they could command. They loved to bait higher headquarters—they conceived of half their job as being to protect the companies from foolishness coming down from regiment—and how they would chuckle when they pulled a fast one! They always loved a joke—practical or verbal—in any circumstances. But when the chips were down, they could team up to get a difficult job done.

The major was an "old war horse." He had been at Verdun and in the St. Mihiel offensive in World War I. He was not very tall, but was a hardened infantryman. He had commanded a company on the old Second Battalion's expedition to the Aleutians. He was the "voice of experience" in the Battalion.

Colonel Thomsen stretched up to this full six feet two inches of height, shrugged his shoulders and relaxed his weight on his right foot. (And that weight amounted to a total of 225 pounds.) Physically, he was of the type of movie actor Wallace Beery. He had been a blacksmith in the Union Pacific Railroad shops in Omaha and he was proud of his enormous strength and agility. This he used to demonstrate back at Camp Butner by walking over to his office doorway and kicking the top of it. He delighted in enticing young lieutenants half his age into trying to imitate this feat. Invariably, they would fail and, frequently, would fall flat on their back in the attempt. His short hair left an island of baldness in the center, which he blamed on the old-type steel helmet he had worn in training during the First World War and the early part of this one.

The colonel always was fixing up some kind of device for added comfort or convenience. Back in California, he had invented an instrument for passing up written messages from a jeep to the cab of a big truck in a moving convoy: It was a clothes pin on a stick. I was wearing a wrist watch whose strap was secured, not by sewing, but by an application of Colonel Thomsen's glue—and it worked. He used his favorite glue for everything—on metal, paper, cloth, wood, or leather; the substance did not matter. This was his panacea for all mending. When a member of the battalion found himself confronted with a broken part of a weapon or a damaged vehicle, he was likely to call out for some of "Colonel Thomsen's glue."

In order that he could have a shelter in which to sit up during maneuvers, he had had an additional strip of canvas sewed to his pup tent, "Now this is a pup-wall tent," he said. Disgusted with the perpetual shortness of raincoats ("The little guys get all the big sizes, which are just about right for them, then we get them up above our knees—just so they will drain nicely into our leggings; did you ever see a raincoat that was long enough?"), he obtained two of the waterproof garments and had the lower half of the second sewed on to the bottom of the first. It fell all the way to the heels of his shoes; when he wore it he looked as though he were peering out of the top of a pyramidal tent. The men would refer to things of the Colonel's by making comparisons in the superlative; an especially large tent or balloon was "as big as Colonel Thomsen's raincoat;" a massive pack or bulk load as "as heavy as Colonel Thomsen's bed roll;" a big collection of papers was as "thick as Colonel Thomsen's notebook;" all the men had known exactly the type of life jacket they were to be issued on the transport ship when Major Weyand told them, "They look just like Colonel Thomsen's field jacket."

Now the Colonel's enormous thumbs were leafing through that famous notebook. That little black volume —known throughout the regiment—contained, in addition to current notes, scores of favorite jokes clipped from *The American Legion Monthly* or jotted down hastily at some meeting. These the Colonel like to repeat at the slightest excuse. And there was a Humphrey scale (for converting rates of march and distances in working with maps), logistical data, engineer data, a table of organization and equipment, a table of the basic loads of ammunition for the battalion, outlines of field orders, an illustrated page of insignia, a protractor, a map scale.

When he wished, the Colonel could command all of the polish and manners ever required of a lieutenant colonel in the United States Army. But he preferred to let his boisterous, swashbuckling nature dominate. His deep voice would carry for a quarter mile. I know that because, once at San Luis Obispo, I was assisting him in conducting some platoon field exercises. I was on a hill some 500 yards away from him as he came down the valley. I had a radio with me, but it was on a different channel from his and I would have to wait for relays from below. However, in this instance I heard his directions, he was speaking into the radio but I was hearing him directly, and when I promptly executed his instructions I heard him turn to the radio sergeant and say, "You see, it is too working; he did just what I told him."

Alfred Thomsen was as strong in his principles as he was boisterous in his talk. He was a "rugged individual" and he would stand firmly against all odds for what he believed to be right. When the chaplain held church services in the battalion, he and the major would always go and sit on the front row. He urged his officers to do the same thing. Once in England, a few days before our departure, we were sitting at the dinner table when he paused for a little while and then said, "We all have our fun with Chappie, but you know it wouldn't hurt any of us to go down to his services and help him out; it is not going to be very long now until we are going to be needing all the help we can get; we are going to be needing help from Somebody up there who is a lot bigger than any of us; then we've got to have something to believe in, to give us hope."

The Battalion commander spoke briefly and to the point while his listeners leaned forward in that hot, stuffy tent: the Third Battalion was to relieve elements of the 115th Infantry (29th Division) as soon as possible; then on the 15th, our First and Second Battalions were to launch an attack through our position. Regimental objective: St. Lô.

The officers stirred with apprehension. "I want the battalion to start moving out of here with Major Weyand in 45 minutes. Ray and Sam and Bruce and Garner will come with me; we'll go down to contact this outfit and make arrangements for the relief—we'll guide the battalion in." Then, assuming a confidential air, he said out of the corner of his mouth, "They picked us to do this because they knew they could depend on Third Battalion to make this relief in the dark, without any prior reconnaissance, and not foul everything up."

Ruby rose to his feet and, groping for the canvas door, muttered, "This is a hell of a time to be moving up—on the 13th!"

Minutes later, four blacked-out jeeps were purring down the road—through the ruins of Moon sur Elle and on down to a position east of a village called Villiers-Fossard. The Colonel stopped first at the 115th regimental command post to check in and get further directions and then we followed him on down to the CP of the 2nd Battalion.

After some searching about, we found it in a deep, well covered dugout at the edge of a field. Colonel Thomsen called down and then we followed him down some narrow dirt steps and crowded into the hole. The light from the gasoline lamp hanging in one corner had grown dim for want of air. This made even more dismal the heavy atmosphere. A pair of dark, tired eyes, set in a gaunt face which was covered with beard and dust, looked up to inquire our mission. The eyes belonged to a major who sat on the floor. He ran his hand through a head of dark hair which evidently had been clipped, but now had grown out. He remained silent; his face did not change its blank, tired expression until Colonel Thomsen spoke.

"I understand we are to relieve you folks," the Colonel said.

"Relieve us? Relieve us?" The major shook a captain who was sleeping beside him. "Did you hear that? They are going to relieve us." It was not very reassuring to us to hear this announcement greeted with such enthusiasm; sounded like we were inheriting a tough assignment. Later we learned that it was common practice not to notify a unit that it was going to be relieved until reconnaissance or advance parties from the relieving unit contacted it. This doubtless was so that such a unit would not be tempted to lie down on the job while it awaited the arrival of its relief.

This outfit had been going with almost no relief since "D" day. The battalion commander had become a casualty and the major had taken over. Arrangements for guides and the other details soon were completed. Garner asked someone if he could see the communications officer.

"Sorry, but he was killed; we can get the sergeant for you."

It got so that one hesitated ever to ask for any particular individual, for it seemed that so frequently that one had been killed.

We went out to the main road to meet the Battalion. It was after 0330 by the time the leading troops started to go up onto the position. We knew that we could not finish the relief before daylight, but were hoping that the most exposed positions could be occupied during darkness. It turned out that all was not completed until about 1030 in the morning, but it was accomplished without incident and without confusion.

Shortly after dawn, the 115th Battalion S-2 came down into the dugout to give me what information he could.

"There are a couple of prisoners coming in," one of the men called down.

"Want to see the prisoners?" the lieutenant asked.

"Sure." I had the same feeling as though I were going up to see a couple of snakes—vicious creatures which were easy to handle, but which might bite you if you were not careful.

After he had questioned the little soldiers in forest green who were posing as supermen, the intelligence officer took me on a tour of the area. "Now keep your head down," he warned. "The Germans are behind that next hedgerow." With a stiff, stubbly beard and dust in his ears and eyebrows, he had the same beaten-up appearance as the others. He was too tired to be nervous or excited about anything. But he was a worker and he did everything he could to help us out all during the day.

"We have made attacks on three separate days and each time wound up in these same foxholes. It's a rough go, but with your fresh troops, you may be able to do it. The men get so they freeze in their foxholes and you can't make them go. The only way the platoon leader can make them get up and go is for him to jump over the hedgerow first and be scout and point and everything; then he gets himself knocked off and there you are."

We walked over to the right. The lieutenant pointed over to the right front. "You see those trees and hedgerows running toward the front? Well, that's that damned sunken road. A Heinie self-propelled 88 pulls up that road and just raises hell in here and before we can do anything about it, he pulls back again. We can't advance down the road because he's got it zeroed in and that leaves our flank open."

We moved back to the rear in order to find a covered route to go over to the left part of the sector. The lieutenant described what a rough time they had had in capturing Villiers-Fossard. In the corner of the field behind the CP, we passed a pile of equipment that included practically everything G I in a battalion. It had come off casualties or had been damaged. There were packs and belts and canteens and mess kits and raincoats and clothing and helmets and weapons. Nearby, were some more dead Yanks. "They got it in yesterday's shelling." Again, there were those neatly laced leggings and shoes on those motionless legs.

When we got back to the CP, the lieutenant borrowed a canteen of water and poured some of it into his steel helmet. He tried to wash off some of the accumulated dirt and dust. As he pulled a dirty handkerchief from his pocket to dry his face, Lt. Col. Boatsman, commander of First Battalion, and Lt. Col. Wilson, commander of our Second Battalion, arrived. They had their operations officers and company commanders with them to make a reconnaissance of the ground over which they were to attack on the morrow. The lieutenant, tired as he was, at once went over and offered his services. Soon he was touring the front again, helping them orient their maps, pointing out terrain features and indicating probable enemy positions.

"Be careful of that damned sunken road," he always would say.

2
"Assemble at Emelie"

Saint Lô was the key to the defense of western Normandy. The town was not a very large one (peace time population: about 12,000), but it was the most important road center in the area. It was the anchor of the German defenses in Normandy. Not only did the main defense line of the Cotentin Peninsula—along the St. Lô-Periers-Lessay highway hinge there, but so did the secondary line—along the St. Lô-Contances highway. About 47 miles southeast of Cherbourg, it lay to the west of a horseshoe bend in the Vire River at the base of the Cotentin Peninsula. It was the capital of the French department of Manche (a name which the French also applied to the English Channel).

American pushes toward St. Lô from both north and east had come practically to a standstill at distances from two to three miles from the city. The British now were meeting the same kind of stiff resistance in the Caen area—the Nazis were holding all along the front. A Vichy radio broadcast on the 12th announced that Von Kluge, German commander in Normandy, was expecting "an all-out American drive for St. Lô." Another German source added that a new German panzer division had been thrown into the battle in the St. Lô area. Those expectations were well-founded.

Colonel Miltonberger received the division attack order at 4:30 p.m. on the 14th and he issued his order to the battalion commanders two hours later. The attack south for St. Lô would jump off at 5:15 with the First Battalion on the right and the Second Battalion on the left. The Third was to remain in position prepared to assist and would assemble on order to continue the attack. All the support that was being concentrated for the attack instilled confidence in all the leaders that their efforts would be successful. Additional battalions of artillery were to lay down a rolling barrage in front of the infantry. Each battalion was to have a company of tanks attached and there was to be a company of TD's (tank destroyers) and Company A of the 60th Engineer (combat) Battalion.

The noisy armor moved up into forward assembly positions during the night, but drew only slight artillery fire. The First and Second Battalions prepared to go.

At 5:15 the artillery opened up and the troops started to move; 115th Infantry on the left, jumped off at the same time to renew its assault from the east. Von Kluge's "all-out American drive for St. Lô" was on.

But the German artillery had opened up as soon as our own. And then German small arms fire. It appeared that the enemy was launching an attack of their own: already men of the Third Battalion, even as they lay in their foxholes, were getting hit.

Men of Company I could see Germans starting to move towards them. Captain Joe Hartung moved up to see what was going on. As he was crouching by a hedgerow directing fire out to stop any counter-moves, the intensity of the enemy shell-fire was stepped up; a mortar shell lit right beside him. He rolled over on his stomach; blood began to ooze from countless wounds from head to toe; but mostly it was his back: hundreds of fragments had torn his field jacket to shreds. His runner, always at his side, tried to help him out, but one gauze bandage was of little use with that many holes. The loyal helper called for medics, got word back to send up a litter team, and then he sat down to watch his captain. Joe could hardly move a muscle, but his mind was clear. In combat less than half an hour and he was knocked out. This thought made him angry; he was an old army man—this was the day he had been preparing for during those years of training, now he could do nothing. Hours dragged by before the litter squad—having a busy first day—could get to him. Shells were still falling. He wondered if they would get him out before another finished him off. A squad of men from "F" Company walked past the blood-soaked captain. Joe heard the squad leader turn to his men and say, "Look at that poor bastard! He's all done. Now that is what will happen to you if you don't take cover."

Ordinarily when the company commander is hit the executive officer—the second in command—immediately takes over. However, only minutes after Joe Hartung had been hit, a high explosive round fell right in the area being used for a company command post. First Lieutenant Billy Guice, executive officer, was wounded. The old top kick—First Sergeant Conners, a veteran of the other war—was wounded so severely that he was first reported dead. This was the first event of a series which was to make Company I the ill-fated company of the Battalion for its company commanders.

When this news reached Colonel Thomsen, he looked around and called for Captain Phil Bauer. Bauer had been assigned to the Battalion back at Camp Butner, and though he was assigned "on paper" as commander of Company M, the battalion commander had retained him at battalion headquarters. He had pinch-hit for a while as S-3 and another while as executive officer and had proved his capabilities. Now the colonel handed him one of the toughest assignments in combat:

"Go up and take command of Company I and get it reorganized."

"Yes, sir."

Bauer did not know a noncom up there; the company was in confusion after losing its C.O., its executive officer, and its first sergeant; as a matter of fact, that shell had wiped out practically all of the company headquarters personnel. But the company's new commander—the third within the space of an hour—went up immediately and got the position reorganized.

Meanwhile the attacking battalions had become engaged in some terrific fire fights. However, artillery kept knocking out the telephone wire, and communications were difficult. So much credence had been given to the stories about radios drawing artillery fire that they had been ordered to be kept silent. This was modified some when a message came down at 6:35

authorizing radios to be used to transmit position locations (in code, of course) and flash warnings.

Shortly before 8 o'clock, a message came down saying that Lieutenant Bill Broadbeck, executive officer of Company L—and schooled under Jim Lassiter—was to report to the Second Battalion to take command of "G" Company, whose C.O. had just been wounded. We later heard that the original commander was killed by a second round as he was being carried away on a litter and, by noon, Broadbeck himself was back at the aid station with a wounded leg.

The First Battalion was having a rough time. It was reported that "C" Company had suffered over 65 casualties in the first three hours and the other companies had been hit almost as hard. However, they were making good progress. At 12:50 Colonel Boatsman reported that his First Battalion had advanced some 2200 yards and were now only 600 yards from the top of strongly-defended Hill 122—key terrain feature before St. Lô and immediate regimental objective. Colonel Miltonberger decided to assemble the Third Battalion to exploit the success of the First. It began to look as though this might be the long-awaited break.

Colonel Thomsen notified the companies to fall into a battalion column down along the Villiers-Fossard – St. Lô road. The First Battalion now was reported to have leading elements in the village of Emelie, a mile and a half from St. Lô. Bruce, gathering up a small party, set off in that direction to reconnoiter for an assembly area. Reischel went up to look for a new motor park for his vehicles.

Members of Battalion Headquarters donned their equipment and moved out with Colonel Thomsen and Major Weyand. For some reason, Sergeant Buckley, Headquarters Company's supply sergeant—whose place ordinarily would have been back with the regimental supply train—was up at the Battalion CP.

Remembering his training habits, Colonel Thomsen called out, "Well, we better have a point out there; Buckley, get a man and act as scouts." Then he turned to the major and said in a lower voice, "We're moving through rear areas—the First Battalion has supposedly cleaned this all out—but we better not take any chances."

We were moving parallel to the front—moving over to the right to find the road. We entered a narrow sunken trail and passed some men who said they were from Company A. That was my old outfit and, naturally, I was keenly interested in how they were faring. I noticed one of the old platoon sergeants. "Well, sergeant, how is old "A" Company doing?" I asked.

The sergeant appeared to be a little shaky. "Oh, sir," he answered, "they're all shot to hell!"

A few minutes later there were some rapid cracking noises over our heads—followed a second later by a similar succession in a lower key. It was one of those hated German machine pistols – a "burp gun." It sounded like the noise of a red-headed woodpecker working at top speed on a telephone pole followed by another working on a hollow tree trunk. The first burst of noise was the sound of the bullets cracking the air overhead; the "echo" a second later, was the report of the gun itself. That is what made it difficult—especially for the uninitiated—to guess from what direction the fire was coming.

Buckley had his carbine at the ready position and began stalking trees which he thought might be likely locations for the sniper. We all began seeking cover behind the hedgerows—all, that is, except Colonel Thomsen. He stood there in the middle of the trail looking around and then said, "Nothing but snipers, let's go."

Soon we dropped down on to a road. It ran in the direction of Emelie and St. Lô all right, but the Colonel was not sure that this was the one which he had pointed out on the map. Now Colonel Thomsen took great pride in his map and aerial photograph reading—there was no one in the regiment who was his equal, but this gravel road was so apparently unused that he was not sure that it was the one he was looking for—there was no way of telling how many roads and lanes there might be on the ground which did not appear on the map.

"Let's go on across and see if there is another road a little farther over," he said, "or at least we ought to run into somebody."

We crossed a couple of fields and then came upon a narrow sunken trail or ditch lined with fox holes. German equipment was piled high all along. This immediately engaged my attention. I turned to some of my intelligence men and pointed out, "Look, there are some of those 5 centimeter mortars we were talking about the other day; you see how they resemble our

60's? And look at that neat little pile of ammunition they left."

"Gosh, the Krauts much have pulled out of here in a hurry," one of the men put in. We crossed another field and found some American soldiers dug-in behind the hedgerow. It was the left flank of the 320th Infantry. Colonel Thomsen found the company commander and got his location established on the map. Yes, the road we had crossed had been the one we wanted. We turned about and started retracing our steps.

"Aren't you traveling pretty heavy?" one of the 320th officers, observing all of our equipment, said to me.

"Yes, but we are just going up to an assembly area."

We re-crossed the abandoned German positions and were going through the next field when the close crackling of a German machine gun sent us all down in the tall grass. We crawled a short way, hesitated, got up, hit the ground again in response to another burst. We finally made it over the next hedgerow by advancing in rushes: four or five men at a time would get up and run at full speed until behind the new cover. This presented too poor a target to draw any more fire.

Going down a gentle slope toward the road, we met Bruce and Reischel.

"Say, I don't know what kind of an assembly area that's going to be up there; I didn't get as far forward as I had hoped, but there were Krauts running around all over the place; we thought we better not stick our necks out any farther," the adjutant said.

"Well, that's probably a few strays that the First bypassed," the Battalion Commander observed.

"I saw some Heinies with a machine gun right over there in those bushes by the road," Reischel added. "I don't know why they didn't open up on us. Let's go down and get them out."

A couple of men with rifles covering him, Elde went back down toward the bushes and tossed a hand grenade. Then he decided the machine gunners had departed.

We got back down to where the road crossed a small creek. The remainder of the Battalion—except Company I, whose location was yet a little in doubt—was waiting in the vicinity. But we could not move a column down that road with that machine gun that had been firing at us still in position. Colonel Thomsen looked around; his eyes came to rest on me. "Sam, take your section and see if you can go up there and take care of that machine gun."

Here was a chance to win a medal on the very first day of battle. But who wanted a medal? I did not think very much of taking a specialized headquarters section out to hunt machine guns. I decided to keep our party to a minimum. My intelligence sergeant, Sgt. Mormance, thought that he had seen the machine gun position and could locate it. I took Fuller, a good intelligence scout, along too.

We walked up the road past a little house with six marked German graves in front of it and on up a slight rise. The embankments and hedgerows were high—perhaps 15 feet on each side of the road at this point.

There was some barbed wire across the road, but it was no obstacle. There were no tracks at all on the road. We had gone two or three hundred yards now and were about opposite the place where the sergeant thought that he had seen the machine gun. There was not a sound of any kind anywhere. "Fuller, you stay down here and watch our rear," I said.

Mormance and I climbed the steep bank and crawled up to the edge of a little orchard. I directed my field glasses toward the spot where he pointed. Then, looking up in the vicinity of the fortified ditch which we had crossed earlier, I could plainly see a German soldier running along. This was not like the book said: in training we had always said that we would very seldom ever see the enemy—that we would have to shoot where we thought he was. And here on the first day, before even making any attack, we could plainly see the enemy running around. He was two or three hundred yards away, but not a bad target for an M-1 rifle. Mormance had brought a rifle. "Shall I fire at him, sir?"

"Sure, go ahead. I'll keep my glasses on him." How much better it would be to pick them off at long range instead of crawling up to throw a grenade! Mormance fired three rounds. It looked like he missed, but the enemy took cover and got out of sight. We waited a little while in the hope of seeing more activity.

The bushes rustled behind us. I turned to see the face of Second Lieutenant Louis Dailey, a Company L platoon leader. "The Colonel is getting impatient;

wanted me to bring my platoon up and help you out; what have you got up there?"

"Come on up." The little lieutenant crawled up to my side. I pointed out where we had seen the activity and where we had been firing. I also pointed to the big tree in the near corner of the adjoining field where we thought there had been a machine gun. "I would suggest that you get some BAR's up to spray those two areas good while you work some scouts forward to get into that corner."

Dailey called his squad leaders up and gave them that information. Within minutes, a line of riflemen and a pair of BAR's were pouring fire into the suspected areas while some scouts were working their way down beautifully in rushes. But this brought a response. Enemy machine gun bullets—in much greater volume than previously—were cracking close over our prone figures. We lay as flat as we could, utilizing every slight depression in the grass-covered ground. A burp gun sputtered close by on our left. Someone was hurt.

Somebody told me Colonel Thomsen was calling. I crawled back to the edge of the bank and looked down to see the battalion commander.

"We're going to move on—we can't let one machine gun hold up a whole battalion. We'll leave Dailey there with his platoon to protect our flank."

I turned back for a moment. The firing had died down. There was a flash and a resounding explosion along the bank.

"Colonel Thomsen has been hit; the Colonel is hit!" I felt a sickening feeling. Often I had wondered how in the world this battalion could operate without the dominating personality of Colonel Thomsen.

I looked down again. The big colonel was descending the bank back down to the road. His face and hands were bleeding slightly; there was another little hole in his leg. "Come on, let's go," he said.

It seemed that as he had climbed up to take a look, someone nearby had fired a rifle having an antitank grenade on the end of it. A high-powered blank always is used to launch a grenade, but this soldier had failed to change the ammunition in the rifle chamber. The bullet then set off the grenade immediately and this is what had caused the slight lacerations to the battalion commander.

The battalion—in columns of twos, one on each side of the road—resumed its march. I left the flank situation to Dailey, hurried back down to the creek to get my big field coat (that was bedroll, shelter, comforter; I would hold onto it at all costs) and made my way back up to the head of the column near Col. Thomsen and operations officer Ray Carroll. Company K was behind us, followed by Company L.

The chatter of automatic weapons broke the silence back around Dailey's platoon. The burp guns opened up in the same vicinity. The battalion continued to march. The head of Company K and the Colonel and his party had reached a slight bend in the road; there was a large brick house some 150 yards beyond on the left side of the road.

And then it seemed that all hell was breaking loose. Machine guns began spraying the road from that house; burp guns rattled to our left and to our rear; shell fire began to drop in to add to the confusion. Small shells were bursting along the adjacent fields, on the tops of the hedgerows, and then down the road...My God, it was those 5cm mortar shells that we had seen stacked so neatly; we had been walking right through the German positions! Larger caliber mortar and light artillery shells began to burst all around—they had a way of hitting the tops of the hedgerow and, bursting in red flame and black smoke, would send fragments and dirt on the men who were seeking cover in the shallow side-ditches below. Wounded men were making their way back to the rear.

The Colonel called over to Carroll, "We've got to get somebody up there and get the machine guns out of that house!"

Ray turned back to youthful Second Lieutenant Ed Kennedy, whose Company K platoon was at the head of the company, "Kennedy, see if you can get two or three men with some grenades and work them up to that house and knock those machine guns out of there."

Two men, assigned the mission, scrambled over the hedgerow on the left. Just as their head disappeared on the other side, a large caliber shell burst at precisely the same spot.

A round of time fire burst over the road, leaving a ridiculous little cloud of black smoke. I crouched against the hedgerow, trying to make use of any side-ditch along the right shoulder of the road. I looked up again and it looked like doom was on its way. A rapid firing, direct fire gun was searching down that shoulder of the road. In quick succession, shell bursts were creeping toward my position. Each burst about three or four yards nearer than its predecessor. I ducked. Another burst—men in front of me were hit. Another round—men behind me were hit. I looked up again. Ray Carroll had his .45 caliber pistol drawn. "What is it?" I called across the road to him.

"Looks like some kind of a damned tank coming down the road." And he was waiting for it with a pistol!

No longer could I see Colonel Thomsen up ahead of me. I wondered if one of those shell bursts had hit him. No, it was not that. He had found an opening in the hedgerow; he had disappeared into the meadow and made his way farther forward. There he saw this armored vehicle, but there was a group of four or five soldiers in front of it—not 50 yards from where he stood. Traditionally, the best pistol marksman in the Battalion, he drew his Colt .45 and took aim; he fired—and missed. He fired six more rounds and missed every time.

Our men were hearing about a tank coming and were beginning to pull back. This obviously was no place for a rifle battalion. Down in this narrow cut, strung out in a column where it could not fight back, with a tank approaching that could lay down withering enfilade fire and automatic weapons and mortars playing on all sides, the Battalion was in a good position to be completely cut up. We all felt sure that we must get back out of there.

Sergeant Mormance came past me holding his arm, "They got me, sir, they got me."

"You'll be O.K.—go right on back to the medics and let them fix you up."

They were taking Fuller back. A shell fragment had torn through his face.

A short distance back down the road, I met Major Weyand and told him what I had seen of the situation.

"Well, there's not but one thing we can do," he said, "and that's pull back and set up a defense." It was after 7 p.m. now.

I saw Payne and his platoon jostling their 57mm antitank guns around down by the little house with the German graves in front of it. "You're just the man we are looking for," I said. "Get set up to cover this road; there is supposed to be a tank coming down this way."

"O.K., we'll be laying for him."

We went back across the creek and directed Company K to set up a defensive position on the right side of the road, with Company L on the left. Then, going back a little farther, we chose a field immediately south of Villiers-Fossard for the Battalion CP. We found some ready-made fox holes behind the hedgerow, though there was a dud shell in one of them.

We tied our telephone onto a line running past there and contacted the regimental CP. To their consternation, we could not at the moment give them an accurate location of the battalion, but we had been out of contact for some hours now and we wanted to report what had happened. At first, they (the regimental commander and his staff) were incensed at the thought that a battalion had withdrawn, but later they saw that there was no other course.

Ray Carroll remained down to check the positions of the companies and, as dusk was coming on, made his way back to our CP. But no one had seen Colonel Thomsen—not since he had gone up to get into that pistol-tank duel. Ray called some men and, forming a patrol, went back to look for him. They returned an hour later with no word of the battalion commander.

We received word that Company I was up on the flank of the First Battalion, which was still attacking for Hill 122. Capt. Melcher tapped in his company phone on the regimental wire to see if he could find out where the rest of the Third Battalion was. And amidst all of this, regimental and division staff officers were discussing sending the Third Battalion into an immediate attack for Hill 122!

At 8:25 p.m. the field phone rang. It was Brigadier General Seabree, assistant division commander. Carroll took the call. He tried to explain our situation, but the General was not anxious to hear it; he considered that we had run into a few snipers.

"You've got to get that battalion down to Emilie where they can be ready to jump off and exploit this thing," he said. "You be at Emelie by 10 o'clock tonight! Then you can dig in for an all-around defense for the night."

"Yes, sir, we'll do our best," Ray said weakly, knowing that it would take more than we had to get up to Emelie that night.

Ten minutes later, there was a violent rustling in the hedge and Colonel Thomsen appeared. He looked over the situation and called the regimental commander to tell him that the battalion now was pretty well under control and he thought that we might be able to assist when the First Battalion renewed its assault at 8:45.

At 10:30, Colonel Boatsman reported that Companies A and B had reached Hill 122, only to be kicked back 200 yards.

There was infiltration and firing going on during most of the night. The Third Battalion was reorganizing: 57 casualties during the day—and that without even being committed to action! It prepared to renew its move toward Emelie on the morrow; but this time it would not be a march in route column for a covered assembly area – it would be an attack!

3
"Attack! Attack!"

The Third Battalion's mission for the next day (the 16th) was to "clear the rear areas in the right zone" (the area through which the First Battalion supposedly had gone) and assemble in an orchard northwest of Emelie. A platoon of tank destroyers was to be attached. Colonel Thomsen tried to emphasize that this was not going to be a question of cleaning out a few snipers and moving up to an assembly area. He had found that out the previous day when the Battalion had been stopped by about a dozen machine guns, he pointed out, and he was expecting a great deal of opposition in this attempt. And Colonel Thomsen was one who leaned over backwards to avoid any accusation of exaggerating his enemy opposition to higher headquarters.

The time for moving out was set for 7:30 a.m.

The Battalion Commander had been hoping to make use of some of the tanks which had been working with the First Battalion. But shortly after 7 o'clock, they indicated that they were going to pull back and his efforts to hold them were to no avail because they were acting on division order. At 7:15 Lieutenant Davoe, our liaison officer from the supporting field artillery battalion—the 161st—called in to request artillery to support the attack. This was refused because the location of the First Battalion was not known definitely enough. The company commanders were at the CP awaiting the final word. It was 7:20 and the attached TD platoon had not appeared. Colonel Thomsen grabbed the telephone and called regiment.

"I can't have any tanks; I can't have any artillery; I've got no TD's. Just how in the hell do you expect me to make an attack? I cannot attack until I get some armor of some kind." He put the phone down and turned to the company commanders. "By God, I'm not attacking 'till those damned TD's show up or we get some kind of armor. If they take all day, we'll just sit here and wait all day."

It was after 10 o'clock by the time the TD's arrived and the Battalion moved off. Companies K and L were in the assault – K on the right – and Company I in reserve. They met immediate and intense opposition, but began to work small groups slowly forward. They were working forward in groups or sometimes even singly. Pfc. Darwin Mohorich found himself and all the other members of his "K" Company platoon pinned down by one of those rapid-firing machine guns. Not content to lie there and take that, Mohorich crept along the edge of the field until he was opposite the right flank of that enemy position. Two hand grenades put an end to that particular trouble spot. Around 2 o'clock, the TD's were getting up there and firing their powerful 3-inch guns into the defended hedgerows with telling effect—ten prisoners came out.

These looked like beaten creatures. They were bareheaded or wore soft caps, their green-gray uniforms were dirty and wrinkled, but they always wore good boots. Most of them carried the cylindrical gas mask container, but it usually had foul cheese and stale bread in it. Most of them came saying, "me Ruski" or "me Polski." We were well aware of the formation of the "East Battalions" in the German army. These units were about two-thirds or more Russian or Polish, but, of course, their leaders were German. Therefore, we were not surprised in running into these Russians and Poles.

But their cries of "me Ruski" aroused little sympathy in the American soldiers.

"Shut up, you sonsabitches, you was pullin' the trigger on that machine gun, wasn't you?"

Whatever the pressure that was brought to bear on them, it was difficult to overlook the fact that they had been shooting our men. And we could not conceive that Russian armies ever ran into any groups of Americans fighting against them on the Eastern front.

We soon decided that about everyone was claiming to be a Russian in order to win better treatment—but they were speaking Russian all right. Of the ten, only one said that he was a German. Haughty and arrogant, he was proud of it. While the others babbled like children in giving all the information they could (sometimes painting the picture rosier for our eyes than it really was), he refused to say anything.

Hostile artillery fire was coming in and the companies were practically at a standstill. Shortly before 3 o'clock, the battalion commander decided to commit the reserve—Company I—in an effort to break through. They were to go in on the left, but intense fire on that flank prevented any maneuver. By 4:30

regimental and division commanders recognized that this was going to take a major attack. Word came down to consolidate and hold what we had.

That evening we learned that we were to renew the attack at 4:30 a.m. With a company of tanks, a platoon of TD's, and a 4.2 in. chemical mortar company attached, the Third Battalion was to make the main effort.

Fog delayed the coming of dawn, but the battalion commander was determined to attack on time. At 4:15 the men were finishing their breakfast unit of "K" ration and were beginning to form up preparatory to the jump-off. It was not necessary to begin to stir very much before zero hour. Sleeping in a foxhole (or slit trench) fully clothed—the helmet for a pillow and the rifle for a bedfellow—and with hair clipped short, there was little else to making one's toilet than simply getting up. Men were traveling light now. Most of the packs had been sent to the rear. Usually a soldier would wear a field jacket during the cool nights, but it would come off during the warm day and be draped around the cartridge belt. The wool O.D. uniform seldom was too warm. Two or three boxes of "K" rations went into the back of the shirt at the small of the back. The bosom and sides probably would be bulging with hand grenades and riflemen would be carrying a couple of bandoliers of ammunition which, slung over opposite shoulders, would cross over the chest. The web cartridge belt was a general catch-all. In addition to its eight pockets carrying clips of ammunition, most of its eyes were carrying hooks for other suspended equipment—most important of these was the canteen of water on the right hip. At the right side was a bayonet or trench knife. Seldom fixed on the rifles, the bayonet was more frequently used as a machete or a can opener than as a combat weapon. On the left side, there usually would be an entrenching tool—a short-handled shovel or pick-mattock. On the left hip (later changed to front) was the first aid packet containing a packet of sulfa "wound pills" and the sterile compress and bandage and sulfa "wound powder." There would be a raincoat hanging over the back of the belt. Certain leaders or designated men would carry other special equipment, like a compass or wire cutters. This belt had to be kept tight in order to hold the field jacket down or keep the shirt tail tucked in; other K rations and hand grenades would be strung all over the field. Officers carried a compass and field glasses, which they like to conceal when in view of the enemy. A net with a few weeds or leaves eliminated the shine and broke the regular outline of the steel helmet.

The hulking figure of Colonel Thomsen appeared from his board and dirt-covered foxhole. He stood up at full height, his mouth slightly open and a wrinkle around his nose, to survey the situation. In his huge hands he carried a map case – a homemade folder of celluloid and adhesive tape. His long field coat was folded over the back of his cartridge belt and it hung down to the back of his knees. He called for his command group—those headquarters personnel who accompany the battalion commander. There was the S-3, the artillery liaison section (officer and radio crew), two intelligence scouts, in addition to the intelligence officer, a radio man carrying the SCR300, a wire crew to follow along stringing wire so that the commander could have telephone communication with the CP and with regiment, four company runners. He called for a message center man to look after the runners. He looked around again, "Drew (Sergeant Major), you had better come along to supervise the men in the group. Leemhuis!. Where's Leemhuis?"

"Yes, sir, right here sir." Bernie Leemhuis, Michigan, had worked back in garrison as the company tailor. But he was a jack-of-all-trades and master of them too. He could fix anything or make anything. He was well-built, with well-groomed sandy hair and a slight, neatly trimmed mustache. And he did not even smoke or swear! Always clean, he never permitted the grease smears of motors or the mud of the roads to remain long with him. His clothes, G. I though they were, were neat and well-fitted. Without being fastidious, he was able to display the same mannerliness in a foxhole that he would in a drawing room. Now he was listed as orderly for the battalion commander.

"Leemhuis, you can get your rifle and look out for us."

The command group was growing to a size too large for a party whose primary job was not actual fighting, but who, nevertheless, would be exposed to movement under enemy fire.

But it was 4:30 and the companies were moving on. Almost immediately they were pinned down by hostile fire. They did not even get away from the line of departure—the creek—before they drew withering fire from those machine guns. The fog was still on and it was impossible to use the tanks with any effect without observation. This fog, likewise, made it impossible for the artillery liaison planes—the little L-4 "Piper Cubs"—to get into the air. There is no question that these observation planes were highly effective in directing fire, but the doughboy came to attach an almost phenomenal importance to them. He wanted one of those Grasshoppers up there all the time – he thought the enemy's artillery would be less intense if those aerial spotters were watching for gun flashes.

"L" Company had been able to advance a short distance, but were hit hard by a counterattack on the left. Colonel Thomsen called in to regiment to see if this was a "hold at all costs affair." Company L's men were falling back. Fire became intense all over the area. We sought what protection we could from previously dug holes—when there were any—along the hedgerows. The Colonel was trying to move Company I up into an effective position, but its platoons became separated as they moved through the hollow—an area thick with trees and bushes down along the creek. Burp guns seemed to be everywhere. Many soldiers declared that enemy snipers transmitted signals by systems of regular long and short bursts of those machine pistols. However that might have been, the Nazis were demonstrating a clever coordination between automatic weapons and mortars. The machine guns and pistols would open up, pinning the troops to the ground and then the mortars would traverse and search over the whole area to exact casualties among the soldiers who were held on the target by the streams of bullets cracking over their heads.

Some had been afraid long before they ever had been under fire; fear mounted in others as they approached the danger zone. Some had conditioned themselves strongly not to be affected by the death and pain which they knew they would see about them; and then suddenly, perhaps after several hours or days of such conditioned nonchalance, the terrifying fact would seize upon them—the next one might be me! Some were horrified at the thought of being mangled like they had seen their comrades mangled. To others, it was not so much death itself that they feared, but it was the thought of the effect on loved ones at home. They wanted so much to live; there were so many things they wanted to do; life could be so beautiful back with their families!

As the fears of combat took different forms, so fear found its expression in different reactions. Some could steel themselves to show little or no signs of fear at all. Others froze and quivered. Many felt an almost overpowering desire to get back—back away from those bursting shells and cracking bullets; a few yielded and became stragglers. Some became angered at their plight and wanted to fight hard—do everything they could to get the ordeal over the right way; those heartbreaking thoughts did not have time to linger in a mind in the thick of active fighting. Many were simply well-disciplined, conscientious soldiers intent on doing their best. Lots of soldiers hoped for a wound—a light one. If a wounded soldier were not doomed to death or to be permanently and seriously maimed, he found little sympathy among his comrades and he considered himself a lucky fellow. Some wanted to lift an arm or a foot up out of a foxhole in the hopes of getting it hit. Those wounds in the foot or hand which had broken bones requiring a long enough period to mend to warrant a return to a hospital in the United States were known as "million dollar wounds." There were a few who resorted to the unsoldierly expedient of inflicting a wound upon themselves in order to find an escape.

Some of the men lay under that fire shaking with fear, unable to move. They lay and let those thoughts race through their heads and that only added to their misery. Others knew they must keep moving to avoid destruction and they intended to do something about it. Some took what comfort they could from a fatalistic view. A great many—probably all, in one way or another—prayed. Aware that they were involved in something bigger than any man, they felt—without stopping to reason out any theories—that they must turn to some Greater Power if they were to find any relief or any escape from certain destruction.

"Oh, Father, if it be thy will, remove this cup from me."

It was nearly 9 o'clock before the tanks started rolling up. By then visibility had cleared. Of the Company's 17 tanks, 15 were in action and ready to go. Demolition crews from the A & P Platoon—the men who knew how to blast a hole through the hedgerows—boarded the leading tanks and they rumbled on down the road across the little bridge spanning the creek and started up the opposite slope.

Bang! A leading tank halted in a flash of flame and smoke. It had hit a mine. The tank was burning and with it, the tank crew and a demolition team.

But others were able to make it into the fields. And the TD's got into firing position. A tank tried to blast its way through a hedgerow with its 75mm gun, but it was to no avail. A well-placed charge of TNT did the trick and the tank roared through to begin covering the opposite hedgerow with machine gun and high explosive fire. Company L was approaching that same large brick house where the battalion column had been held up two days before. Jim Lassiter called for the 4.2 inch chemical mortars to put some white phosphorus shells onto the place. Minutes later, the mortar officer called "on the way!" and we saw huge billows of that thick, white smoke rising.

"Beautiful," Lassiter called back. A TD moved up and started blasting away with its 3-inch gun. The troublesome enemy machine gun was silent. But the enemy was not ready yet to give up that advantageous position—another machine gun crew was running to the house from the side. The alert TD gunner noticed in time and put an end to that.

We got a few prisoners around noon. They were concerned mostly in being assured that we were not going to kill them. They wanted to get back someday to see their wives and families. They illustrated their devotion to their families by displaying dozens of photographs. One little German, who looked to be about 40 years old, said that he used to live in Chicago —out by the stockyards—but that he had returned to Germany in 1935 and this was where he wound up.

"L" Company was starting to move again. Leading the attack was 2nd Lt. Lou Dailey and his platoon. Dailey was of small stature and—as a second lieutenant is supposed to be—young. He was another who had served as an enlisted man on the old Second Battalion's expedition to the Aleutians. He was up at the head of his platoon now, leading up against those next hedgerows. It was drawing fire, but the platoon kept on moving until it had driven a wedge into the enemy's position. This brought down intense mortar fire. And Lou Dailey, leading his platoon, died in that mortar barrage.

Now over on the right, Company K was moving. Melcher had moved his company wide to the right, so Colonel Thomsen called for Company I to move up on his left and Company L reverted to reserve. By early afternoon, they had advanced 500 to 800 yards beyond the creek which had been such a hot spot earlier in the day.

During these attacks, Company M's machine gun platoons had been attached to the assault companies. The heavy machine guns were being mounted on light machine gun mounts or on improvised bipods or, with no mounts at all, were fired by laying them on the tops of the hedgerows. By this time, however, the heavy weapons company had become practically a "light automatic weapons company." Through battle-field recovery, salvage, repairing and shrewd trading in the rear areas (of enemy pistols or machine guns for U.S. automatic rifles), executive officer Virgil Hyde had been able to replace most of the heavies with light machine guns or with BAR's—a popular favorite in the hedgerows—and he had added a few Thompson submachine guns for good measure.

Supporting this advance on the left was Second Lieutenant Halley Dickey's First Machine Gun platoon. Dickey was a handsome young officer, intent on getting his job done. He so wanted to get back home to his lovely wife, but he wanted to do it by getting this nasty job finished. Devotion to his wife had ruled his whole being. The whole battalion had noticed with admiration back at Camp Butner when they used to stroll hand-in-hand through the camp on Sunday afternoons. They had lived near New Brunswick, New Jersey, and when the battalion arrived at Camp Kilmer preparatory to going overseas, Halley had found a spot in the camp where he could see the house in the distance. He had been able to visit home a time or two while there and after that, he would go to his selected spot each evening at an appointed hour and with his field glasses he would watch his wife waving and he would wave back—all day long he waited for that moment. When we arrived in England and other officers began to go out in the evening, Dickey always would stay alone in his room to write letters to his wife.

Halley had been wounded during this action, but he refused evacuation so that he could get his platoon organized. Then, noticing a wounded soldier lying out in the open exposed to enemy fire, Dickey crawled over to him and dragged him to cover. But now he found himself in the midst of a field of "S" mines – those deadly "Bouncing Betties!" Fine trip-wires were running all along the ground. Dickey lay quiet.

Major Weyand, growing impatient back at the CP had walked up forward to see the reserve company. He heard about Dickey's plight and immediately got some medics with a litter and went over to where Dickey lay. A team had evacuated the man whom Dickey had dragged back. Now they put him on a litter and Major Weyand walked alongside. Then that tremendous blast of a mine beside them. Only the Major was able to walk away, but fragments had torn painful wounds into his arm—now he added a Purple Heart from this war to the wound stripes he already wore. His only concern was for the men still back there in that minefield. Other medics and some pioneers went back to get them out. While they were dressing his wounds at the Aid Station, the Major kept asking, "How is Dickey and how are those two medics?"

Dickey and one of the medics were dead.

As the afternoon wore on, there seemed to be no diminishing of the enemy resistance. There would be lulls, to be sure, and sometimes there would be minutes of silence so complete as to be almost as frightening as the loudest noises. But each time that the companies would begin a new movement, they would find themselves "stirring up a hornets' nest."

Company I, coming up on the left, had lost contact with Company K. Lieutenant Norman Wardwell made his way over to the right to make contact and establish the relative positions of the two companies. On his return, he found that Captain Bauer had been hit. With enemy fire still falling in the area, he knew that they must move forward to get out of it. Quickly organizing the men in the vicinity, he led them forward. They moved forward steadily, over one hedgerow, then over another. Wardwell moved on out in front. A small cluster of farm buildings looming ahead appeared to him a likely site for an enemy strong point. He crouched behind hedgerows and worked his way on forward. He saw no sign of life; he ran quickly over to the barn—then, edging his way around to the back, he came upon a German 81mm mortar. It looked as though the crew was preparing to make a hasty departure. Reaching in his shirt, he brought out a hand grenade and pulled the pin. Other men were coming nearer now and the Germans started to leave. But Wardwell's grenade stopped most of them—they would not be back to fight another day.

Meanwhile, Company K was making good progress on the right. It made good progress as far as a road which ran across its front between LeMesnl-Rouxelin, a village on the right, and Emelie on the left. Then it was another of those wicked machine guns. Firing from the right flank, the German 42 had the whole company pinned down. Captain Dick Melcher moved up to determine the trouble. He saw that the machine gun fire was coming from the edge of the village (LeMesnl).

His whole company frozen in place, Captain Dick started after the machine gun himself. He found himself going through a real "infiltration course"—more trying than those of Camp Rucker and Camp Butner combined. When he saw that the fire was coming from a church, he had to creep and crawl through an open field—under the machine gun's stream of bullets—in order to get to it. He got out three hand grenades and laid them on the ground. He lay quiet for a moment. He was breathing rapidly and sweat was running through his dirty four-days' growth of beard. Dragging oneself across a field like a reptile was exhausting enough in itself—not to mention the nervous strain of stalking a deadly machine gun! Dick raised himself up and in rapid succession hurled the three grenades through a church window. Result: complete destruction of the enemy.

It was growing dusk, but the companies moved on another two hedgerows before consolidating their positions for the night. They were on a part of Hill 122. Colonel Thomsen moved up with the command group to a sunken trail near the farm buildings which Company I had overrun. One of the buildings was on fire. Almost immediately an enemy direct-fire gun—a dreaded "88" began firing. Its shells, bursting every few feet on the ground and sometimes overlapping, pockmarked the whole field. Most of the men could recognize the "88" (88mm gun—tank gun, antitank gun, or dual purpose antitank, antiaircraft gun) now for its loud "zip-bang." There was no long whistle of the shell. In fact, the shell arrived first and then would come the sound of the gun. At first, every enemy bursting shell—mortar, howitzer, gun—was attributed to the "88." But the effectiveness of the gun was second only to the stories about it.

In two days the Third Battalion had gone a mile and a half to Emelie—two days after the general had made his demand.

The hard fighting was finished for that day, but that did not mean that the work was finished. There were supplies—ammunition and rations—to be brought up. Preparations had to be made for attack on the morrow. No, no orders had been received. But there was no question about it—it would be attack, attack until St. Lô had fallen.

Twilight was adding its shadows of gloom to the already grotesque pattern of shelled and torn Villiers-Fossard when someone came up the road near the battalion CP to say that there were some wounded men in a knocked-out tank about a thousand yards to the front. The tank still was exposed to enemy fire. Immediately, Edward Thill, a technician in the medical detachment, volunteered to go get them. Without allowing time for any refusal, he jumped into his jeep and took off. Once a Milwaukee taxicab driver, "Mouse" Thill now drove his jeep with as much disregard to mines and enemy fire as he would have given to yellow traffic lights. Two considerations demanded speed: to get the wounded men back to the aid station as quickly as possible and to limit the time of exposure to enemy fire. Thill felt no reluctance to apply speed. Flying a red cross flag over the radiator, the jeep sped down the road until he neared the tank. Then, disregarding the enemy fire, he raced to the tank and was able to extract two wounded men. He got them into the jeep and, half- standing, half-sitting on the back of the seat, he came roaring back with his precious cargo. This feat won a silver star medal for Thill. His work was typical of the medics. All of them had won a high regard for themselves in the hearts of the doughboys. This regard was especially keen for the company aid men—three (one for each rifle platoon) when they were fortunate enough to be at full strength —who, unarmed, went right along with the rifle platoon and crawled from one wounded man to another to administer first aid; and for the litter teams who came up to evacuate the wounded.

As night fell, the periphery of the glowing light from the burning house up near Emelie extended farther and farther outward. The flames became a reference point which could be seen for miles in the clear night. Then ammunition in the house began to explode. This fireworks display continued sporadically almost all night.

Engineers were working on the road to remove mines from the vicinity of the U.S. tank which had hit one. Third Battalion's supply train—a jeep and trailer for each company—started up from the motor park. Leading the column, Company I's truck started to pull around the tank. A quaking, sickening explosion… men, dead or mauled: jeep twisted to destruction.

Men from the Regimental Antitank Company's Mine Platoon and engineers tried to find another route, but met with no success. Engineers went to work on the main route again. But at 6 a.m. Colonel Thomsen had to call in to say that he had been unable to get his supplies up yet. Finally, motor officer Reischel was able to get over a detour route which the First Battalion had used.

"On to St. Lo"

4
On to Saint Lô

The attack on the 18th was a continuation of the previous day's. The companies were able to advance a couple of hedgerows and then it was the old story of confronting those well dug-in, coordinated positions.

The doughboys had been apprehensive about the presence of tanks in the attack at first. In fact it seemed at first that men of the First Battalion did not want to attack without tanks, while men of the Third Battalion did not want to attack with them. Actually, the Third Battalion soldier wanted the tanks around, but not in his own particular sector. He was afraid of the way they would draw enemy fire. This fear was deepened this afternoon when men of Company I found themselves under the machine gun fire of our own tanks. If there is anything worse than stalking a firing German machine gun, it is approaching an American machine gun. There is the same danger, but the danger cannot be eliminated with a hand grenade. But Technical Sergeant Milton Bates, recognizing the slower-firing weapons as American, braved the bullets to go back to the tanks and have them call off their fire.

Company L moved up to the assault position in place of Company I, on "K" Company's left. Both companies pressed forward. It was hard going. There were no men who were unafraid—unless it was Colonel Thomsen—there were strong men who had the courage to go in spite of fear and there were some weaker men who could not go on. It took discipline of the highest order to keep going in the face of that machine gun and artillery fire. It was a question of which side could give the most and take the most. Company L's light machine guns were sputtering out their support for the advance. Always, they became priority targets for enemy artillery fire. When one salvo came in, one of the company's machine guns stopped firing. Private

Thomas Hudson was hit in the shoulder. He looked up and found all the other members of his squad wounded. But those enemy riflemen had to be kept pinned down in their holes if "L" Company's men were to keep going. Hudson moved the gun to an alternate position and opened fire. He had to handle the ammunition and keep the gun firing all alone. He kept spraying the hedgerows, supporting the attack, until he collapsed from loss of blood.

By 6 p.m. the attack had carried well down the forward (southern) slope of Hill 122. This was not a tall, forbidding hill, but it did command the northern approaches to St. Lô and the well-organized Nazi defenses made it forbidding enough. It was regarded as the key to the situation. If there ever was a full regimental job, the taking of this hill seemed to be that. As a matter of fact, the 2nd Battalion of the 320th Infantry was attached to our regiment for this day's attack on the hill. It was something of a disappointment to men of the Third Battalion later (they were not concerned with such things at the time) when only the First Battalion was given credit for capturing the hill in a "Presidential" Unit Citation. They recognized that the First did a magnificent job—company commanders riding tanks and leading their companies on—but it seemed that the blood and work of their own battalion had not been recognized equally in the effort. This was to their particular chagrin when a re-examination of the map showed the crest of Hill 122 to be within the zone of the Third Battalion. However, at the time, any argument for credit seemed petty and so did it seem again when time began to leave it farther behind.

This advance left the Third Battalion hardly a thousand yards north of the edge of St. Lô. Colonel Thomsen was as anxious as higher headquarters to push on and complete this big initial assignment; he could look down and see shattered roof-tops and spires beckoning to him. He notified the companies to reorganize and then go for St. Lô at 7:30. However, they were cautioned to go only to the edge of town and not on down to the principal parts – the 29th Division was attacking from the east and they were to have the honor of entering the town which had been marked as their objective originally. More than that, there would be danger of mingling troops and getting into each other's fire if both divisions had troops going into the town.

Pairs of Thunderbolts had gone in earlier to drop their pairs of bombs on the already much cratered town. The time was growing near for the renewal of the attack.

Dick Melcher and Jim Lassiter, captains of the assault companies, met down at the junction of sunken trails.

"Dick, I don't know whether my men can make another attack or not."

"Well to tell you the truth, Jim, I don't think mine can move another yard. I told the Old Man that, but he insists that we make one more try. Well, it's about time to go; let's give it a try. Stick right with me."

"O.K., I'll guide on you. Let's go."

Melcher returned to his company and passed word down to the platoons to get ready to move. He took a few puffs on a cigarette and threw it away. He looked at his wrist watch—it pointed to 7:30.

"Let's go!" he shouted down the lines of foxholes. The weary men did not move. He called again and started over the hedgerow, but he was all alone. He walked back a few feet.

"All right, you guys, we were ordered to make one more attack this evening, and by God, we're going to make it!" He lowered his Tommy gun and let a burst go down the hedgerow.

"Now, goddammit, let's go!"

They were jolted into action: over the hedgerow they went and started moving for the opposite one. Melcher looked to his left. He could not see Company L moving. "Dammit, Lassiter, let's go!"

"L" Company was having the same trouble. Days of fighting were beginning to tell. Weariness had taken the edge off the discipline of the men which forced them to go forward without regard for themselves. Yes, it was just as that 29th Division intelligence officer had said—"They freeze in their foxholes and you can't do anything with them."

But now, one of "L" Company's platoons was leading out. First Lieutenant Francis Greenlief had his platoon on the way. They went over the hedgerow and started across the next field. When a man hesitated, "Fluff" Greenlief called out to him. "Now keep going," he shouted. His voice could be heard above everything else in the area. Big, well-built and strong, Greenlief already had demonstrated his aggressiveness. Poor eyesight made strong eye glasses necessary, but he had nerves of steel and a complete self-discipline. Fluff Greenlief wanted to get home just as much as anyone else; the same fears played upon him that haunted the privates of his platoon. But he was an officer; he could not fall behind. He was a platoon leader; men were looking to him for guidance—they were afraid. But he always had insisted on discipline.

As "L" Company's First platoon advanced across the field, a German machine gun 42 suddenly opened up with a long burst from an opposite corner. It caught most of the platoon. Four of them fell dead. The remainder of the platoon hit the ground and froze. Fluff shouted to urge them on, but they could not face that machine gun. He crawled to a wounded soldier and picked up his Browning Automatic rifle—always a favorite weapon. The big platoon leader, still shouting to his men, jumped up and opened fire—firing from the hip. He stood up and sprayed the whole hedgerow ahead of him and then, still firing in order to keep the Germans' heads down—he knew they would "freeze" as much as his own men—he rushed to the corner where the machine gun had been firing. He went in fast and destroyed the entire enemy crew. With the immediate danger removed and such an example of heroism as this, the men could no longer remain down.

They began moving all along the line. Each took confidence as he saw his comrades moving with him. Now they were moving in short rushes, from cover to cover. No longer was it a pair of scouts or half a squad working forward along the hedgerow—it was fire and movement all along the battalion front. Tired men forgot their fatigue. Scared men forgot their fear. All of them, brave men now, kept shooting and going forward.

An "L" Company man leaped over the next hedgerow, but he dropped his rifle on the wrong side. When he looked up, he saw three Nazi soldiers standing beside him. They were as surprised as he; but they had one important advantage—they were armed. Acting quickly—almost by reflex—he grabbed a burp gun from the hands of his nearest adversary and with a single burst, shot all three of them.

Dolan Boggs' usual place was with the CP or command group of Company L, for he was the communication sergeant. But he wanted to help to get the company moving on this drive. He volunteered to man a BAR. Soon after he had moved up behind a hedgerow and opened fire, an enemy machine gun burst hit him, but he kept on firing—kept on until his wounds forced him out of action.

A frightened German jumped up in front of Company K and fled over a hedge. "Get that rabbit! Get that rabbit!" Two or three riflemen paused for a shot; he fell on his face with such violence that his helmet rolled out ahead of him and his long hair strung out in front.

The call carried on down to Company L, then someone started yelling the old war cry, "All hell can't stop us!" "Lah We Lah His!" The Kraut was on the run and when he was on the run, he could not very well shoot back.

Company commanders cautioned their men to halt at the edge of the town, but the assault was now out of their hands. It swept into the outskirts of St. Lô. Over in Company L's zone, Private First Class Buster E. Brown was spearheading an assault of his own. When a short platoon of Germans sought to make a stand in a St. Lô house, Brown went right after them with his grenades. Soon he had cleared out a fair sector of the north part of the town for himself. He was standing at the point of the Third Battalion in the key town of St. Lô. To Buster Brown of the Third Battalion's Company L went the Division's first Distinguished Service Cross.

After some effort, the company commanders were able to recall their men back up to the edge of town and organize a defensive position. During the night, the keeper of the regimental S-3 journal made these entries:

2400 - Blue 3 wants to be sure liaison planes will be in the air at day-break.

0115 - Capt. Heffelfinger (First Battalion S-3) reports Strader (C.O., Co. A) tied in on to Lassiter in St. Lô – cemetery on outskirts – out of our boundary. Strader is requesting AT guns to be there by daylight.

0130 - Called Blue 6 – Lassiter is tied on a church about 1000 ft due N of St. Lô – K is on his right. Strader and Davis on the left.

FO #7

XIX Corps defends along line Vire R. – St. Lô – 35th on right, 29th on left.

134th w/ Co A, 60 Engr. Complete occupation of St. Lô in zone; organize to defend line of Vire R. – St. Lô in zone. Establish limiting point on MLR (Main Line of Resistance), RRL (Regimental Reserve Line). Tie in w/ 29th Div.

Being on the regimental right, the Third Battalion was assigned the mission of maintaining contact with the 137th Infantry on our right and of operating foot patrols along the horseshoe bend of the Vire River from a point south of St. Georges—Montcocq to the right flank of the First Battalion in St. Lô. This necessitated a reconnaissance of the river bank.

Colonel Thomsen called on me to get an officer from each company during the afternoon, make the reconnaissance, and get the patrols started. I met the officers along the sunken trail serving as a front line trench and, getting into patrol formation, we set out for the river. The only information we had was that earlier in the day Lieutenant Strader had been wounded while with a Company A patrol down in that direction.

We moved quickly, but cautiously, down the sunken trail to the church where we entered a gravel road and followed it a few yards down to the asphalt—paved St. Lô – Pont-Hebert-St. Jean De-Daye Highway. The afternoon sun shone brightly and as we turned our backs to the debris that was St. Lô, the countryside was almost beautiful. But as we went back north almost half a mile, we were not free from the marks of war. There was wire and we were suspicious of mines. We paused once while one lieutenant went up to investigate a tank-looking vehicle which turned out to be only a huge truck.

We made a left turn to follow another gravel road on to the west for another half mile. A lone steel helmet lying along the road spoke of the tragedy that had preceded us—yes, at a road junction was a jeep in which someone had ventured too far forward.

We turned into a meadow and soon found ourselves on a bluff overlooking the horseshoe bend. We located ourselves on our map. The view below us looked like a skillfully-tinted enlargement of the aerial photograph in our hands. We just lay there to take in the view. This was the first time that we had been able to see beyond a hedgerow or two. Barney Blackburn, Company M's mortar platoon leader, was adding to the color by sending out a few rounds of white phosphorous shells whose smoke rolled upward from the railroad buildings a thousand yards away.

Finding a trail down the bluff, we made our way down toward the river and followed it back toward the town. Foxholes dug into the side of the bluff commanded the valley, but we were relieved to find them abandoned. We pointed out landmarks along the trail which would serve as connecting points for the regular patrols.

Soon we were back amongst the rubble of St. Lô. We climbed up on some broken stones that once had been a house and tried to find some of the streets shown on our map. But the streets were as unrecognizable as the house where we were standing. Buildings had been flattened to spill rubble into the streets to the same level as that remaining above the old foundations. A map was of little use in this sameness of destruction. About the only reference point to be seen was the church. It was badly hit, but the tall steeple yet was standing.

Enemy artillery began to fall; it was doing its bit to make rubble of the rubble. We waited beside a garden wall until it subsided and then started on up to find the highway. An automatic weapon opened up to our rear —sounded as though the Germans had one of our BAR's or a similar weapon of their own. However, no one was hit and, hugging the wall, we kept moving.

It was dusk, which meant that it was well past 10 o'clock by the time we got back to the battalion area. As we entered the mouth of the sunken trail we heard sounds of aircraft overhead.

"Too late for our Air Corps to be up," someone said. "They are all in bed by now – between sheets."

Just then, a bright flare caught us. "Freeze!" I called. We felt as though we were standing there completely naked. It seemed that the flare would never burn out and that we were the only persons in the world whom that Nazi pilot could see. We remained rigidly in the positions in which the flare caught us. That was a result of the training of the old school. The soldier always had been taught to "freeze" in place—whatever his position—when caught in the light of an enemy flare. More recently, though, a newer teaching had directed that everyone should hit the ground. It was held that the time required for eyes to adjust themselves to the bright light was sufficient to permit this action without being seen and this had the added advantage of affording some protection from hostile fire.

"If he starts shooting, we'll hit the ground," I called back.

This I had hardly said until it was accomplished. We were on the ground by the time we heard the first bomb explode some distance to the rear. Then machine guns began to chatter. We could see red and green tracers racing across the now darkened sky. At first, it seemed that machine guns in the rear were sending up antiaircraft fire, but no, those red balls of fire were coming down—he was strafing the hedgerows. Two members of the battalion were hit.

Back in Service Company—in the regimental kitchen and supply area—he was working with greater damage. A bomb dropped in the area killed one, injured five or six; strafing caught two more. Rocky Stoneburner, Third Battalion S-4, was in the kitchen area and, like everyone else, ducked for cover behind a hedgerow—and lost his steel helmet. Groping about in the dark to try to find his helmet, he started crawling back along the hedgerow. He bumped into someone and looked up into the bespectacled face of Lieutenant Joe Friedal, onetime Third Battalion S-2. Joe was crouching low as the machine gun bullets cut through the tree leaves and the jarring thud of bombs kept coming.

Stoneburner quickly looked about and said, "I can't find my damned helmet." Joe yelled into his ear, "Here, Rocky, you can share mine!" His head alongside the S-4's, Friedal lifted his helmet to cover partially both heads.

Quiet returned with the departure of the airmen, but locally it soon was to be interrupted by another incident. It was shortly after midnight when a wild scream of terrified pain echoed through the dark orchards and meadow. Comrades of Battalion Headquarters Company rushed to the stricken man. They found him in a foxhole, a nasty cut in this thigh. He said that he had been bayoneted. This remained an unsolved mystery. The only explanation ever offered was that a lone German soldier had been hiding in the bushes and had rushed upon the American sentry, grabbed the rifle from the hands of the surprised man and turned to stab the sleeping man. Amidst the resulting confusion, then, he had been able to make his escape.

The next day was the first since coming up to the front that there had been any relaxation possible. To be sure, the patrols had to keep going, the enemy remained on the opposite side of the river, and artillery shells came in usually in the early morning or evening—but now for the first time, everyone had a chance to shave in the cool water of Normandy wells and Rocky could bring up hot chow.

Colonel Thomsen even directed that the Battalion CP move into a large house standing in a lot adjacent to the orchard where the Pioneers had dug out a shelter for the CP. This was the first time that any part of the Battalion had occupied a building. Fear of booby-traps and fear that they would be artillery targets had put a taboo on all buildings. There were signs of anti-personnel mines in this yard, but none was discovered in the house. This made much easier the installation and operation of telephones and radios and working with maps and notes.

One change had taken place in the view to the front: the tall church steeple had toppled over—and only the preceding evening the regimental S-2 had been discussing putting an OP (observation post) in it.

Occupying this position on the high ground at the edge of the town, the Third Battalion had reverted to a reserve position, with the First and Second Battalions occupying the main parts of town. After three days in this position, the Third Battalion received orders to relieve the First. The companies moved down to occupy basements and occasional lower rooms in the shattered houses and building – an undamaged building was not to be found anywhere.

The Battalion CP took over from the First Battalion in a small tomb or mausoleum in the cemetery near the northeast edge of the town. Telephone lines ran down the marble steps to the crypt where officers and assistants crowded over maps in the light of a gasoline lantern. The vault left little room for movement about the sides, but in spite of its stone-carved figures, it served as a desk for maps and papers and as a table for "K" rations. The air was heavy with carbon dioxide. Colonel Thomsen had his bedroll brought up and this, put down at the foot of the vault, served as a mattress for staff members to take turns at taking a nap when the situation permitted.

Some of the men slept in the small upper room. Others preferred to dig foxholes outside—some were digging their own graves.

Even the dead could have no rest. German artillery was more furious than ever. Usually it seemed that the Germans tried to send in the artillery during early morning and evening when they thought chow was coming up, but it was coming at all hours now. Going between companies, or between the Battalion CP and the companies, was a precarious undertaking—everyone dreaded "running the gauntlet" down the street past "88 corner." Bursting shells crumbled tombstones and dug craters among the graves. The mausoleum itself proved its worth by sustaining a number of direct hits.

Each night supply parties would have to carry rations, water ammunition, radio batteries from a quarry about a mile outside of town.

One afternoon a shell went through the roof of a small house in the valley behind the cemetery and wounded all the occupants who happened to be present. This included Shuster, the Colonel's jeep driver. But a replacement was available immediately: Leemhuis.

Finally the Colonel decided to move the CP back about 300 yards to get out of the cemetery and back behind the hill. Once more the Pioneers and all hands dug in.

War had left its marks along this highway which ran out of St. Lô to the northeast. The body of an old woman in a black dress and bonnet lay along a shoulder of the road. A little farther up was another knocked-out jeep of the 29th Division. A damaged winery stood down by a small creek 300 yards on beyond the CP site. On its walls, scrawled in big letters, was the motto of our predecessors in this sector: "Let's go 29th!"

We knew that this defensive situation could not last much longer. We heard that "something big" was up. I made a trip back to the regimental CP to see how the "big picture" looked. Friendly, helpful, efficient Ed Keltner, assistant operations officer, explained what was up. They were going to try for a break-through as soon as we had a good flying day. Infantry and armored divisions—the first mention of armored divisions—were "stacked up" behind us.

5
Moving along: Conde-sur-Vire

"Come out and look at this: Boy this is really something!"

The 3,000 planes—fighters to Flying Fortresses—were in the air. Their bombs began to fall. One could feel them almost more than hear them. They kept coming in a seemingly endless stream. It appeared that some of the bombs were falling very close to friendly troops.

"Looks like the 30th may be catching hell."

For 75 minutes, the great air assault continued to loose its 6,000 tons of bombs. Reports came in that the attack was going well and that the armor was on its way. Obviously, we would have to maintain pressure to our own immediate front in order not to permit the transfer of any troops to the area of the main break-through.

On Thursday morning, the 27th, we were surprised to see officers from the 28th ("Keystone" - Pennsylvania) Division coming up to the Battalion CP. They had orders to relieve us. This seemed a little strange, but we thought perhaps we were going to follow-up the break-through while this newer unit would take over the defensive mission. Hardly had these reconnaissance parties left until a call came from regiment.

"Previous instructions on relief canceled; we jump off at 1500."

The 134th Infantry was to make the main effort in taking the high ground to the south of St. Lô. Nineteen battalions of artillery were available to support the attack.

Colonel Thomsen took his command group and moved down through the rubble to Company I's CP. Passing the old, once beautiful, Church of Notre Dame, men paused to point out to those who followed an inspiring curiosity of the ruins: stone dust had clouded what was left of the beautiful blue and white and gold of the interior—most of the roof was demolished, the walls were crumbling—but in the center of this destruction, resting on the only opposing pillars which had been spared, rose the great crucifix unscarred.

In a thin single-file, the battalion column moved over the deep rubble which filled the streets, wound down narrow steps to get down to the river level, and then moved down along the highway to the southwest. A small field of Teller antitank mines laid on the road surface near the edge of town suggested that the German withdrawal had been a hasty one.

A TD platoon had been attached to the Third Battalion, but it was unable to move through the rubble of St. Lô. A tank reconnaissance officer went down to look over the conditions and estimated that it would take two days to get any armor through St. Lô. Division engineers went to work with bulldozers and shovels and trucks—and mine detectors. Though the principal route had been heavily mined, the debris had covered the mines so completely that they could not be detonated. The engineers worked through the night to clear a vehicular route in record time.

Company L deployed on the left of Company I and the Battalion moved warily ahead more than a thousand yards before running into any trouble. Here, after a brisk fire fight, Company I knocked out a machine gun and took some prisoners. Now leaving the highway upon which it had been guiding, the Battalion moved southeast through orchards and hedgerows. Here and there the Battalion would run into a pocket of resistance and then move on. Prisoners in groups of four or five to 20 were taken and, of course, more men were getting hurt.

It was such a pocket of resistance that the Battalion encountered as it crossed another of those sunken roads. During this series of fire fights through the hedgerow terrain, it was difficult to maintain contact. Colonel Thomsen had gone forward to contact Company L and members of the command group, left to wait in the sunken road, were not sure of his whereabouts. I met Lieutenant Sid Davis, a big well-mannered Texan, looking for part of "K" Company. We found a gate out of the sunken road and started forward to see if we could find what parts of the Battalion were up there. After walking only a few steps, we ducked instinctively to the very low whistles of artillery shells coming from the rear. Four deafening bursts of red fire and black smoke hit in the meadow little more than 25 yards in front of us.

"That's our own damned artillery!"

We made a hasty retreat back to the cover of the sunken road and got on the field telephone to call about the artillery falling short. A burst of small arms fire cracked overhead and cut through the tree leaves. Radiomen and telephone men lifted their rifles or carbines. We started to move around a slight curve in the sunken road: there was another burst of fire from the other direction. Now the volume of fire grew intense. Men had to fight off panic as that sickening feeling of being caught like rats in a trap sought to possess them.

"Wait, listen," Sid Davis said. "By God, that all sounds like American weapons." He looked around, "Yes, a platoon of "K" and a platoon of "L" are shooting the hell out of each other!"

We were in the sunken road between the two platoons. We hurried to the radio to get word to the two companies to cease firing. In due course, this was successful before there had been actual casualties on either side.

Division orders were to continue the attack until 10:30 o'clock. At that hour, the Third Battalion was in another brisk fire fight and darkness had applied its own envelopment before quiet returned. Then, with the Companies' assigned hedgerows surrounding two fields and the Battalion CP along the middle hedgerow, the Battalion "tucked in its tail"—formed a "wagon wheel" all-around defense—for the night.

Hardly had the men dug their foxholes before that bothersome German airplane was circling overhead. Again came those brilliant yellow, everlasting flares and then the bombs and then the machine gun bullets. It was awe-inspiring to watch, as long as he kept at a safe distance, but when he came over our own orchard, it was more comforting to hide the head ostrich-like in the foxhole and shut out that disrobing light. This night he seemed to be interested particularly in our supporting 161st Field Artillery Battalion. One bomb tore a huge crater in the very center of a field, which scattered mud all over trucks and guns around the edge. So regular had these visits become—11 o'clock each evening—that everyone referred to the hostile airman as "Bed-check Charlie." And men were asking: where was the famed "Black Widow" night-fighter?

A regrouping of troops during the night (27-28 July) brought the 29th Division out of the line and shifted them, by motor, to a sector on our right. This move was to carry that division down through the Brittany Peninsula. The 35th now was in Major General Leonard T. Gerow's V Corps; withdrawal of the 29th left the 2nd Division on the left.

Moving off at 10 a.m., the Third Battalion deployed on either side of the road leading to Ste. Suzanne sur Vire and Conde Sur Vire and met only scattered, slight opposition. Colonel Thomsen was moving behind the assault companies with the same energy as always. Sometimes he would give his command group, and especially the wire crew, a fit as they tried to keep up. Often it took something more than mind reading to know when to follow and when to wait for him. The wiremen and messengers, of course, could carry only a limited amount of wire—even with the light wire, it could be no more than three or four miles and the wiremen had a difficult time of it in trying to follow the Colonel as he would zig and zag from one Company's zone to the other. Sometimes he would say, "Wait here, I'll be right back," but he would just keep going. It got to be a game to try to cut across his turns in order to save wire and keep up with him—and he always insisted on having that telephone wirehead with him.

Approaching the village of Ste. Suzanne, the Colonel decided that he was nearing the day's objective —the high ground between Ste. Suzanne and Conde sur Vire—and he called the Company commanders to meet him on the road. "Melcher, you come out to the road and we'll be along there in a minute."

The command group continued on down the road. There was a German platoon wagon and its very recently killed horse in the road just outside Ste. Suzanne.

"I wonder what got this," the battalion commander said. "The outfit on our right, over across the river, must have seen them withdrawing and given them a shelling."

The First Sergeant was examining the cargo. He extracted a couple of tall bottles and put them in his bosom, "We'll have to check into this stuff this evening; might be lighter fluid."

As we entered the village a mortar smoke shell burst in front of us.

"Why, that's white phosphorous—can't be Kraut!"

Another shell burst behind us.

"Boy, he's got us bracketed."

A third was a hit on a house very near us.

"It's that damned 30th Division shooting from across the river," someone cried. "Why the hell can't they keep their fire in their own sector?"

We moved on through the town, but saw no signs of life anywhere.

"I wonder where the hell Melcher is?" the Colonel said.

Barney Blackburn came along looking for positions for his mortars. He and a couple of men went up to the left of the road and then on down toward Conde.

"Sam, go back along the road and see if you can find any of "K" Company." The Colonel sat down on the shoulder of the road.

I went back through Ste. Suzanne and about two hundred yards on the other side I saw Captain Melcher coming up the road.

"Where have you been—where is the Colonel?" he said. "I have been waiting here for over 20 minutes."

"Is this "K" Company right along here?"

"Yes, along there on the right of the road. Lassiter is right up there on that hill."

"Holy smoke! The old man is acting as the point; he is sitting up there along the road about four hundred yards in front of everybody."

Melcher laughed slightly. "Well, I'm glad to hear that the town and everything up that far is all clear."

Just before sunset, the Battalion moved up on the high ground and reported "On objective." Taking over some abandoned German foxholes (theirs were always better than ours—deeper and with thick coverings) and digging some new ones, the men prepared for the night.

The First Sergeant dropped to the ground and leaned against a hedgerow. He withdrew one of the German bottles from his bosom and smiled eagerly as he removed the cork. He lifted the bottle to his lips and breathed deeply to take a long draft. However, he cut it short in wild sputtering and violent language. "White lightning!" he cried.

During the afternoon, the First Battalion had been held up and this had left a big gap—both in width and in depth—between the two battalions. Accordingly, the Second Battalion, in reserve, had been ordered to move up on the left of the Third and take over the objective originally assigned to the First Battalion.

The Battalion was getting organized on its position when there was a close, nerve-racking burst from a burp gun. Always it was difficult to distinguish between the sound of the bullets and the sound of the weapon and the use of smokeless powder made a German weapon a hard thing to locate. Men started looking for a sniper. There was nothing hated worse than a sniper—an enemy who would hide himself in a tree or in a house or in a chimney to shoot down Americans until his ammunition was exhausted when he would come down with his hands up to expect mercy (and usually found it).

Some American weapons began firing in the area. Colonel Thomsen ordered all firing ceased so that we could hear this sniper.

A man came up to me. "Sir, I think I see him. Shall I let him have it?"

"Wait and let me check—where is he?"

"Right there in that tree." He pointed and other men along the hedgerow lifted their rifles towards the tree. I adjusted my field glasses. Just then a man jumped out of the tree and looked around at all those rifles trained on him—it was Johnson, one of our intelligence scouts!

By this fear of snipers in trees, we denied ourselves the use of trees for observation—one of the few means at hand for taking a look over the hedgerows.

An increase in the tempo of the firing to our left rear told us that there was something more than a sniper or two back there. The Second Battalion, coming up, was encountering real trouble in an area immediately to the left of the route over which we had come up. The firing was intense on both sides now. Company F's Captain called for his 60mm mortars. They went into position and prepared to fire.

"I'm afraid we don't have clearance right here sir," the gunner called. "We've got a tree in the way."

"To hell with clearance!" shouted the Captain. "We've got to get those Krauts out; fire!"

The assistant gunner dropped a shell into the tube – back out it came to begin its high arc, but its course was cut short. Yes, there was an overhanging bough. The shell burst. The Captain was dead.

Not till the next morning were the three battalions able to make contact with each other. By that time the Germans, now following a regular pattern, had withdrawn. But there was no intention of permitting the enemy any respite.

An "L" Company patrol reported at 6:50 a.m. that an enemy tank had moved in alongside the church in Conde sur Vire. The attack moved off without any opposition two hours later. Another patrol at 10:20 was able to describe the steel monster as a self-propelled 88. Company K was moving in at the same time and now the Battalion Antitank Platoon was looking for a place to get in a shot with a 57mm gun. The result was a couple of antitank rockets (from "bazookas") from one group, some antitank grenades from another and some 57mm slugs from the third. No one was quite sure who delivered the knock-out blow, but the Battalion had "bagged" its first tank. Company L found the tank crew in the church and routed them out.

At 4 o'clock, orders came down to continue the attack—the regiment was to keep going until it had taken the town of Torigni-sur-Vire. Lieutenant Jack Campbell of "L" Company took a patrol on through Conde sur Vire to reconnoiter the ground beyond. He found no enemy on the high ground to the south. The 35th Cavalry Reconnaissance Troop was working down the highway to his right.

By 7 o'clock the companies were through Conde. But once again, darkness was overtaking an attack. The Companies moved forward about a thousand yards during each of the next two hours. At 9:30 they passed through a small cluster of farm dwellings and barns noted as "le Bust" on the map. French people – men, women and children – came out to greet them. Here, for the first time, French families were found occupying their homes. Villiers-Fossard had been almost completely abandoned, St. Lô a ghost town, Ste. Suzanne and Conde sur Vire practically lifeless. But not this little farm hamlet—its people were out to greet the Yanks.

Fifteen minutes later there was machine gun fire up ahead, but it was of short duration. The Battalion commander directed the companies to "tie-in" and await order. He walked over to the wirehead and picked up the field telephone to call regiment.

"Our orders are to keep going until we take Torigni," the regimental commander told him.

"Yes sir, but by God, sir, we are going to hit something when we move out of here and I think it's a hell of a poor idea to try to attack in the dark without any kind of reconnaissance."

The regimental commander was wholly in sympathy with the objection to a night attack without any prior reconnaissance and, after another telephone conference with the Division Chief of Staff, he was able to have continuation of the attack postponed until 9 o'clock the next morning.

I had remained with Captain Bruce and the rear elements of Battalion Headquarters at the hedgerow CP north of Conde. While the Battalion was moving into its position in the sunken road and hedgerows through the orchards immediately south of le Bust, we, with the Battalion's "tail," were moving down through Conde to join the forward echelon.

"It's almost 11 o'clock," Bruce said. "We're going to have to step on it to beat 'Bed-check Charlie.'"

We quickened our pace, but it was 11 o'clock and darkness was upon us when we reached a group of buildings—a large farmhouse and outbuildings—midway between Conde and le Bust.

"Here comes Bed-check," someone called. "Don't you hear that old putt-putt washing machine motor? It's Kraut all right." The plane, motor idling, was soaring over head.

"Get covered before the flares come!" The men were scattering among the buildings; the Second Battalion was moving along the road beyond a railroad underpass ahead of us, scattering along the hedgerow, when a string of flares cast its bright yellow light over the landscape. There was a short burst of machine gun fire from over across the railway. The airplane answered by swooping down low with its machine guns strafing over the Second Battalion—a bomb sent tremors through the earth.

I found myself in a half-wrecked room of the big farm house. There also were Bruce and Sergeant Novak, communications chief.

"Well, I have read in the papers how the English civilians get under a heavy table during an air raid," I said.

"Here's a table." Sergeant Novak started throwing refuse aside. We joined him to push the table up against the most substantial looking wall and dived underneath. We grasped each other to cultivate the reassurance of comradeship and sat quietly. We could hear an occasional burst of machine gun fire—the slow turning motor began to sound louder. Then we could hear a high-pitched screaming whistle—it was a crescendo, violent tone whose intensity heightened as it came closer. Then the shrillness was lost in an engulfing reverberation. Bits of masonry fell onto the table over our heads; plaster dust fell down our necks.

"Boy, that must have got the house."

We waited a few minutes and then, as the overhead drone became faint, crawled out for a look around. A quick check disclosed that none of the men of our immediate group was hurt, but we heard that the Second Battalion had been hit hard.

"I don't see why in hell they don't get some night fighters up," said Joe Morhan, one of the intelligence men. He adjusted the 300 radio on his back. "This is the way it is every night, always the same time, but no one ever up to meet him—our air corps can't get away from those clean sheets and warm bunks...bankers' hours. You never see them out before 10 and they are always in for tea at 4—."

Someone interrupted to cry, "Say, he got a bull's eye. Did you see what he did to the bridge?"

We walked a few yards up the road to see the bridge —it was, or had been, over the railroad. The bomb, rather than hitting the nearby house, had made a direct hit in the very center of the bridge; crumbled stone from the demolished span lay amongst the twisted rails below.

It was necessary for us to climb down into the deep cut and out again over the rubble on the other side.

When we arrived at the site of the Battalion CP, Sergeant Drew came out to meet us to explain where the other members of the Headquarters were located. Then he led me over to a spot along the hedgerow next to his foxhole and I began to dig.

"Sir, you should have been up here this evening. The French people came out with fried chicken and wine and it was good! The Germans made them fix it, but we ate it!" I thought of how we used to have orders in California to refrain from accepting food from strangers, but now the awareness that death always was lurking near at hand overshadowed any fears of gastric sabotage.

"How did you make out with your school French?" I asked.

"Oh, I could get along."

Even under the roughest conditions, Drew's speech and manners betrayed his education: he had taught English in Chicago after graduating from Loyola University. His features were not visible in the darkness of the night, but he was of more than average height and slender in build with light, curly hair. At the termination of Tennessee maneuvers, he had risen from Battalion clerk to Battalion Sergeant Major – T/5 (equivalent to Corporal) to technical sergeant. He was a highly efficient administrator. He was a keen observer, a good thinker, and a ready wit. I always enjoyed talking with him.

"Some of these men around Battalion Headquarters make me sick," he was saying. "They don't realize what a better deal they have than the boys up in the rifle platoons…some of them are feeling bad about losing some of the boys, but God, we can't go around wearing everybody on our cuff or we'll all go crazy." He hated to see anyone act afraid and he was vigorous in expressing his disapproval.

We talked a long while there in the middle of the night—philosophizing on fear and death or recounting the happenings of the day—while I dug into the side of the hedgerow and he dug his hole a little deeper. We discussed the visit of "Bed-check Charlie"—it appeared that the Third Battalion had suffered a few casualties during the raid, but parts of the Second had been hit hard. We told how a system of green flares, apparently fired into the air from the ground, practically had outlined the battalion area just prior to the air attack. We wondered if some of these people might be disguised Germans or German sympathizers.

I walked over to pull some bunches of grass and threw them into my slit trench, then snuggled down in my field coat to claim a few short hours of nature's escape from warfare.

The drone of an airplane overhead interrupted my sleep. I rose to look about and saw to the front a green flare; soon a similar flare burst to the right side—then to the left—finally to the rear. "They have us surrounded," I thought. Then came the bright yellow flares from the plane as he searched for prey. Fortunately, there was no firing on our area. "We must have good camouflage," I thought.

6
"Bloody Sunday"

Having finished eating their "K" ration breakfast, the men were putting on their equipment preparatory to moving off with the 9 o'clock attack. I had just put on my harness and belt and picked up my map case when my intelligence sergeant came up.

"Sir, I would just as soon go with the command group today," he said. In order to be able to spend some time at the CP and be more free to move about without being pinned down helplessly for hours at a time along a hedgerow, I had decided to alternate with the sergeant in accompanying the battalion commander. Thus, one of us would be available to handle prisoners, distribute maps, coordinate and report information of the enemy.

"No, that's all right," I answered. "I was with the CP yesterday, so it's my turn with the Colonel today."

"No, really sir, if you don't mind I would just as soon go – I would rather go if it's all right with you."

"Well, it doesn't make any difference, I guess. Go ahead if you want to."

Colonel Thomsen walked up to the corner of the field, plastic map case in one hand, long field coat slung over the back of his belt, paused momentarily to collect his command group, and moved up a hedgerow to a sunken road where he stopped to direct the attack.

The companies jumped off at 9 o'clock, but the German withdrawal pattern had been altered: there were immediate bursts of hostile fire all along the line. The enemy added artillery to his small arms fire.

An hour and a half later the situation had not improved. "K" and "L" Companies unable to advance, Colonel Thomsen send Company "I" around to attack on the left of "L," but there was no flank and "I" was under fire before it even came abreast. All companies were suffering casualties and were gaining nothing. Artillery fire had cut our telephone lines and we were out of communication with regiment. Captain Ray Carroll called over, "Sam, maybe you had better go down and give them our situation."

I went across the road to call Bernie Haas. He drove the jeep out of the barn and we took off down the dusty road. The regimental CP had moved into the buildings where we had stopped during the previous night's air raid. We drove down as far as the destroyed overpass and then I went afoot down a sunken trail to the west and then followed a path down across the tracks. As I came up the bank on the opposite bank, I came across a dead German; he was lying on his back, head toward me. His head was lying in dried blood and his glassy eyes seemed to gaze upward.

As I went into the operations room to report to Colonel Miltonberger, I was aware of my three-day's growth of beard, of my wrinkled and dirty uniform—even in these circumstances, I remembered the Colonel's insistence on neat dress and personal police. The Colonel was a big man—in the six feet plus, 200 pound category. As I approached him, his brown eyes looked past my beard and dirt and searched into my own for news of the Third Battalion. I explained how the opposition was and that we were going to have to add something to be able to go.

"Yes, I understand," he said. "The attrition of taking those casualties is weakening you all the time; now if you can hold what you have got, we'll be able to get some tanks up there early this afternoon."

I told him about the flares preceding the air attack. He was very much interested and he called upon the S-2 to investigate. The Second Battalion had made a similar report and they had found French children with burp guns and ammunition—apparently the Germans had supplied them liberally and told them to shoot all they liked.

The Colonel laughed slightly and said, "Now we have 'Reveille Pete' to visit us as well as 'Bed-check Charlie.'"

When I arrived back at the Battalion CP, I saw that the medics were busy there. A litter team was lifting the battalion clerk from his foxhole onto their litter. He had painful wounds in his arm and thigh. Someone lit a cigarette for him and he thanked them cheerfully as he was carried away. Carroll was over in the corner, but I saw no one else about until Johnson lifted his head up and said, "Sir, you just missed it. We have been catching hell here—those awful tree bursts. Lieutenant Garner got hit bad…there is his coat, it was torn to ribbons—looked like he had a pierced lung…they don't know whether he'll live or not…The tank officer who had come up to coordinate was in that hole there and he got hit...Captain Carroll had gone up to see Colonel Thomsen and you were down at regiment. I was the only one here who did not get hit. Look at that man over there—"

There, a few feet away, was one of our messengers sitting in his foxhole—dead. He looked as though he were sitting there asleep. I remembered joking with him only the previous evening. Carroll held up his coat for me to see—it was full of holes. "I'm sure glad I was not in this," he said.

Shells began coming in again. I looked at Johnson, "You say your hole is the only one that was not hit?"

"Yes sir, I guess I was sure lucky."

"Move over, Johnson, I'm coming in."

Meanwhile, the Companies were trying hard to advance. Company K was still on the right and trying to make the next hedgerow. Technical Sergeant Paul Forney of Nebraska, platoon sergeant, had found himself in command of his platoon when the lieutenant had been hit. He led the platoon out across the orchard toward the next hedgerow. Moving through enemy fire, Forney was wounded; but he kept right on going to throw his hand grenades over the next hedgerow. He rallied his men to continue the assault, but the next burst of fire killed him. Pfc. Edward Abraham of Ohio was a little more fortunate. When his platoon was pinned down by an enemy machine gun, he leaped over the hedgerow and, although wounded, he crawled down near the German gun and destroyed the crew with a hand grenade.

Four automatic riflemen were wounded in quick succession at a vital position protecting the left flank of Company L's 2nd Platoon. Immediately, Pfc. Luverne Strand of Minnesota and Robert Hanlon of Washington D.C., ran up to take over the BAR. They opened fire and kept the weapon going until a direct hit from an enemy mortar killed both of them.

Over in Company I, one platoon had been able to drive a short gain, but heavy enemy fire from front and flank forced it to give this up. Technical Sergeant Leonard Oseik of Ohio, the platoon sergeant, grabbed a light machine gun to cover the withdrawal of his platoon. He remained in position until all the other members of his platoon had taken cover behind the hedgerow to the rear. Then, firing the machine gun from his hip, he walked backwards until he reached the hedgerow. But as he started to climb over it, enemy fire killed him.

Colonel Thomsen was becoming worried over the Battalion's situation. Tanks were coming up; they were able to cross the railroad over a grade crossing about a half mile to the west of the knocked-out overpass, but the sunken road which ran parallel to the railroad was too narrow for them in some places and there it was necessary for pioneer demolition crews to blast openings in the hedgerow. All of this was taking time and, in the meantime, the accurate enemy fire was sapping the Battalion's strength. The Battalion Commander was hoping that Colonel Miltonberger would commit the Second Battalion, which was being held in regimental reserve.

I made another trip to the regimental CP. As is customary, the reserve commander, Lieutenant Colonel Wilson, commander of the Second Battalion, was there. Colonel Miltonberger turned to him and told him to get his battalion ready to move in on the left of the Third. Colonel Wilson made no response, but sat as though in a stupor. Concussion from the previous night's bombing had broken his ear drum.

The Second Battalion's executive officer was near nervous exhaustion and it was not until the Colonel got hold of the S-3 (operations officer), Captain Frederick Roecker, a young West Pointer, that he was able to get any action.

As the jeep approached le Bust on the return trip, we heard shells coming in again. We stopped.

"Shall I park her here somewhere or drive back up into the barn?" Bernie asked.

"Better pull in here somewhere for now," I replied.

He backed up to an opening and turned into a meadow behind a high hedgerow. We crouched in a side ditch.

Another shell came close. We lay there and mentally dared one to come closer. It did. It left our ears ringing and our nostrils filled with the odor of burnt powder. I glanced up the road to the group of farm buildings on the left. A long whistle announced the approach of another shell. It burst on the barn where Bernie was going to leave the jeep. Splinters of wood, timber fragments, smoke and dust rose high into the air. Members of the Pioneer Platoon came running out of the old building; several were injured—Lieutenant Hall had a gash in his hand.

The Battalion medical section was having its busiest day at the aid station which was in a small building about a hundred yards off the road to my immediate left. Now a barrage hit the aid station. One man was holding out his hand having a finger bandaged; a big shell fragment took off the hand. Wounded men lying helplessly on the floor wounded a second or a third time; medics were wounded so that they could not care for them. The assistant surgeon gathered up the party and started down the road while Matthew jumped in his jeep and went on down to find another site. A pathetic group it was that emerged from the damaged building and filed out to the road. Bloody bandages fluttering from arms or heads or shoulders…wounded medics carrying men on litters who were unable to walk… everyone in a hurry, but no one could run…out to the road to join a stream of God-forsaken human beings… the walking wounded from the Pioneer platoon, and additional ones coming from the companies, added their number to the battered column…French civilians from the little hamlet—the ones who had been so gay the night before—now added to the general confusion by coming out onto the road pulling carts stacked high with bedclothes, utensils, what foodstuffs they might have. They all trudged down the dusty road in the hot sun toward the railroad. Doc set up his aid station in an orchard along the tracks.

It took some time to get any part of the Second Battalion started up, but presently Captain McDannel approached the area of the battalion CP with Company E. (By this time, I was back up in Johnson's foxhole.) They were coming up in single file. McDannel directed the leading men to cross the hedgerow to our front and go ahead to the next one until they contacted the left of the Third Battalion. He yelled at the men to take cover as they went when we told of the shelling we had been getting. But another barrage was on the way.

Tree bursts sent leaves and boughs fluttering to the ground and sent steel fragments about the men below. An "M" Company mortar crew was knocked out on the other side of the hedgerow to our right. Other shells hit on top of the hedgerow and one the ground beside it— they cut down that column of men. Wounded men were writhing all along that hedgerow in our field. Some were shouting.

"Oh, Jesus, help me, help me, my God, My God, isn't anybody going to help me?" one of the men called out in a loud voice. "Oh, Jesus." He was mortally wounded in the back, but he remained fully conscious until death relieved him within a few minutes. Others died more quickly.

It was nearing 5 o'clock now and Colonel Thomsen was worried about the situation. He chafed at being unable to advance; he was impatient that neither the tanks nor the Second Battalion had been able to give any assistance and he was concerned about the loss of men. There had been nearly a hundred casualties so far during the day. Captain Jim Lassiter of Company I had been seriously wounded in the abdomen. Colonel Thomsen was standing behind a tree in the sunken trail.

A barrage burst among the trees to scatter its lethal fragments on the sunken trail. Lou Mormance shook himself and coughed. He looked up and saw that about everyone in the command group had been hit. A 300 radio on his back, he began running up and down the hedgerow. He saw that Colonel Thomsen was wounded; he sat down to report on the radio what had happened. He knew that Captain Melcher of Company K was near and he called him over.

Captain Carroll went up to take over. Medics were at work quickly, but they had a big job on their hands. Colonel Thomsen was unconscious from a wound in the head, the artillery liaison radio had been destroyed, and all the members of the liaison group wounded. When I first heard about what had happened, I sensed without even asking that Sergeant Drew had been killed. Yes, as he lay in a slit trench up there, face down, helmet down low, a huge shell fragment had torn into his side.

My intelligence sergeant was wounded, but when the medics came for him, he refused to be evacuated until all the other wounded men had been cared for.

I went back down to regiment to report again. I told the Colonel that Colonel Thomsen had been hit.

"Is it serious?"

"In the head."

"My God," he said. "Well, tell Carroll to take command for the rest of the day; you'll have to help him out with the S-3 work. I'm going to have the Second Battalion relieve you tonight so that you can pull back to an assembly area and get reorganized."

I left the jeep at the same place as before and started walking up the road. A sniper's burp gun directed me to the side ditch for a few minutes. I met Lieutenant Ruby. The "M" Company commander was working everywhere that day. He was evacuating wounded with his jeep, bringing up ammunition, getting information, making reports.

"You probably better get up to the CP as soon as you can," he said. "I just left there and Jack Campbell from "L" Company is there, but no one else is around."

"Right."

I got up and ran to the sunken trail which bordered the small field in which the CP was located, but I had to stop and turn back. As I rounded the corner, I came suddenly upon a mass of blood, of human flesh and limbs—they were torn beyond all recognition. Here, the only time during the war, I came upon a sight so repulsive that I could not pass it. I saw Lieutenant Reischel over near the barn. He already had found those dismembered bodies and had found some dog tags – it was my intelligence sergeant and the two medics who had been carrying him out on a litter.

Throughout the day, we had been receiving shell fire from time to time from the rear. We could hear the report of the gun distinctly and the shells would come ripping through with deadly effect. Immediately, we had accused friendly artillery, but thorough investigation showed this not to be the case. We concluded that there was an enemy mobile gun somewhere in the rear area, but we never were able to actually find it.

Carroll came back to the CP and soon Ruby came up, and we went into a huddle to plan for bringing the Battalion out. Ruby said that he would find an assembly area back to the east of Conde sur Vire, have a wire crew string a line from the regimental CP, and would post guides all along the route at every turn so that the weary men could find their way back there in the dark.

Carroll went back up to confer with the Company commanders and I went across the road to the barn to discuss the relief with officers of the Second Battalion, who now had moved their CP up to that location.

I talked with the Second Battalion executive. He spoke slowly and in a low tone with apparent calmness, but it was the calmness not of strength, but of complete fatigue.

"We are beginning to look like the 29th Division," I thought.

The major said that he would have the Company F and G commanders go up right away to make a reconnaissance and would get the Battalion ready to move.

I returned to our own CP and waited. After an hour's wait there in the twilight brought no results, I went back to check with the Major. He had forgotten to notify his companies. Captain Roecker was there then. He had been up to our forward positions and was acquainted with the situation. He got the Company commanders and went up to talk with Carroll.

It was dark before the relieving companies started up and it was a slow process. Elements of our companies had become intermingled during the heavy fighting and it was a task to get the platoons reorganized so that they could move out in an orderly fashion. And any intimation to the enemy that a relief of battalions was going on would have invited disaster.

Ruby had taken the available members of Company M, as well as much of Headquarters Company, to act as guides. At last, members of Company I came back to the vicinity of the farm houses, formed a column, and set off down the muddy sunken trail and turned into the dry gravel road. The night was calm and clear with a partial moon and it was cool, as always. We waited another hour—sweating out "Bed-check Charlie." Fortunately, we received word that there would be friendly night-fighters up and Charlie missed a call. Presently the sticking, slippery sound of feet upon mud told us that Company L was coming out.

It was well after 5 a. m before all the Battalion was back in the assembly area. Lieutenant Colonel Shepard, regimental executive officer, was sitting by a lamp in a dugout. He was to remain with the Battalion until its new commander arrived.

Members of the earlier companies already were asleep when the later ones started digging their foxholes. Some men had to be sent up to outpost the gap between the First and Second Battalions. Everyone was physically and mentally exhausted. Men had seen about 115 casualties leave the battalion during the day; they were wondering when their turn would be – percentages looked well enough when the figures were dealing with the whole Army, for most of the Army does not fight, but in the fighting elements of an infantry battalion they began to see that they had no odds in their favor. It was becoming a question, not <u>if</u> they were going to get hit, but <u>when</u> and <u>how badly</u>. Would he be one of the lucky ones or would he be killed or permanently maimed? During these two weeks of combat, the Battalion had suffered 574 casualties – 86 were wounded fatally.

7
Pinched Out Across the Vire River

There scarcely can be any greater stimuli to a soldier's morale than hot food and mail. Both items came up for the Battalion on that Monday morning following "Bloody Sunday."

Yet, in spite of its desirability, mail could have the effect of magnifying one's sense of frustration. Now when one had a few minutes to reflect on the happenings of the preceding day, he became keenly aware of the odds against him. But letters from loved ones reminded him that all this would affect more than merely himself; he wanted so much to be back with them again, but they seemed so very, very far away. He wondered if he even dared hope.

The mail brought a crumpled, mud-stained envelope containing a verse card:

A PRAYER FOR YOU IN THE SERVICE OF OUR COUNTRY

God is our refuge and strength. Ps. 46:1

God keep you safely
Day after day
Show you His power
As help and stay,

Light up your pathways
With hope and cheer,
And keep His presence
Forever near!

What more appropriate time for such a message than the day after "Bloody Sunday"?

Some men received packages of candy or cakes in the mail and they hastened to eat them quickly, for tomorrow might be too late to enjoy them.

Earl Ruby was up early moving about to get his company reorganized. A group of replacements had come up to replenish partially the weakened companies. Ruby was good for a chat or wisecrack under any circumstances.

"By God, Sam, if I live through this thing, I think I'll be a preacher," he said. He did not mean that. He never had professed to be particularly religious and could command as violent language as anyone, but he was expressing a sentiment which could be felt in the Battalion. "You know, for every one of those shells that come down, there are about fifty prayers going up the other way; we are all laying there saying our prayers; this will make Christians out of lots of the boys." He laughed and moved on.

At 8 o'clock, Lieutenant Colonel Robert E. Moore of Missouri arrived in the area to take command of the Battalion. He had been assigned to our sister 137th Infantry back in the States, but then had gone to an assignment with higher headquarters. A veteran of World War I, he had been clamoring for action—he wanted to command an infantry battalion. Now he was going to have it. Colonel Moore was of less than average stature, but well-built and his hair and mustache were gray. He did not propose to introduce any radical changes into the way the Battalion operated.

Two hours later young, stocky Captain Harlan B. "Butch" Heffelfinger of Beatrice, Nebraska, came walking down the shaded path. I had worked with him under Colonel Coonley and Major Thomsen in the First Battalion and knew him to be a highly competent officer. Now he was leaving his place as First Battalion S-3 to be our executive officer.

Lieutenant Snyder of New York, who had been First Battalion communications officer, was with Captain Heffelfinger—Snyder was to take over the same job in the Third.

The injury of Captain Bruce had left yet another vacancy in Battalion headquarters: S-1 (adjutant). This I was to take over for the time being. We called Sergeant Buckley up from the supply section to take over his old place as Sergeant Major and sent a message back to Division Headquarters, rear echelon, to have a young clerk there named Bartash return to the Company as Battalion Clerk.

During the morning, everyone took advantage of this opportunity to shave and wash. But the luxury of relaxation never could last very long. A telephone call came from regiment, "Can you be ready to move by noon?"

"Yes, sir."

Failure to follow up an advantage to make a victory decisive or to exploit a favorable situation vigorously has been a weakness of military commanders—like McClellan at Antietam or Hooker at Chancellorsville—all through history. Commanders in this war were determined from the start not to be guilty of this shortcoming. Therefore, the watchword was "push, push." The enemy must be allowed no respite.

Apparently the Germans had been hurt as much as we had during the previous day's fighting, for when the First and Second Battalions jumped off at 12 o'clock, the opposition had withdrawn from the front.

A change in boundaries gave the city of Torigni-sur-Vire to the 320th Infantry and by evening it was cleared out.

Our advance continued the next day without any real opposition. Down the sunken trails, over unused highways, across hedgerows, through meadows and orchards, the columns moved through the Bocage country. During one temporary halt, an artillery liaison plane, fluttering earthward like a stricken sparrow—the pilot was trying to land with the greatest possible speed—gave notice that enemy aircraft were approaching. Seconds later, two Messerschmitt 109's streaked across the sky. And then, two Thunderbolts—recognizable only through field glasses—appeared and shot down one of the intruders; the other one turned about and sped in the opposite direction in the greatest exhibition of air speed that we ever saw.

Opposition on the ground did not develop until evening when the First Battalion ran into some small arms fire. The Third was able to go up on the left of the First to dig in for the night, but at twilight there were heavy barrages of artillery and mortar fire. This was somewhat disconcerting for the column of replacements coming up. Other shells fell into the motor park. This knocked out a jeep and hit an ammunition trailer, which quick work by the A&P men saved, and forced the aid station to move to the rear.

Colonel Moore said that he was through with having his CP in a hole behind a hedgerow and he directed Battalion Headquarters to move into a small farm house and its outbuildings—we soon discovered that a house was better protection against artillery than was a foxhole. Quilts and comforters over the windows provided the necessary blackout and the farmer's kerosene lamps (we frequently burned gasoline in them) gave the necessary light. An old dining table, covered with a blanket (we were careful to protect it from scratches and spots, although a few shells might have reduced it to splinters at any moment), afforded a place to install telephones and work over maps and notes.

Hardly had the command post been set up when the regimental S-3 came down to visit the battalion commander. The regiment had orders to continue the attack during the night to seize the Vire River line. Lieutenant Ruby and one or two of the other company commanders happened to be in the CP. The reaction was quick.

"By God," Ruby said, "it's easy for these people to sit back at Division and get some wild hare notion like that; that's damn foolishness to go wandering around out there in the dark over ground you've never had a chance to look at." He was talking to the other commanders and battalion staff officers there, but he was speaking in a loud voice for the benefit of the regimental operations officer.

The visitor asked if he might speak with the battalion commander, S-3, and executive officer alone. But these three were quick to voice their opposition to any plan calling for a night attack without any prior reconnaissance. "Of course," Colonel Moore concluded, "if it's a direct order, we'll have to go – we'll go with the others." After the visitor had left, he turned to Carroll and said, "We'll guide on the right battalion – when they go, we'll go, but I don't intend to stick my neck out."

Jeeps and trailers came up with hot chow—hot meals, whenever at all possible, was another "must" of the new battalion commander—and then the companies were told to be alert and prepared to move at 2 a.m., the time given for the night attack.

At 2 o'clock, Colonel Moore reported to regiment that he was ready to go, but was waiting on the First Battalion. He had one of the companies send out a patrol and kept in close radio contact with Red Battalion.

"Hell, they're fighting a battle on the radio," the executive said.

"Well, we'll stick right with them."

Actually, the main body of troops moved out sometime after 7 o'clock. We encountered French people returning to their homes and interpreted this as a good sign. The Pioneers had to clear a big tree which had been felled across the road before the vehicles could come up, but no other obstacles barred the way, and by noon the battalion had reached high Hill 201 overlooking the Vire River Valley. A main highway leading to Villedieu-les-Poels and Avranches ran across the front.

Higher headquarters were getting excited about crossing the Vire River: the V Corps Chief of Staff was at the regimental CP, the Division G-3 was making calls to regiment and soon General Baade, the Division Commander, came down to visit the battalion. "There's nothing out there," he said, "and we must cross that river this afternoon; stop for nothing; the enemy is withdrawing." The objective was the city of Vire, some 10 or 12 miles away. That always was the depressing thing about capturing an objective—there always was another, bigger and farther away than ever.

It was true that there had been no opposition to the advance during the morning and there was no shell fire of any kind now, but the battalion commanders were apprehensive of going down into that deep valley to face those commanding hills (the river itself was reported to be narrow and shallow here—no obstacle to foot troops) without any preparation or reconnaissance. They determined to take enough time to make a short preliminary reconnaissance.

Colonel Moore came back and called for an officer and three men from Company I—he was going to lead a patrol himself to check on a route down to the river. Having lost one battalion commander already, we did not look upon this project with much favor, but the

Colonel was determined to go. Lieutenant Wardwell reported with his men within a few minutes and the patrol set up. They carried a 536 hand radio and were able to relay messages back through Company I. However, they were soon out of range when they started down the hill.

After they had been gone long enough to arouse considerable anxiety, the battalion commander and his party returned. The Colonel was carrying a German burp gun slung over his shoulder. As the patrol had been moving along down near the river, the alert Wardwell suddenly had lifted his rifle to fire into a bush and out fell a would-be assassin whose machine pistol had been pointed directly at Colonel Moore. Three or four of the assassin's associates had fled. But now the Colonel was able to report it all clear to the river.

The battalion column—I, K, L—in single file, wound down into the valley like a huge serpent. Communications men had to carry the 284 radio by hand. Machine guns and ammunition became greater loads as their bearers filed down the slopes.

Here, for the first time, it was possible to find an observation post from which one could watch the Battalion's advance. Captain Heffelfinger and Lieutenant Barney Blackburn remained here to observe. Should the Battalion run into trouble, Barney could open fire immediately with his 81mm mortars and the executive officer could call for artillery or other assistance. It was another bright day and observation was good.

We followed the path—if there was no path originally, there was one by the time these companies had passed in single file—down through shoulder-high grass and bushes to the water's edge.

"Is this the Vire River?" someone said. "Hell, I can spit across this." But there was a feeling of dread throughout the Battalion. We looked at the high, commanding hills on either side of us as we started down the side of the valley.

"What just one machine gun on each of those hills could do to us," we said—it would be like being with General Braddock or with Custer at Little Big Horn. It was difficult to imagine why the enemy should not defend these heights.

Still, without any kind of enemy opposition, the column followed along the side of the valley toward Pont Bellenger, 1500 yards to the south. As "I" and "K" Companies uncovered from behind the nose of the hill and began to approach the town, the enemy opened up. Machine guns and rifles sent bullets crackling through the valley and shell fire was quick to follow up. Mortars searched the column all the way back to the stream. Fortunately, the enemy had failed to set the trap at his disposal and there was no direct fire from the tops of the riverside hills. However, that coming from the vicinity of Pont Bellenger was sufficient to be costly. Company I, in the lead, had 25 casualties within a few minutes. Nearly the whole battalion was pinned down.

Barney Blackburn, observing from the high ground on the other side of the river, had his mortars open fire on the town with white phosphorus and high explosives.

Captain Dick Melcher crawled up to his 300 radio man, but as he reached for the handset, a shell fragment tore away the mouthpiece and killed the radio operator.

Colonel Moore and most of his command group were pinned down in a little shed. Just outside in the meadow lay Elton Ridge, one of the new intelligence men. Ridge had come up with the replacements the day after "Bloody Sunday" and now was getting his initiation. He was a neat, blond, well-built man who was almost overly conscientious; he had been a farmer and a school teacher of social studies back in Missouri. Company I men were coming back and Ridge was crawling toward the relative safety of the little shed where he would join the other members of the command group when an "I" company sergeant came upon him.

"Where the hell are you going?" the noncom yelled. "Stay up there and shoot!" Naturally, all the new men in the companies had not had a chance as yet to become acquainted with each other and the sergeant apparently thought Ridge one of his own replacements. At any rate, the new intelligence scout found himself on the "I" Company firing line blazing away. Men still were falling about him…rapid bursts of machine gun fire barely grazing over his back…a shell hit within ten feet and set his ears to ringing and made him cough. He glanced up and saw a wounded man lying a few yards ahead of him out in the meadow. In spite of all the natural fear which was crushing down upon him, Ridge crawled out under that machine gun fire and amidst the shell fire to drag the stricken man back to safety. The wounded comrade looked up and said, "What's your name, soldier? That was a great thing you did."

The companies withdrew back around the nose of the hill to reorganize. Captain Craig, who had been commanding Company I, had been killed. Lieutenant Bickford, who had taken over command, had been wounded—a machine gun burst had broken his leg. A Second Lieutenant who had come up only the night before—he was one of those about whom I got that horrible feeling when I first met him, that feeling that he would be killed—had been killed. Lieutenant Wardwell, a highly capable officer, was left, but he was badly shaken up and felt that he could not assume the command. That left Company I without a commander and the Colonel was determined to renew the attack. Captain Carroll, Battalion S-3, volunteered to undertake the tough assignment of taking over a strange, disorganized company and lead it into an attack.

Colonel Moore shifted Company L up to the left of K in assault and left I in reserve for the new attack at 8:30. By this time, the Second Battalion had come up on the high ground to our right and the opposition subsided. The assault companies reached the edge of Pont Bellenger within an hour and the battalion dug in to wait for renewal of the advance at 8 o'clock the next morning.

Bridging difficulties made it necessary for carrying parties to take up ammunition, water, and rations during the night. "Bed-check Charlie" made his usual visit, but inflicted no local damage. The sister regiments continued to advance; the 320th came up on the high ground to our left—and in a confusion of challenges shot one of our sentries—and before 7 o'clock the next morning the 320th reported that it had men on high, commanding Hill 203 to the southeast of Pont Bellenger and the 137th had elements on Hill 193 to the southwest of Pont Bellenger. Now it did begin to look as though enemy opposition was broken.

The Battalion moved out the next day following the road through Pont Bellenger—the pioneers had to mark a route around a mine field there where one man already had been killed—and continued southward over the nose of Hill 203. There the odor of broken tree limbs, torn green leaves, and burnt gun powder—an aroma which now had become so closely associated with death—was heavy in the air where terrific artillery barrages had pounded this key terrain feature all during the night. Careful of mines which might lay concealed beneath the fallen leaves and branches, the column moved on.

There was some resistance down near the town of Annebecq—the town received a terrific German shelling while the Battalion remained safely to the left (east) of it—in the evening, but the advance moved on at 6:30 the next morning without difficulty.

Rumors had been coming down that Vire no longer was to be a Division objective—that the British and the Second Division were to take it. The 134th had heard so many rumors in the course of this campaign about being "pinched"—that is have other friendly units maneuver across the front and thus cut off contact with the enemy—that the term had become a popular byword. Now, however, as the battalion advanced, queer-looking British vehicles began to appear along the roads to the left. Before noon, orders came down to hold up. The elements of the Second Armored ("Hell on Wheels") Division were approaching from the right; they were heading for Vire down the Tessy-Vire highway. The Battalion went into a defensive position in some orchards and meadows; the command post set up in a farm house which had escaped the destruction of war.

It felt as though a tremendous weight had been lifted from the shoulders. Men washed up and shaved, built small fires, got fresh water (always putting in the purifying halazone tablets, of course), and basked in the warm afternoon sun. For the first time, there was something besides enemy out in front. For the first time in nine days, it looked as though there would be no order coming down calling for a resumption of the attack. We knew that the Third Army was racing across the Brest Peninsula; the situation now called for a change in sector for the 35th Division and we speculated on the possibility of mounting trucks and returning to the Third Army to follow Patton's armor.

While we were stimulating our own morale with such speculation, Colonel Moore suggested that nothing could help his morale better than a fried chicken. We were delighted when he pointed out that untended young fries were running about just asking to be caught.

He turned to me and said to go out and find someone to fry them.

I stepped out into the orchard and looked around. My eyes fell upon a man of obvious Chinese extraction, sitting under a tree. "May be just what I'm looking for," I thought.

I called to him, "Hey, soldier, what's your name?"

"Hon, sir," he said as he stood up and saluted.

"Where are you from?"

"Chicago."

"How did you happen to join the army?" I asked.

"My draft number was 158, the first number drawn. They wrote all about me in the Chicago papers."

"What is your assignment here?"

"I'm 'K' Company runner."

"What did you do in Chicago before the draft?"

"I worked at Golden Pheasant."

"What is Golden Pheasant?"

"A good restaurant."

"A restaurant! Well, Hon, from now on you are the colonel's mess orderly. He says he would like some fried chicken. Do you think you can arrange that?"

"Of course. But what about my Company K?"

"I'll take care of that. You take care of the chicken."

Looking out through the clear night, members of the Third Battalion could see Vire burning in the distance and the flashes of artillery barrages, but the sounds were scarcely audible. They munched on chicken and rabbit and contemplated on the end of the Normandy campaign.

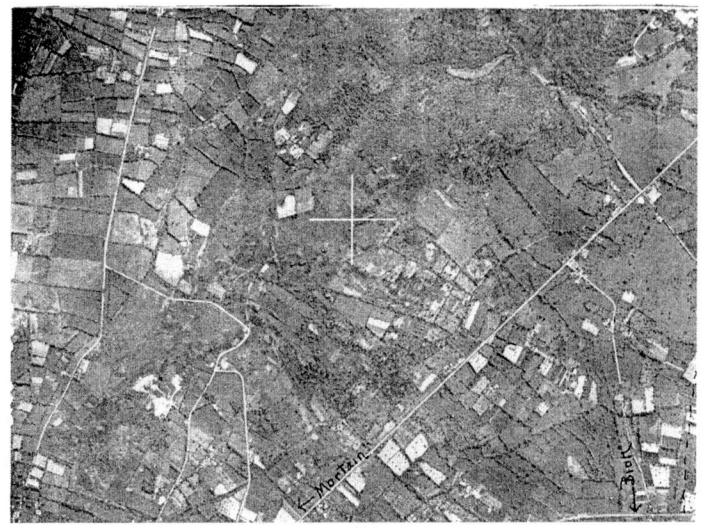
St. Jean du Cordl, near Mortain

8
Detour to Mortain

The Battalion moved into its assigned assembly area along the hedgerows northeast of Annebecq after a rapid, warm afternoon march from its latest defensive position on August 5th. Indications were that the 35th Division would be moving by motor late the next day to join in the spectacular drive of the Third Army.

So far removed from the scenes of combat that the roar of cannon were now reduced to peals of distant thunder, the feeling of safety added to the brilliance of the sunshine on that bright Sunday morning. Everyone seemed to be intensely conscious that he was alive.

This was the chaplain's first opportunity to hold any kind of a church service since the Battalion had entered combat. The Catholic Chaplain, Father Hayes, who was accompanying the Second Battalion, came over to the Battalion area to hold a service at nine o'clock and then Chaplain Walker prepared for his Protestant service at ten o'clock.

As the hour approached, men began to gather at the designated spot in an open meadow. This was near the center of the battalion area and streams of men came from all directions. Trained never to be without their protection, the men were wearing their steel helmets and carrying their rifles—it reminded one of the Pilgrims going to church back in Plymouth Colony.

It appeared that every man in the Battalion was attending church. The Chaplain almost was overcome as he stood up to face his greatest military congregation. Actually, it was too large a group to have together this close to the front, but no one was afraid. Several hundred male voices joined in singing some old hymns and then the solo voice of Corporal Cross, battalion medical technician, carried clearly across the countryside in a special number.

The men sat in that sun-bathed meadow looking at the hills in the distance. A pair of airplanes flew over the hills and flashed their sides in the sun as they circled back – they were friendly. Here was the beauty of quiet such as had not been experienced in three weeks—in three weeks which seemed longer than months. The monotony of continuous violence of attack, the sameness of fear and pain, had been exchanged for the serenity of quiet worship.

"We are all very much aware of how fortunate we are to be able to come together for worship on this beautiful morning," the chaplain said, "and we remember in our hearts and in our prayers our comrades who are not here today. We turn to the only source we know to find strength to see us through the trials in the days to come."

The chaplain ran short of bread and wine when nearly the entire group remained for Communion service. As Ruby had said, those few weeks "made Christians out of lots of the boys."

Rocky brought up a football and a softball and bats to make it a real Sunday afternoon. Colonel Moore was the most enthusiastic of all. He peeled his shirt and led a group—officers and men—to start passing the football, then he retired to the shade of an apple tree and fell asleep while the others carried on. The sandlot baseball picture was completed when someone hit a fly through a truck windshield.

That truck was one of some 20 (the fighting strength of the Battalion was down to less than 400) of the sturdy 2 ½ ton 6x6 cargo trucks which had arrived to move the Battalion that evening.

Considerations which usually would dictate a night move actually called for a daylight move under the circumstances then existing in Normandy. The Germans always had made their withdrawals and troops movements at night in order to escape our air forces.

No one ever explained why it was that our own air forces could not operate with flares at night just as effectively as a few scattered Germans could, but the fact was that in that sector, the air at night usually was left for the enemy—not only did our aircraft refrain from carrying out any offensive operations at night to our front, but they even refrained from sending up any defense most of the time. Regular as he was, "Bed-check Charlie" never seemed to run into any night fighters. The Germans then found that most of the time, they could fill the roads with troops and wagons at night in perfect immunity. We, on the other hand, never had any trouble from German air attacks during the daytime.

Whatever the reason might have been, we played ball and rested during that Sunday until evening. Then we boarded the trucks. The destination was in the vicinity of Louvigne. Lieutenant Hall had gone ahead with a quartering party to select an assembly area and then guide the Battalion in.

No one was surprised when the familiar slow drone of an enemy airplane came over the motor column about 11 o'clock. Fortunately, the Third Battalion's trucks were able to find some concealment in the shadows of high hedgerows and bushes along the narrow road. The plane's particular target was a bridge which we had crossed about a mile and a half to the rear, but he missed that. However, he was able to inflict some costly casualties on some of the Division special troops in the vicinity.

By August 7th it was reported that six American spearheads were driving eastward on a 53-mile front less than 135 miles from Paris. But on this same day, it also was reported that four German armored divisions had opened a "large-scale counter-offensive" toward Avranches and the sea. Aimed at seizing that key point at the juncture of the Cotentin and Croton Peninsula, the Nazis already had recaptured Mortain and penetrated three miles toward the sea.

Avranches was the focal and critical communications point between the supply bases at the beaches and at Cherbourg, on the one hand, and the fast-moving columns of the Third Army which were racing across Brittany and turning toward Paris. Hitler was making a desperate gamble. If successful, it would cut off the Third Army from its supplies. Lieutenant General Omar N. Bradley, commander of the American Army Group, decided to match Hitler's gamble with one of his own: the Third Army's columns would race on—he would divert other troops to meet the counter-offensive—an Army and a campaign were at stake.

Now the 35th Division, in assembly areas near Louvigne, awaited word to continue its move to join the Third Army. But the big gamble required that it be diverted first to the Mortain sector to help stop that dangerous German drive. Actually, the Division had been teamed with General Jacques Leclerc's 2nd French Armored Division in the XX Corps of the Third Army, but now was returning to the First Army for a few more days. It was 3:20 p.m. on that same August 7th when the Battalion's motor column began to move back north. Within 30 minutes after its receipt of orders, the Division had formed into its three regimental combat teams.

Smaller units—doubtless because of lack of time—had not been very well oriented nor given very clear orders. As we rolled through St. Hilaire and headed east and southeast toward the area marked on the map as our "goose egg," we were not sure whether we were moving up to an assembly position preparatory to attack or into a defensive position, or to await further orders. We only knew vaguely that there was some kind of German counter-offensive on: we were told that there was a "pocket of resistance" in the Mortain area.

We began to notice civilians in greater and greater numbers trudging along the roads pushing carts or pulling small wagons stacked high with their effects. Were these people returning to their liberated homes or were they fleeing the German offensive? One inquiry was sufficient to clear up this question. They would point to the direction whence they came (i.e. the direction in which we were going) and cry "Boche!" One civilian report had no less than 80,000 Germans in the Foret de Mortain.

The Battalion went into a defensive position on some high hills above a small creek. The attached 2 ½ ton trucks were to be retained and they assembled in the protection of the valley. However, we very soon learned that it was not the American policy to meet a counterattack with defense – but with attack. At 8:20 o'clock that same evening, the Battalion received orders to move. Hardly more than an hour later, the Battalion, mounted in the trucks, was back on the road. We were to move tactically by motor as far as practical and then dismount and continue on foot to an area just west of Notre Dame de Touchet. Lieutenant Ed Kennedy of Company K was out in front with the point.

In the vicinity of Villechien, where the 35th Reconnaissance Troop had reported enemy less than half an hour before, the Battalion now came upon scores of armored vehicles—some turning around, others starting and stopping in a road and a cloud of dust, others sitting quietly—of the 2nd French Armored Division. It was necessary to infiltrate through that armored column to get to the Notre Dame road. As we turned to the east – toward Notre Dame – machine gun bursts could be heard and tracers could be seen streaking across the road to the north. We heard that a cavalry unit was involved in a brush up there.

Trucks were released a mile or two short of the objective, and then the companies moved up to the edge of Notre Dame without any difficulty.

It was a little surprising when the Battalion resumed its advance at 6 o'clock the next morning, went through Notre Dame, and on down the warm dusty road toward its objective beyond the Barenton—St. Jean du Cordl Highway—without meeting any opposition. Object for the greatest resentment of the marching doughboys was a platoon of tanks which moved through the column churning up choking dust over the dogfaces. Tanks were regarded as another of those things which "you can't get along with and you can't get along without."

During a temporary halt after our three hours of marching, a formation of high-flying B-17's—Flying Fortresses—appeared overhead. The regular pattern of faint silver crosses presented a striking beauty against the bright blueness of the sky. But the picture of innocent beauty was marred presently by a series of dark blotches. Antiaircraft shells were bursting beneath the big bombers; soon it became intense—puffs of smoke appeared all through the formation. But not a plane wavered from its course; straight through the flak they flew. Then we saw that one was crippled, it lost its speed, seemed to pause for a moment there in the air and then its nose turned down and it plunged earthward. There was no spinning, no turning, no pauses; in ever increasing speed it fell straight down until it disappeared behind trees on the horizon. Seconds later, there was the noise of a tremendous explosion and a pall of smoke rose above the trees. "How well put," we remarked to each other, "'Queens Die Proudly.'"

"Yes, aren't they beautiful creatures there in the sky …didn't see any parachutes open—there was a squad of men in that plane."

As the Battalion neared the highway, other planes appeared. This time they were the fighter-bombers— three pairs circled over a high, wooded hill southeast of Mortain. First the P-51's (Mustangs), guided by smoke shells, went in to dive toward the positions and drop their bombs and then zoom upwards. Heinie hardly had time to shake his head after that before the P-47 Thunderbolts came in to "lay their eggs." And that was not all yet; most beautiful of all (thought members of the Third Battalion who had made their acquaintance in California) were the P-38's (the twin tail boomed Lightnings) diving down, then streaking up again as an earth-shaking roar came across the valley and clouds of dust and smoke billowed into the air.

The Third Battalion went into position on its objective before noon and sat down to await developments. The only trouble there during the day was in the afternoon when parts of the Battalion were moving farther forward to better positions and drew some shelling. Tree bursts caught parts of Company L coming down a sunken road and killed one man and wounded some others. But when trouble is not at hand, we go looking for it.

The other battalions had not fared so well during the day. They had run into strong opposition and had made little progress in their attack toward St. Jean du Cordl. Young Captain Frederick Roecker, who had succeeded to the command of the Second Battalion, had been wounded during the morning. Now the Third Battalion, alone on the objective, was sticking out like the proverbial sore thumb. Anxious to take advantage of this favorable, if precarious, position, the regimental commander made a plan to have the Third Battalion form a task force to take up a position to the southeast of St. Jean where it could cut off any enemy withdrawal and annihilate him as the First and Second Battalions attacked from the west.

A part of Company I, with some "M" Company machine guns and a platoon of tank destroyers, moved up the highway and deployed to the southwest of St. Jean.

The Battalion CP was set up in a small, fragile shed. Other headquarters men moved into a nearby barn. In trying to converse with some of the French farmers, I decided that I needed an interpreter. I went back to the barn to see if there were any men there who could speak French. The First Sergeant knew of an "L" Company messenger. Again, we knew that "L" Company would not think much of losing a man to Battalion Headquarters, but I said that we would just borrow him for a little while.

Vlascious was a little, dark-haired, dark complexioned fellow of Greek extraction. He had picked up his French around a New York shoe factory. He was neat in appearance and spoke with the speed of a stammerer which ought to delight the Frenchman. He fell into helping out with odd jobs around the CP and soon paired off with Hon. This team—the Chicago Chinaman and the French-speaking Greek—became an indispensable institution in Battalion Headquarters.

There was another fellow out in that barn who also was growing into something of an institution. T/5 Bartash was breaking into the work of a clerk up with an infantry battalion after he had been performing clerical duties under more quiet conditions with the personnel section at Division Rear Echelon. He was keeping close to Sergeant Buckley, the sergeant major.

"Hey, Buck, what does an 88 sound like?"

Just then came a jarring "zip-bang!" and a thunderous explosion just outside the barn.

"Like that," Buckley said.

The men huddled low in a circular concrete feed trough.

During the afternoon and evening of August 8th, the enemy showed no signs of letting up. Groups of enemy infiltrated into the rear of the First and Second Battalion. They captured the Second Battalion's aid station, chaplain and some motor personnel. At 8 o'clock, tanks were reported in the First Battalion's motor park. Another enemy group approached the Third Battalion's task force, fired a few rounds and withdrew. All this was enough to keep most men on the alert during the hours of darkness.

The Division order which came down the next morning was the kind which one learned to expect in those situations where attack was meeting attack. (The Division had been assigned to the VII Corps the previous day.) The 320th Infantry was to go in on the north of the 134th; the 3rd Battalion, 137th Infantry was attached to the 134th Infantry and took over the First Battalion's mission, while the latter reverted to reserve and was to follow closely behind the Second Battalion. The Third Battalion, alone on its objective, was attached to the 137th Infantry which was operating northwest from Barenton. The Third Battalion, however, was to remain in position for the time being while the rest of the Division launched a new attack at 9 a.m.

The task force did become active enough to draw fire, though it had to be careful not to move into the zone of one of the battalions coming from the other direction. Colonel Moore went up to direct the fight and had a narrow escape from machine gun bullets. The artillery liaison officer, Lieutenant Vernon Freitas of California, went up to see if he could assist the effort. Freitas climbed up on a house top and there found that he could see St. Jean—the focal point toward which all these attacks were directed. He set to work to bring some observed fire down on the town. However, his own position became perilous when enemy shells began to fall in the area and then the machine gun fire started up again below. Some of the men pulled back from the vicinity of the house to seek better cover. But Freitas, out in front of his own infantry, remained there to bring in the artillery on the enemy. This proved to be effective and he was able to get back to the CP without injury.

Meanwhile, the First and Second Battalions were in trouble again. It was another counterattack. The regimental commander sent Captain O'Keefe, regimental assistant operations officer, up to find out the situation and report back. O'Keefe arrived as tanks seemed to start closing in from all directions. Colonel Boatsman, First Battalion commander, reported the number to be anything between "15 and 50." The Second Battalion was pinned down on a sunken road to the front and now the enemy tanks, attacking the rear of the First, had both battalions cut off. We had heard that there was a "lost battalion" of the 30th Division surrounded in or near Mortain. Now it looked like there was to be a pair of lost battalions here. Radio communications were good, but it was not wise to give too much of a bad situation over the air. Colonel Miltonberger was getting impatient. He went to his regimental radio and contacted Captain O'Keefe at the First Battalion.

"O'Keefe, you get back here right away," he said.

"Yes sir, I would sure like to but I am afraid it would take an armored division to accomplish that right now."

A German tank came up to the First Battalion's motor park and, pointing its long gun over the hedgerow, fired right down the line of jeeps in the other field. First Battalion lost four attached tanks and three tank destroyers, five jeeps and five other vehicles.

Heavy artillery fire and vigorous fighting back forced an enemy withdrawal during the night.

All of this was happening to the west of the Third Battalion. To the east were some units of the 2nd Armored Division and they, too, were receiving an attack by the next morning, but here the situation was a little different. The tankers heard the enemy preparing for an attack and set themselves for it. Light and medium tanks were deployed all along the forward slope of the hill but, concealed behind hedgerows and shrubbery, they were not visible to the enemy in the dim light of pre-dawn. The enemy came rushing across the field in an old infantry charge. The tankmen held their fire until the shouting Nazis were within 200 yards and then 30 caliber machine guns, 50 caliber machine guns, 37mm guns, and 75mm guns opened fire all down the line. This quickly broke the crazy charge and left about 200 dead Germans on the field.

How the Third Battalion escaped all these attacks remained a mystery. The Battalion was having casualties every day, to be sure, but it had been able to march right up on its objective and remain there free of strong counterattacks while the other units were having a most difficult time making any progress at all. We had taken several prisoners—they were from the vaunted S.S. "Das Reich" and "Deutschland" divisions. From our observation post we could look across the valley to a high enemy occupied hill and plainly see enemy activity. It was most trying to watch German vehicles going up the road or troops on bicycles pedaling around the curve and then be unable to get artillery on them. Other sectors had the priority for artillery just then. One afternoon, however, the commander of the Division's medium artillery battalion (155mm howitzers)—the 127th F.A. Bn.—came up to visit our OP. As a matter of fact, our observation post was so good that it attracted all kinds of "brass" visitors; when an OP has too many visitors, they are likely to draw fire and then it becomes useless—we nicknamed this one "Yankee Stadium" and swore that it was a sell out every day. At any rate, the artillery's Old Man was in good spirits this day and he wanted to shoot.

"I'll give you all the artillery you want," he said.

He saw the activity out there and fired several volleys. Then he sent one last message down for another—"Make that TOT," he said.

This was a new term for us. I turned to Sergeant Joe Morhan who had taken over as intelligence sergeant. "We don't want to appear too dumb to these people—see if you can find out from our artillery sergeant what he means by TOT."

A while later Joe returned to say, "We don't need to feel so bad; the artillery boys couldn't tell me what it was, but the sergeant wasn't in." Later he found out that TOT meant "time on target"—all the guns of a battalion, or a dozen battalions, were fired at such a time that all shells would hit the target at the same moment. Thus, the whole target was covered in an instant and there was no chance for victims to run for cover.

Attached to the 137th Infantry, the Third Battalion moved late in the afternoon of the 11th to join in attack of that regiment. The Battalion assembled back along the St. Jean-Barenton Highway and marched off to the southwest through Barenton then followed the main Barenton-Mortain Highway back northwest. A turn off the highway to the left would take us to the west and we would be heading for that hill on which we had been firing artillery from the opposite direction.

Vehicles of the 2nd Armored Division were all through Barenton and strung out along the highway which we followed out. An ammunition truck had been hit at a particularly "hot corner" ahead of us and this delayed the march for a few minutes. Shortly after, the Battalion left the road, and with Companies K and L abreast, advanced in the direction of our hill objective. But by this time, dusk was closing down.

I came upon a platoon of Company K as it prepared to move off through a farm yard. The men crouched behind a hedgerow awaiting their orders. One of them turned up to me.

"Sir, will it be very rough? I just came up and I don't know much about it," he said quietly and seriously.

"Well, sometimes it's not so bad, but other times it gets very rough; but I think we're going to come out all right this time." I was anxious not to frighten him by drawing too dark a picture, but at the same time, I did not want him to think it was going to be anything easy. Most never had thought how heavy the casualties were going to be.

"I'm afraid I may not know just what to do all the time," he continued.

"Do you know you sergeants—your squad leader and assistant squad leader?"

"Yes sir, that's my squad leader right over there."

"Well don't get too far away from them and do everything they tell you to do. When in doubt, ask them; then you do everything as much as you can just like they taught you back in training—that will work all right."

The companies moved out across the meadows and tied in for the night on the edge of a woods. The Battalion CP was established in a pile of rails – the center rails were pulled out and raincoats spread out to insure blackout.

As we were walking down a small lane toward the CP, we heard a strange, weird sound in the west. It sounded like some gigantic spring cog winding up. A loud, awe-inspiring scream and then a huge flash of light—like sheet lightning—came up behind a hill to precede a rapid series of thunderous explosions. It was the "screaming meemie" rockets. Immediately there was an answer. From the rear came the hollow-sounding reports of a rapid-firing gun—it was a sound which had become familiar in nightly harassing and interdiction fire back at St. Lô—none of us had been able to see the weapon, but we heard that it was a recently developed 4.5 inch gun and the bursts of its shells sounded to be at the precise spot whence the sounds of the "winding up" had come. We heard nothing more from the screaming meemie that night.

The attack was scheduled to be resumed at 7 o'clock the next morning, but Colonel Moore felt that a little night activity might make the task easier. He determined to send a combat patrol—a full rifle platoon —to the hill which was our objective. If they ran into opposition, they were to return to the area, but if they could sneak up the hill without hitting anything, they were to set up an all-around defense to hold it and radio word back to the Battalion. The Battalion then would move up the next morning quickly. A few hours after the patrol's departure, the reassuring word came over the 300 radio—it had reached the hill without opposition.

Only a few stray Nazis were to be found in the path of the Battalion the next day as it moved up to occupy its objective. The command post moved into a small, but neatly-built farm house. Its sole occupant—at least on this day—was a tiny, white-haired old woman. She was happy to see the Americans come. She led some of the men up to a loft in the little barn where they found some discarded German uniforms and equipment. The old woman could not understand any English, but she was keenly interested in the friendly soldiers. When we broke out our "K" rations at noon, she insisted on clearing off part of her long board table for us to set our cardboard boxes and tins on. Then she set to building a fire in her fireplace so that we could heat our food until we got it across to her that smoke from the chimney might bring in shells from the Boche.

As a matter of fact, it was not long until shells started to come and they were shells of large caliber. One of the men brought in a fragment so that we could see how large they were. This yet-hot, jagged piece of metal was longer than a man's forearm and three or four inches wide. The old lady looked on with interest and then suddenly her face lit up and she hurried outdoors. We did not notice her until she returned a few minutes later struggling with something heavy. It was a dud! She sensed that something was wrong when we all scattered from the unexploded shell. She set it down on the concrete floor. Finally, ammunition expert Charlie Hall picked up the dangerous missile and carried it to a safe spot.

Shells started coming in again and the frightened old French woman knelt beside her fireplace to pray for most of the afternoon. From time to time she would look up and her eyes would search our faces for some sign of reassurance.

Captain Butch Heffelfinger decided that the shelling had subsided enough to permit him to make a visit up to the positions of the forward companies. He took a messenger and an intelligence man and started up the hill. They were nearing the top when the whistle of a low shell came in fast upon them. It was coming right for them. The messenger winced and fell to the ground; the shell bounced crazily on down the hill. Unable to get up, the man found that he had a broken leg. The shell had hit his leg! But its angle had been just the precise one which left the leg reparable and yet prevented the shell from exploding. Had the round hit the ground, it is probable that all three men would have been killed.

Later in the afternoon, Lieutenant Clyde Payne came bounding into the CP with a bundle of papers. He laughed and said, "Look what I've got here!"

He had found a stack of Nazi propaganda leaflets. Apparently they had been intended for dropping among British and American troops, but the German withdrawal had made the planned distribution impossible. However, distribution within the Third Battalion was now very rapid.

The leaflets were well-illustrated with skillful drawing and photographs. One pictured a British soldier leaving his wife:

When you left your wife – you tried to console her in the belief that by "this very last, great effort of all Allies together"

the war will definitely be over within a few months

Well-in between perhaps you already changed your mind a bit, getting the first, slight impression of what means

Invasion

In order to preserve you from any further disappointments you ought to know:

You are facing German soldiers now, defending the forefield of their home.

They are equipped not only with new weapons (and you will have the honor to make their acquaintance) but also with the experience of three years war against the Bolshies.

Besides the Jerries have been rather busy in this country and by no means only in the coastal area – you certainly heard about "German accuracy."

And don't forget:

The men, you're facing now, don't defend territorial or economical or any other sort of material interests, but a very simple and elementary thing;
  The life of their women and children and their national existence!

Do you think there is only the slightest hope on a German capitulation?

Happy end in a few months?

Then beside a photograph of a German soldier in the lower corner:

"I tell you, these Germans are damned good soldiers."

Statement of General Montgomery quoted by Wendell Wilkie in his book, "One World."

Did you write home already? Do it at once! A few hours from now, it may be too late!

Another was supposed to represent an American sergeant with an English girl who was saying:

"You Americans are sooo different!"

And on the other side it pictured a British soldier's grave and said:

British Soldiers!

You are fighting and dying far away from your country while the Yanks are putting up their tents in Merry Old England. They've got lots of money and loads of time to chase after your women.

While the Third Battalion waited on its objective, another dramatic episode was reaching its climax to the northwest.

Two days earlier the 1st Battalion of the 320th Infantry had been assigned the mission of making contact with a battalion of the 120th Infantry (30th Division) which was surrounded on a hill at the edge of Mortain. At 3 p.m. on the 10th, men of the 320's 1st Battalion, under command of Major William G. Gillis, Cameron, Texas (former West Point football star), mounted tanks of the 737th Tank Battalion to drive up a steep, narrow road in a move to rescue the "lost battalion." The attack was almost due north—right angles to the direction of attack of the remainder of the regiment.

With the advantage of observation, the Germans began hitting the tank column with artillery even before it started. American planes came in to bomb.

The tanks were in column and the road was deeply hedged. There was no possibility of leaving it on either side. The Germans hit the column with everything they had. "By nightfall, the identification panels on the tanks were shredded until they looked like lace." About half of the tanks were knocked out, but the column reached the hill and got part way up. When darkness stopped the heavy fighting, they were on the outskirts of Mortain. There was wild confusion all during the night and hard fighting all the next day. Finally on the 12th, they made contact with the beleaguered troops. Two men loaded a Quartermaster Company truck with supplies and water and headed for the position convoyed by three tanks. They dodged enemy fire, raced down rutted roads to reach the battalion with supplies intact. On the return trip, 20 seriously wounded men were evacuated.

Another order, with a new objective for the Third Battalion, came down later in the afternoon. Colonel Moore assembled his command group and went down the sunken trail to the road. The companies would attack generally northward along that road.

The luck of the Battalion in encountering relatively light resistance thus far had run out. There was opposition almost from the first and it was vigorous – small arms and shell fire. The aid station was busy. When talking with Carroll on the telephone, I could hear the crack of machine gun bullets very plainly.

Captain Butch was on the phone.

"My God. Was it bad?"

A mortar shell had come in on the command group. Colonel Moore, Captain Carroll and Lieutenant Freitas, at least, were hit. None of the wounds was fatal, but they would be out indefinitely.

Roads Without Birds

"Come on, Sam," Butch said, "let's go up and take over."

The battalion commander and the artillery liaison officer already had been evacuated by the medics when we arrived on the scene, but Ray Carroll still was there. His wounds were not serious, but the scores of lacerations all over his body doubtless would be painful once the excitement of battle had subsided. Ray would not leave until he was sure that everything was under control.

We established the locations of the companies and, as darkness approached, began to tie in for the night. The command group established itself in a room which Company K was occupying. We took a few minutes to open a "K" ration supper when a call came from upstairs observers that some Germans were approaching. It was a group of about 25 coming in to give up. It looked as though their resistance might be breaking.

Soon after, a party of officers from the 4th Division came in. They were to relieve us during the night.

At 10:30 the next morning, the Battalion moved out once again in route column. It was moving back to an assembly area near Notre Dame.

Spirits rose as the troops marched down the road on another bright day. It had been depressing to come back to another week of Norman hedgerow fighting after we had been on our way to join the Third Army's spectacular drive. And this long week had not been without its cost. There had been another 250 casualties in the Battalion.

When we moved into the assembly area, we learned that once again we were to mount trucks to join in the Third Army's drive. The 35th Division was to move to the vicinity of LeMans to join the XII Corps.

One bit of news dampened our high spirits: Colonel Thomsen was dead. After he had been evacuated on "Bloody Sunday," the surgeon had given him a 50-50 chance. He even had been able to write a letter and we had heard that he was getting better. But, no, he was dead. We knew that this rugged leader—the symbol of the Third Battalion in the battle for St. Lô—must have gone down fighting. But his influence would persist throughout.

JUILLET 1994

Ce petit lopin de terre du bocage est dédié à la mémoire de la 35th division.

En reconnaissance de ces combattants qui ont libéré dans le courant de la 4ème semaine de Juillet 1944 les villages qui bordent la route du Bust, haie par haie. Quelques mètres en sont reconstitutes avec une tranchée individuelle semblable à celle que ces courageux fantassins utilisaient pour se protéger.

Le village de la Plotinière fut libéré le 31 Juillet 1944. L'infanterie passa pendant quelques heures en file indienne, une distance de 10 mètres séparant chaque soldat.

Nous étions en bas de l'avenue proposant un verre de cidre.

Les américains étaient le 28 Juillet au village de la Belinière, depart de la route du Bust (auprès du bourg de Condé).

Le front fut rompu à quelques haies à l'ouest du village de la Couvane.

Un chef fanatique allemand est venu se faire soigner de ses blessures 3 fois au village de la Couvane avant d'être tué.

De là, dans le courant de la nuit du 30 au 31 Juillet, les forces de la Vehrmarcht se sont mis en retraite avec des chevaux attelés sur banneaux volés, suivis d'une trentaine d'hommes.

Etant en position favorable, ce petit peloton d'Allemands avait tenu tête face à un nombre bien supérieur de combatants américains munis d'un fort matériel.

JULY 1944

We have dedicated this small piece of Norman land to the memory of the 35th American Division, in order to show our gratitude to the Boys who on the fourth week of July 1944 liberated, hedge after hedge, this part of our country.

We have tried to reconstitute there, a small part of the battle site as it looked then.

Growing a short hedge and digging an individual trench, similar to those our brave GIs used to protect themselves.

La plotinière was freed on July 31st 1944. On that day we saw American soldiers filing across our farm and offered them glasses of Norman cider.

On the 28th of July, American troops were at "Belinière" near Condé-sur-Vire, on their way to "le Bust".

They went through the front line a few hedges before "La Couvanne".

A wounded fanatic German officer came three times to "la Couvanne" to be treated, before he was killed there.

During the night from July 30th to July 31st some German soldiers tried to resist but the Americans were more numerous and better agripped so the germans retreated with stolen horses and carts.